NEEDS ASSESSMENT

NEEDS ASSESSMENT
A Creative and Practical Guide for Social Scientists

Edited by
Rebecca Reviere,
Susan Berkowitz,
Carolyn C. Carter,
Carolyn Graves Ferguson

Taylor & Francis
Publishers since 1798

USA	Publishing Office:	Taylor & Francis
		1101 Vermont Avenue, N.W., Suite 200
		Washington, DC 20005-3521
		Tel: (202) 289-2174
		Fax: (202) 289-3665
	Distribution Center:	Taylor & Francis
		1900 Frost Road, Suite 101
		Bristol, PA 19007-1598
		Tel: (215) 785-5800
		Fax: (215) 785-5515
UK		Taylor & Francis Ltd.
		1 Gunpowder Square
		London EC4A 3DE
		Tel: 171 583 0490
		Fax: 171 583 0581

NEEDS ASSESSMENT: A Creative and Practical Guide for Social Scientists

1 2 3 4 5 6 7 8 9 0   B R B R   9 8 7 6

This book was set in Times Roman by Harlowe Typography, Inc. The editors were Holly Seltzer and Heather L. Jefferson. Cover design by Michelle Fleitz. Prepress supervisor was Miriam Gonzalez. Printing and binding by Braun-Brumfield, Inc.

A CIP catalog record for this book is available from the British Library.

∞ The paper in this publication meets the requirements of the ANSI Standard Z39.48-1984 (Permanence of Paper)

Library of Congress Cataloging-in-Publication Data
Needs assessment:a creative and practical guide for social
    scientists/edited by Rebecca Reviere [et al.].
        p.   cm.
    Includes index.

    1. Social surveys.   2. Needs assessment.   I. Reviere, Rebecca.
HN29.N39   1996
300′.723—dc20

96-21821
CIP

ISBN 1-56032-375-2 (case)
ISBN 1-56032-376-0 (paper)

Contents

Contributors

Susan Berkowitz, Ph.D.
Westat, Inc.
1650 Research Boulevard
Rockville, MD 20850

Carolyn C. Carter, M.S.
Fairfax Area Agency on Aging
12011 Government Center Parkway
7th Floor
Fairfax, VA 22035

Carolyn Graves Ferguson, M.A.
Arlington Area Agency on Aging
1801 North George Mason Drive
Arlington, VA 22207

Robin L. Miller, Ph.D.
University of Illinois at Chicago
Department of Psychology
Mail Code 285
1007 West Harrison Street
Chicago, IL 60607

Rebecca Reviere, Ph.D.
Howard University
Department of Sociology and Anthropology
PO Box 987
Washington, DC 20059

Elizabeth E. Solomon, B.S.
Harvard University School of Public Health
1639 Tremont Street
Boston, MA 02127

E. Walter Terrie, Ph.D.
Florida State University
Center for Population Studies
Tallahassee, FL 32306

Preface

A well-planned, methodically sound needs assessment can and should be a powerful guiding force for change. As a type of applied social research, needs assessment is meant to foster program development and policy-making. Needs assessments can be used as information-gathering tools by a wide range of organizations, agencies, and social scientists at local, state, regional, and national levels, and can be conducted under a variety of arrangements. This book provides a comprehensive guide to the entire needs assessment process, from conceptualization through implementation and dissemination of findings.

Chapter 1 introduces the concept of needs assessment and describes the benefits it can provide. It presents a broad framework in which to consider needs assessment and emphasizes the inclusion of key stakeholders throughout the process. In addition, the chapter stresses the importance of enhancing the methodological sophistication of needs assessment and utilizing findings for program and policy ends.

Chapters 2, 3, and 4 cover research design and selection of methods for a needs assessment and can be read as a set. Chapter 2 demonstrates working principles for developing a sound, well-integrated research design. It discusses the basis for choosing the methods or combination of methods to be employed, and whether to use primary or secondary data or both. Chapter 3 describes the quantitative sample survey approach to primary data collection, including framing the research question; probability sampling; selection of mail, telephone, or in-person survey modes; instrument development; and data analysis. Chapter 4 considers qualitative approaches to primary data collection, mainly focus groups and intensive interviews, and shows when these methods are most appropriately used. This chapter covers the types of research questions best addressed by qualitative methods, purposive sampling, use of intensive interviews versus focus groups, designing interviewer guides and focus group protocols, and analyzing qualitative data. The final part of chapter 4 shows when and how to combine qualitative and quantitative methods creatively in a needs assessment study.

Chapter 5 discusses the process of planning a needs assessment from two perspectives: the strategic plan and the project plan. Strategic planning involves identifying factors that are both internal and external to the system in which the needs assessment is being carried out and assessing the potential impact of these factors on the project. Details of the various steps used in planning the project are also presented. This chapter emphasizes the importance of producing a clear, simple, and coherent plan to alleviate many of the difficulties that can arise in undertaking a complex project and discusses how to facilitate problem solving when conflicts emerge.

Chapters 6, 7, and 8 present case studies of actual needs assessments, illustrating the application of different methods to different target populations. The case studies document the real-life contexts of the needs assessments and present a framework for understanding the decisions to use particular methods and focus on specific target populations. Each chapter provides a detailed account of the impetus for and procedures used in the needs assessment project. Service providers, policy makers and researchers in different fields share commonality in the kinds of issues they address with their clienteles. In the spirit of bridging disciplinary boundaries, the case study chapters are aimed at readers in a variety of fields who might wish to apply one or more of the described methodological approaches to their own target populations.

Chapter 6 is a fascinating account of a project, sponsored by a community-based organization, that took a multimethod approach to assessing the AIDS-related needs of women in a low-income, urban neighborhood. Chapter 7 describes a county-level assessment of maternal and infant health needs using computer-based techniques to analyze census and vital statistics data. Chapter 8 discusses two distinctly different approaches to assessing transportation, health, social service, and recreational needs of elderly populations: one approach is a longitudinal survey of suburban elderly; and the other is a qualitative assessment of the needs of homebound African-American, Hispanic, and Vietnamese elderly.

Chapter 9 deals with the use and dissemination of needs assessment findings and examines how to make the transition from research to application. It discusses the importance of early identification of the audience in terms of who they are, what they want or need to know, and how they can be approached to ensure that the needs assessment is shaped appropriately from the early stages of planning. This chapter also shows how well-developed strategies for dissemination increase the audience's chances for using the findings to create policy, develop programs, or increase or modify service delivery.

Chapter 10 summarizes and integrates the earlier chapters, with an eye toward future efforts. The final test of a needs assessment is the impact of its findings. What steps can be taken to ensure that a needs assessment will make a difference, and be worth the effort? This chapter documents how a variety of constituencies can potentially benefit from a well-conducted needs assessment. It presents an overview of the necessary foundations of a successful project, the processes that support it, and alternative approaches that might be considered in the future. This final chapter closes with a discussion of needs assessment as an ongoing, forward-looking process, suggesting proactive strategies for anticipating the changing needs of target populations over time.

This book is designed for a variety of audiences. For example, administrators may be interested in this book to make better decisions concerning how to use needs assessment to target limited staff or resources. Planners may want to know how to use needs assessment to identify what services are most needed by their clients and which segments of their client population most need the services provided, or to justify the groundwork for new programs and services. Students will read this book to learn the fundamentals of the methods and applications of needs assessment. Researchers and consultants will find this a useful guide for deciding on the most viable and reliable approaches for gathering the information they need, and for learning effective ways to present their findings. Although readers may use needs assessment for disparate reasons, they will find clear guidelines, relevant examples, and creative solutions in this book. This is a practical guide for anyone who is asked to implement a needs assessment.

Rebecca Reviere
Susan Berkowitz
Carolyn C. Carter
Carolyn Graves Ferguson

Acknowledgments

Thanks to our families and loved ones for their tireless support, understanding, and assistance. We appreciate the contributions of our employers and colleagues from the Arlington Area Agency on Aging, the Fairfax Area Agency on Aging, Howard University, and Westat, Inc.

1

Introduction: Setting the Stage

Rebecca Reviere
Susan Berkowitz
Carolyn C. Carter
Carolyn Graves Ferguson

Needs assessments are tools. They are tools designed to identify what a particular group of persons lacks to achieve more satisfactory lives. Despite the absence of a single standardized methodology or cohesive body of guiding theory, needs assessment has become increasingly popular. Because families and other informal support networks are unable to satisfy all of an individual's needs, people are turning more often to professionals and public and private agencies for assistance. Formal organizations must know what services and programs will adequately remediate or solve these problems. Along these same lines, agencies must know if and how well their programs are working. In addition, because today's population is increasingly diverse, service providers and social scientists can no longer assume that what they have done in the past remains appropriate for their present constituency.

These changes in assistance and population patterns are further complicated by limited funds. Scarce monies make underwriting a needs assessment project more difficult, but also more necessary. As finances become tighter, resources are increasingly targeted to the most needy, and accountability becomes paramount. Data acquired from needs assessment are necessary to help organizations make educated decisions in planning programs and allocating resources.

Although the type of information required to assess need and its intended uses may vary widely, many organizations will find, at some point in time, that they must assess needs to achieve their goals. Today organizations at all levels are undergoing some form of restructuring, streamlining, reinventing, or reorganizing. Public, private, nonprofit, and proprietary systems are beginning to recognize that services can no longer be provided in the same manner or to the same populations as in the past.

The impetus for conducting a needs assessment can come from a variety of levels. First, it can come from within the community. County citizens may express a desire for improved health and sanitation facilities, and a needs assessment will be required to determine the amount and location of services. At another level, the need for information may emerge from within an organization. For example, a lean budget year might create a need to justify the reasons why certain programs should be maintained (i.e., not cut). A third reason for carrying out a needs assessment may be political. For example, federal mandates may require documentation of needs for maintaining or expanding the allocation of funds for a particular program.

Needs assessments are tools used by a variety of organizations, agencies, and social scientists with differing needs for information. Governments employ needs assessments to outreach to their constituencies, keep in touch with community sentiments, and decide how best to allocate funds. Social scientists are interested in needs assessments as a means to track population status, analyze statistics, and answer basic questions. Service-providing agencies assess the extent of service use and the gap between need and use to plan for the future. Advocacy groups use needs assessments to justify their activities.

Similarly, needs assessments are conducted under a variety of arrangements. A legislative mandate to an agency dealing with the elderly could be conducted by an in-house researcher. A foundation concerned with child welfare might be interested in the needs of its constituency and contract with a consulting firm to carry out the assessment. A human service agency concerned about the mental health needs of its clientele might write a grant to a funder to conduct the project. A state governmental agency might decide to underwrite a study investigating needs of the disabled population as it implements new laws. Because needs assessments occur under various structural conditions, terms may vary from situation to situation. Here the terms *agency* and *sponsoring organization* are used interchangeably and specify the organization housing the needs assessment.

BROADENING THE SCOPE OF NEEDS ASSESSMENT

This book is designed to further professionalize the field by broadening the scope of needs assessment in several ways. First, this book challenges readers to rethink basic assumptions and definitions of needs assessments, and to enlarge the idea of what types of endeavors can properly be called needs assessments. This book demonstrates that a variety of different perspectives can be taken on how to conceptualize needs assessment, all of them legitimate and potentially mutually informing. Whether a given project is viewed as a needs assessment depends, in part, on the vantage point, or "slant," that one takes.

A broadened conception of needs assessment is also required because, as chapters 6–8 of this book show, needs assessment methods are being applied to widely varied populations, some of them marginal to the middle-class mainstream. Individuals in these groups may lack the experience or ability to articulate needs in a way that makes sense to the dominant culture and to traditional service-providing agencies. Yet these groups are more likely than middle-class mainstream populations to be the subjects of needs assessments. Bearing this in mind, the chapters that follow sensitize readers to the importance of creating a suitable fit between the definition of needs assessment used and the characteristics of the population whose needs are presumably assessed.

This book also enhances the perspective on needs assessment by expanding views on the range of methods that can legitimately be used, and creatively combined, in assessing need. The tendency has been to rely on the same methods used in previous efforts, even when this is not technically necessary. In contrast, asking which methods or combinations of methods are most suitable for answering the questions at hand can open the methodological vistas of those who design and conduct needs assessments. Creative thinking about which methods might work best provides the most interesting opportunities to examine different dimensions of the question at hand.

This book also broadens thinking about the practice of needs assessment by showing that there are different kinds and levels of audiences for needs assessments. Policymakers might not be interested in the specific findings for a particular county, but might want to see how that county compares with other counties. Researchers might want to know more about how and why the needs assessment was conducted to determine whether application of similar methods would work for a totally different population in another part of the country. However, most needs assessments have been limited projects designed to provide local decision makers with information on specific populations or groups. This has obscured the common basis of needs assessment and has helped foster a somewhat haphazard approach to needs assessments. This book creates a much larger potential audience for needs assessment efforts by moving beyond the usual emphasis on the empirical findings to setting the results and methods in a broader framework.

This book also consciously moves beyond the segmentation by discipline or by "interest area" that currently exists in the field; it does so by demonstrating how needs assessment methods can be applied to a wide variety of groups. For example, gerontologists doing needs assessments of the frail elderly may be largely unaware of efforts to evaluate the independent living needs of disabled or deinstitutionalized mentally ill persons. Those who deliver services to these superficially different groups actually confront similar issues. Thus, there is much of potential interest and use to gerontologists in what professionals in disabilities or mental health are doing and vice versa.

Although virtually everyone agrees that simply producing data has little effect, relatively little systematic written attention has been paid to practical and strategic issues of how to effectively disseminate and use the results of need assessments to make a positive impact on policies and practices. This is especially surprising in a field with such a strong applied orientation. Why else are needs assessments done but to provide information useful for implementing policy decisions or program changes? In keeping with its practical focus, this book illustrates how researchers can facilitate the effective utilization and dissemination of results by early involvement with the various constituencies interested in the results, and by developing recommendations that are concrete, realistic, action-oriented, and tailored to the specific context and policy environment.

CONCEPTUAL ISSUES

One purpose of this book is to broaden the working definition of and to supply a conceptual model for needs assessment. Defining and evaluating need is not as straightforward as might be assumed. On the surface, it seems a simple matter of finding out what people need. The underlying assumptions are either that existing data will be self-evident in this regard or that people will know what they need so that all one has to do is ask. This begs a host of questions. What does it mean to say that a person or community needs a particular service? What is the difference between need and want? It is relatively easy to decide that a starving person needs food or a homeless person needs shelter. But what if an assessment points to areas of need that are not acknowledged by the individuals themselves, who may believe they need something else altogether? What if the target population and the service providers in the community recognize different areas of need or disagree as to what will best meet that need?

DEFINITIONS OF NEED

Needs are relative to the life experiences of individuals as defined within the framework of a reference group—the group against which status and performance are measured. Specific historical antecedents condition individuals to certain levels of expectations, which, in turn, influence how they define what is needed or necessary to meet some basic standard. Individuals who lived through the scarcities of the Depression, for example, may experience need very differently from ones who came of age during the affluence of the Baby Boom. Age also shapes conceptions of need. For example, although many older individuals clearly experience poorer health than younger persons, the former have a tendency to rate their health relatively highly based on their perceptions of their own health compared with the health of other older people (Stoller, 1984). Estimations of needs would be expected to work similarly, in that they are defined in the context of one's individual and generational experiences.

If standards of need are assumed to be relative, for the sake of comparison, there must be a base group to serve as a standard against which to evaluate levels of need. In needs assessment, the comparison group is most appropriately the relevant community of which the target population is a part. Although national standards do exist for some needs and programs, it is unrealistic to expect standards to apply equally to urban areas of northern California and rural parts of southern Alabama.

Various writers have discussed the concept of need. One of the best known is Abraham Maslow (1954), who developed the notion of a "hierarchy of needs." Based on ascending levels of more complex needs, Maslow hypothesized that, once a lower level need is met, humans move on to other higher order needs. Basic needs for sustenance and safety give way to higher needs for love from others, self-love, and self-actualization. Often criticized for simplicity and linearity, Maslow's model nevertheless suggests that needs are knowable, and that meeting one set of needs may leave a person open to experiencing another set of more complex needs.

Bradshaw (1972) developed a taxonomy of four types of social need. In this scheme, normative needs are those defined by professionals in given situations; as such, they are likely to be paternalistic. Felt need is equated with want and may not truly represent need at all. Expressed need is felt need turned into action; in other words, it is demand. Finally, comparative need is the gap between service receipt between two similar groups.

York (1982) politicized the definition of need as a social problem when he stated that "social concerns come to be defined as social problems through a political process in which varying actors have stakes in divergent outcomes" (p. 53). McKillip (1987) suggested that need was a "value judgment that some group has a problem that can be solved" (p. 10). Introducing the concept of values into the discussion of needs pushes the discourse onto a different plane. Although the importance of measuring needs is generally accepted in social science research, many early social scientists loudly denounced the inclusion of values, however implicit or explicit, in their work. More recently, scholars have criticized the very idea of value-free research, and social scientists are increasingly willing to openly state and address the values implicit in their work.

Values

Simply stated, *values* are ideas about what is good, right, and desirable. Although abstract, values are generally thought to be a central basis for judgment and behavior. The subtle, yet significant, role of values must be recognized early in the decisions and definitions surrounding needs assessment. "Professionals" often believe that, given enough money and freedom, problems can be found and eliminated. However, considering the diversity of interpretations of need, it is important to recognize and be prepared to work with this variety of values and value assumptions. The time to acknowledge and examine any underlying value conflicts or differences in basic assumptions is during the planning stages of a needs assessment. A "consumer" model of needs assessment works best for well-educated, mainstream middle-class adults who are reasonably practiced in expressing their needs as individuals. It breaks down, to one extent or another, when applied to groups that live on the periphery of mainstream culture—be they homeless, people with serious mental health problems, or poor. As needs assessment is increasingly focused on the disenfranchised, it becomes more important than ever to allow these groups to speak in their own voices and to hear what they say without imposing preconceived notions. In a needs assessment, values must be discussed openly by the researchers and others involved throughout the process.

Need

Need is defined as a gap—between the real and ideal conditions—that is both acknowledged by community values and potentially amenable to change. This definition has three parts. First, a gap must exist between the real and the ideal conditions in a community. Differences will always exist, and individuals will always be arranged on a continuum from more to less needy. None-theless, narrowing the gap is a positive goal. Second, this gap must be per-ceived and acknowledged as a need by a community. Few, if any, communities have only one consistent or recognizable set of values. Many agencies and organizations, however, assume that they can and do make life "better" for their clients. One task of a needs assessment is to check this assumption, ensuring that all involved groups agree on the direction in which to move to achieve improvement. Third, the gap must be amenable to change; needs must be potentially satisfiable. If no change is possible (i.e., walking after a spinal cord injury), energies should be focused on conditions that are modifiable (i.e., designing a better wheelchair).

Definitions of Needs Assessment

Needs assessment has been defined in many ways. According to the United Way of America (1982), "needs assessment is a systematic process of collection and analysis as inputs into resource allocation decisions with a view to discov-ering and identifying goods and services the community is lacking in relation to the generally accepted standards, and for which there exists some consensus as to the community's responsibility for their provision" (p. 2). York (1982) stated simply that needs assessment is a "measure of how much of what is needed." For McKillip (1987), needs assessment is a process of "ordering and prioritization" of community needs.

These definitions implicitly assume that needs assessment is basically a method of data collection or population description. The present approach differs. Needs assessment is defined here as a systematic and ongoing process of providing usable and useful information about the needs of the target pop-ulation—to those who can and will utilize it to make judgments about policy and programs. Needs assessment is population-specific, but systemically fo-cused, empirically based, and outcome-oriented. Needs assessment, then, is a form of applied research that extends beyond data collection and analysis to cover the utilization of the findings.

THE ORGANIZATIONAL AND POLITICAL CONTEXT OF NEEDS ASSESSMENT

Needs assessments are not carried out in a vacuum, but in an organization that may be facing external as well as internal political pressures of various kinds. These multiple political forces are real and must be considered, along with the purpose of the information gathering, from the beginning. Rarely do agencies develop, plan, and operate their services and programs without sig-nificant input, restrictions, and modifications from the political context in which they operate. These political constraints can influence such things as budget, personnel, and resources available, and scope of the problem investi-gated.

In addition to external political pressures, the internal apparatus of the organization has an impact on the project. Internal pressures may come from constituents, clients, and coworkers. Agencies are political beings; they were organized through political bargaining, and staff members come to work with their own agendas (including keeping their own jobs). Further, the assessment is done to facilitate decision making concerning policies and programs that will exist in this same political arena and impact different individuals in different ways.

Guba and Lincoln (1981) suggested that evaluation is always disruptive of the prevailing political balance. The measurement process has impact primarily because the findings are interpreted and acted on. Therefore, other political forces may come into play. If housing is needed for the elderly, monies may have to be channeled away from transportation. Rearrangements of resources and priorities resulting from the needs assessment can ultimately impact intra- and interagency relationships in a shifting political field.

Just as support may come from various places, resistance to carrying out the needs assessment may also develop from different sources. For example, divided political loyalties may impinge on support for a needs assessment. Other persons within the organization may feel that their territory is being threatened by the project and attempt to sabotage it. Service providers may believe that research interferes with their primary goal of service delivery. Posavac and Carey (1989) listed other possible sources of resistance: (a) those who fear change (e.g., their program may be eliminated), (b) those who fear the information may be abused, (c) those who resist quantification, (d) those who resist the cost of the project, and (e) those who resent needless work (e.g., those who believe nothing will come of it anyway). These pressures must be acknowledged and confronted when the purpose of the needs assessment is first articulated. Methods for examining the possible impact of internal and external factors are discussed in chapter 5.

STAKEHOLDERS

One means of negotiating the maze of issues that arise; of clarifying and separating definitions of *want, value,* and *need;* and of grappling with the external and internal political and organizational atmospheres is to involve as many "interested" people on as many levels as possible. It is popular to talk about the *stakeholders* of a particular program or policy. This term usually refers to the clients, or those who receive the service. In reality, clients, as well as service providers and management, community members, certain politicians, the funding source, business/trade associations, and the actual research workers are invested in the process, outcome, and implementation of the findings. These stakeholders are a subset of the larger audience of the findings, which, in turn, is composed of the totality of all those interested in the needs assessment, including those who will find the project useful to their cause.

Those who will be service and program users, either directly or indirectly, should be involved in the initial stages of defining, targeting, and carrying out the research because they will be the group most intimately affected by the findings. Because cooperation from every quarter is crucial, those carrying out the needs assessment should attempt to involve representatives from every possible and relevant group in as many stages of the project as meaningfully and practically possible. "Ownership" fosters responsibility and encourages cooperation if all partners are given a chance to help shape the product from inception to dissemination and implementation. A philosophy of inclusion, rather than segmentation or exclusion, best guides the investigation. This inclusion must be coupled with the belief that stakeholders possess the competence and ability to carry out significant project functions (Iutcovich, 1993); otherwise, it is an empty and meaningless exercise.

Berkowitz (1993) outlined three primary rationales for utilizing stakeholders. First, the utilization rationale suggests that active participation in the needs assessment by those who are affected by it will generate a sense of ownership that, in turn, will increase the likelihood that the findings will be put to use. Second, the decision-making rationale suggests that the diversity of stakeholder input better informs the different decisions that will be made throughout and after the project's completion. Third, according to the empowerment rationale, participation in a research project can be a vehicle to empower previously marginalized groups.

Johnson and Meiller (1987) suggested that there are four main functions of public, or stakeholder, involvement: (a) informational—giving and getting information; (b) interactive—working together on problems; (c) assurance—ensuring that public views are taken into account; and (d) ritualistic—satisfying legal requirements or social norms. Although stakeholders will not fulfill all rationales or functions in every needs assessment, it is crucial to recruit involvement for as many uses and in as many ways as feasible and logical in the context of a particular project.

METHODOLOGICAL ISSUES

In the current state of the art, when compared with the range and level of sophistication of methods used in other types of applied social research, needs assessment stands out as something of a methodological stepchild. A limited, often apparently ad hoc collection of methods has been applied in assessing needs—ranging from holding public hearings or informally surveying service providers to conducting a population survey with a probability sample or utilizing census data. This eclectic assortment of approaches, often coupled with widely varying levels of rigor and scientific acceptability, results partly because these efforts are not always designed by or carried out in conjunction with trained researchers. Under pressure to supply quick answers, policymakers or practitioners with limited backgrounds in research methods may have to improvise as best they can. The idea that the project is only a one-time endeavor of purely local interest and implications would also militate against paying much systematic attention to methods because issues of generalizability or wider applicability would seem fairly moot.

Needs assessment is a type of applied social research. As such, needs assessments involve a methodological design to collect and analyze data that adhere to the guidelines of social science research. Further, methods that are available to other applied social researchers are also available for needs assessment.

Various factors have served to obscure this basic and seemingly obvious point. As Lareau (1983) noted, part of the issue is that needs assessment grew out of practical, rather than theoretical, considerations. In the absence of a true theoretical foundation for needs assessment, the individual practitioner has been left with the responsibility for defining and operationalizing the concept. This has created a situation in which different types of studies are conducted in the name of needs assessment and "practitioners required to conduct needs assessments find little consistent guidance about what to do and how to do it well" (Lareau, 1983, p. 518). This has reinforced the tendency to look to past efforts as models and, in turn, restrict the range of methods considered appropriate for needs assessment to those already in common use. The result has been that, for the most part, needs assessment methods have not kept pace with the development of methods in other areas of applied social research.

Lareau (1983) identified five major types of methods used by State Units on Aging (SUAs) to conduct needs assessments. They were, in order of relative frequency: (a) surveys of elderly respondents; (b) examination of already gathered data, including both raw data and "digested findings"; (c) reliance on key informants, or persons active in the community believed to have knowledge and understanding of the problems, needs, and desires of the target population; (d) use of group process/public hearings that involve either holding meetings at which interested citizens provide public testimony or assembling interested persons to reach a consensus on service or need priorities; and (e) examination of service user statistics generally supplied by providers.

In a follow-up survey, Harlow and Turner (1993) found largely the same methods in use. This basic constellation of methods identified by Lareau is not unique to needs assessments of the elderly. There is almost complete overlap with Warheit, Bell, and Schwab's (1979) survey of the five general methods commonly employed in assessing health needs. Although needs assessment methods have matured somewhat over time, changes have largely been in elaboration of the basic models, rather than in breaking new ground.

However, even within the limited range of methods commonly applied, needs assessments are often not done well. For example, in their evaluation of a national sample of needs assessment documents produced by agencies serving the elderly, Lareau and Heumann (1982) found more than three-fourths "of such low quality . . . they could not provide meaningful input to the planning process" (p. 518). Lareau's (1983) further analysis of these documents uncovered problems with sampling, data reporting, questionnaire design, and inappropriate use of secondary data. Most important, she found only a loose fit between the method(s) employed and the conclusions produced. Put differently, in many cases, the methods used were inadequate or inappropriate to justify the conclusions reached. In addition, when used together, different methods were rarely combined correctly, let alone most wisely (Lareau, 1983).

Later research has suggested that the quality of needs assessment research has not greatly improved (Harlow & Turner, 1993).

Although Lareau's (1983) and Harlow and Turner's (1993) studies focused on needs assessments of the elderly, needs assessments of other target populations are no less free of methodological problems. For example, during the same period in which Lareau conducted her research, Robins (1982) surveyed a sample of various human service agencies in Wisconsin. Agencies were allowed to define what they considered to be a needs assessment; but to qualify as having done one, they had to have produced a written document describing the findings. Robins found that only 30% of the agencies had produced such a document during the prior 3-year period. Most agencies that had not conducted an assessment felt a formal study was not necessary because they kept in constant touch with the community's needs through an informal process.

This presumption of many community and state agencies—that they already know the needs of their clientele—may also help explain the relative lack of critical attention paid to the methods used to ascertain need. Implicit in the concept of "research" is a commitment to "look again" at something in a systematic, verifiable way. The results may or may not confirm the expectations of agency personnel; needs assessments may raise unanticipated new issues or uncover serendipitous findings that challenge the assumptions and self-images of even the most well-meaning agency personnel.

The primary purpose of the agencies in Robins' sample that did undertake a formal needs assessment was to identify and describe needs—either to estimate the size and scope of certain problems, develop a list of the needs of target groups, or both. However, identification of needs was rarely the sole purpose of the assessment. Secondary goals included publicizing the agency's services and activities, promoting awareness about the needs of target groups, and providing information on service availability to prospective clients (Robins, 1982).

Sample surveys were the most common data collection technique employed by these agencies. Although personnel perceived that surveys were more reliable, valid, and objective than other needs assessment approaches, Robins (1982) rated fully 70% of these assessments of low quality methodologically. Even when these agencies recognized the desirability of conducting technically sound needs assessments, they apparently still lacked the knowledge, skills, time, and resources to do so. This theme was echoed in Cheung's (1993) research on the use of needs assessments by Area Agencies on Aging, which found a notable difference between the methods agencies actually used and those they would have preferred to use. The discrepancy was mainly due to a lack of personnel with the appropriate methodological skills. Agency respondents strongly agreed that hiring a research consultant to assist in developing the assessment would have been helpful.

Some of the methodological weaknesses in needs assessments can clearly be attributed to the fact that they have been conducted or overseen by agency personnel and others with little or no training in research methods. The best option for many agencies is to obtain expert assistance to conduct a sound assessment. In lieu of hiring a consultant, knowing more about methods in general can eliminate common errors that can invalidate a well-meant effort. Several alternative methods are available to social scientists embarking on a needs assessment project. These are outlined in later chapters.

FINDINGS: HOW TO MAKE THEM EFFECTIVE AND USEFUL

In general, agencies and individuals utilize needs assessments for two reasons: descriptive and policy/program purposes. The first reason is appropriate for organizations that simply want to document existing conditions. Although the acquisition of basic knowledge is laudable, description is most appropriately seen as a first step, rather than an end in itself. Data that serve to justify the status quo are efficacious only when the status quo is available, accessible, and desirable to all. Knowledge serves little purpose if it is not put to use. Therefore, the second reason to implement needs assessments is to utilize the information to actually make changes in existing policy and programs.

Too often, needs assessment findings are treated as ends in themselves, not as essential means to an end. Examinations of published needs assessments reveal lists of findings and statistical analysis, but little comment on the policy and practical implication and impact of the findings (Kimmel, 1977). In a review of the literature on educational projects, Thompson (1981) found little evidence that research findings informed decision making. Thompson also found a related widespread frustration among administrators with the waste in time, money, and effort when research findings were not used. Even the most well-designed study is often published without implications for services or suggestions for decision makers. Clearly, however, a needs assessment does not end with a simple enumeration of needs or problems; evaluation of data and integration of information should result in informed decision making on recommendations, policy, and programs (McKillip, 1987).

If policies and programs need to change as a result of the needs assessment, how does this change take place? If further funding is needed to put new procedures into place, where does it come from? Will the community stand behind the results? Issues such as these must be discussed early in the process of designing and planning a needs assessment. In addition, they should be worked out in conjunction with community leaders, advocates for the constituency groups, and members of the groups whose needs are being evaluated. More input from various groups and more rigorous planning on the front end of the task makes the back end more manageable. Iutcovich (1993) illustrated this dilemma well in her discussion of the research consultant "scrambling for time" before a town meeting where findings were to be discussed. The researcher was pushed to complete addition analyses at the last minute because earlier contact with the advisory group was insufficient to clearly define their expectations. Effectively utilizing the results of a needs assessment requires a strong foundation; this includes a sound conceptual and methodological base and a supportive commitment from stakeholders in all crucial phases. Utilization is also dependent on the quality, appropriateness, and accessibility of the data obtained. Useful implementation is not facilitated by a presentation of statistical findings that is not linked to the lives of the individuals involved and that fails to demonstrate policy and practical implications. Yet researchers may not know how to provide these results in a way that is technically accurate and accessible to the various audiences. To ensure that study findings will be useful, the research questions must be relevant to the information needs of the primary audience, and answers must be a result of sound methodological design (Newcomer, 1994).

Even with a well-planned approach, problems invariably arise in implementing the study findings. However, a proactive strategy to ensure the effective use of findings involves anticipating likely barriers. For example, some considerations may need to be addressed in the early stages of planning. Economic factors might include cost of program initiation and/or modification. Political forces might develop in competing demands for use of funds needed to implement recommended changes. Administrative difficulties could arise because of resistance to new approaches that require making changes in established structures and practices. Identifying internal and external forces that could impact on both the conduct of the study and implementation of the findings is an important contribution of strategic planning (discussed in a later chapter); it influences both the method of data collection and the dissemination and utilization of findings.

The results of a needs assessment can be utilized in many ways, not all of them immediately obvious. Examples include (but are not restricted to) support for specific grant awards, development of task forces, modifications to budget decisions, creation of new programs, changes in direct service to clients, and even introduction of new legislation. Needs assessment findings are sometimes unexpected and may lead to new and nontraditional approaches to meeting those needs. With effective dissemination and utilization, the consequences of a needs assessment can be far-reaching, long-term, unanticipated, stimulating new ventures. This is part of what makes needs assessments so exciting and rewarding, if also quite exhausting at times.

I

UNDERSTANDING AND DEVELOPING NEEDS ASSESSMENT

2

Creating the Research Design for a Needs Assessment

Susan Berkowitz

The method or combination of methods selected to conduct a needs assessment is vitally important. The choice of methods determines what kinds of data will be collected and what can legitimately be concluded about the findings. This chapter shows why careful and systematic consideration should be given to creating the research design that will serve as a blueprint in carrying out a needs assessment study. It illustrates how to design a successful needs assessment by using a master matrix approach integrating the research questions, data elements, data sources, and analysis plans in a logical, coherent format. The chapter provides a working example of how to think about research design by delineating possible research strategies and demonstrating their respective strengths and weaknesses in relation to cost and resource considerations, the goals of the particular project, and the audiences to whom the results are directed. Chapters 3 and 4 develop the master matrix example further by presenting detailed discussions of sample survey and qualitative and mixed method approaches to needs assessment.

NEEDS ASSESSMENT AS APPLIED SOCIAL RESEARCH

The key point to keep in mind when considering which method or methods to use in assessing need is that needs assessment is essentially one type of applied social research. To say it is a type of *social research* means that needs assessment entails a systematic process of conceptualizing a research design, and gathering and analyzing data according to commonly accepted standards of social science. To say it is *applied social research* means that the results of needs assessments are used to inform policy and program development. Consequently, the range of methods that can be used in needs assessment is potentially the same as that available to all applied social researchers.

Needs assessment methods are divided into two basic groups: those employing secondary data and those using primary data. Needs assessments that rely on *secondary data* are based on information that has already been gathered, usually by other researchers or agencies. These are usually collected for purposes other than or broader than those of assessing the particular need or needs of the specific target group or groups.

Judicious, appropriate use of secondary data has an important role to play in most needs assessments. Analyzing secondary data is usually less costly than collecting primary data because it eliminates the need to pay for data collection. However, the major disadvantage of relying on secondary data is loss of control over precision of definition of relevant variables because the data are not gathered expressly to suit the purposes of the needs assessment at hand. Examples of secondary data sources include:

- the U.S. decennial census—the census of the entire population conducted every 10 years by the U.S. Census Bureau, which contains data on demographic characteristics such as age, race, ethnicity, and household composition for various levels from the nation down to individual census tracts and neighborhoods;
- vital statistics registers (containing a variety of statistics on births and deaths, marriages and divorces);
- national, state, or local population-based sample surveys carried out for government agencies (e.g., the National Health Interview Survey);
- city or county police department, health department, or social service department records; and
- service utilization data, such as hospital discharge rates.

Needs assessment methods that use *primary data* rely on direct collection of information concerning the needs of the target population in question expressly for the purposes at hand. Specific primary data collection methods include surveys, intensive interviews, and focus groups, all of which are described in later chapters. Using primary data means that data collection can be fit to the specific requirements of the study, enabling strategic decisions on how best to collect which information and from whom. Primary data collection, however, can be expensive. It also takes time to properly collect and analyze the data, and may require hiring, coordinating, and supervising a variety of personnel. Thus, before deciding to conduct a needs assessment utilizing primary data collection methods, it is wise to weigh the costs, time, and labor requirements against the "value added" gained by acquiring greater control over the definition and execution of the effort.

Primary data collection methods can be quantitative or qualitative. *Quantitative* data collection and data analysis methods involve the collection, aggregation, and analysis of numeric data or data that can be expressed in numeric form. In needs assessment, the most common quantitative primary data collection method is to survey a sample of the target population (e.g., frail elderly, low-income families, female-run households) and/or a sample of service providers, local government officials, or other stakeholders. Chapter 3 examines the use of sample survey methods in detail. *Qualitative* methods focus on collecting, synthesizing, and interpreting data and attributes of data as expressed in words rather than numbers. Qualitative analysis is directed at uncovering and explicating themes or patterns in these data. Although employed less often than survey methods, qualitative methods such as intensive interviews and focus groups as discussed in chapter 4, can also be used effectively in needs assessment.

There is no methodological reason to confine any needs assessment study to exclusive use of either secondary or primary data, or to restrict primary data collection to only quantitative or qualitative approaches. Careful and artful combination of secondary and primary sources, and of quantitative and qualitative methods, greatly strengthens a research design.

DEFINING THE RESEARCH QUESTION(S)

In needs assessment, as in any type of research, the methods used should be driven by the research question(s) to be answered and the reasons for asking these questions. The *research question(s)* are the questions about needs the study seeks to address. They should be distinguished from the *interview questions,* which may be directly asked of respondents to obtain some part of the information to answer the research questions. Because the methods employed in a needs assessment are only the means to the end of answering specific research questions, it is impossible to make an intelligent decision on which method(s) to use without being clear on the research questions to be addressed.

The concept of "needs assessment" is too generic to provide more than a starting point for posing the research questions. Considerable refinement and fine tuning have to occur before the exact research questions for any needs assessment can be clearly defined, even if these questions and their underlying rationale appear self-evident at the outset. For example, suppose a state child welfare agency wants to assess the need for parenting education in its state. On the surface, this seems a relatively straightforward proposition. The research question becomes: What is the need for parenting education in the state? But why does the state agency want this information? Is it proposing to launch a new parenting education program to supplement existing programs, or perhaps thinking about replacing other services with parenting classes? Are certain groups or types of families targeted as primary recipients of these services? Depending on the answers to these and other concerns, the research questions for the needs assessment necessarily become more precisely focused.

After some fine tuning, the overarching research question might be changed to: What is the need for additional parenting education among at-risk, low-income families in the state? If parenting education classes are viewed as a possible replacement for other parenting education services, an auxiliary research question should also be posed that weighs the relative need for classes, rather than another type of parenting service in this target population. The research question might be amended further to read: What is the need for additional parenting education classes, as compared with the need for intensive in-home family-preservation services among at-risk, low-income families in the state? As a logical extension, the policy question to be addressed is: Given the relative need for these two services among the at-risk target population, if only one of the two can be funded, which should it be? An apparently simple matter of asking about the level of need for a given service thus becomes considerably more complex and layered as the underlying rationale for the needs assessment is clarified and placed in politically and analytically relevant context.

Although some refinement of the research questions as the study proceeds is to be expected, it is inadvisable to attempt wholesale redefinition of the research questions while the needs assessment is in progress. The result may be answering the wrong questions or not knowing which questions the data do answer. In selecting needs assessment methods, it is important to be as precise, concrete, and unambiguous as possible about the research questions, and to be sure that they cover the full scope of the intended study. A good test is to ask: Whose needs are to be ascertained, and why?

The first issue is to determine the *target population,* or the group whose needs will be assessed. A precise definition of the target population, based on a clear rationale for that choice, is essential both to formulating the research question(s) and creating the research design. For example, to project service needs for families in a given state, the target population should include the entire state and not just one locality within it. However, it may only be important to know about the service needs of a subset of all families in the state, such as low-income families with young children. The rationale might be that these are the families most in need of social services and to whom the bulk of public services will be directed. Although it might be informative to know about the needs of higher income families, public agencies are not likely to be able to address these needs. Hence, for the purposes of an applied needs assessment, it makes sense to focus only on the low-income families as the target population.

It is always useful to examine whether greater precision can be achieved in delimiting the target population by more clearly defining demographic characteristics, such as age, residence, gender, socioeconomic status (SES), marital status, race and ethnicity, national origin or immigration status, religious affiliation, or household composition. Health and/or social characteristics that can be presumed to relate to areas of service need might also be specified in defining the target population. For example, it might be relevant to investigate the needs of homebound elderly for in-home supportive services, or to assess at-risk, low-income families' needs for parenting education services.

Selection of the target population for a needs assessment is also an eminently political process. Depending on a variety factors, including the funding source for the needs assessment, how the effort is portrayed, and the extent, level, and nature of publicity surrounding the project, selection into the target population for a needs assessment may be seen as beneficial or burdensome and even stigmatizing. Bounding the target population too narrowly may be perceived as exclusionary, and thus may undermine some potential or actual bases of support for the project. At the same time, advocates for the poor may complain that low-income families have been overstudied and that action, rather than more research, is what is really needed. Consequently, it is probably necessary to carefully weigh a mixture of both methodological and political considerations to achieve agreement on the appropriate target population(s) for the project.

Deciding on the target population has important ramifications, in turn, for the choice of appropriate methods for conducting the needs assessment. The best methods to use in determining the parenting education needs of low-income families may be different than those most useful for a target population of all families in the state. For example, if the target population of low-income families is composed of many different groups of non-English speaking minorities, use of a standardized survey instrument may be difficult.

As with selection of the target population, appreciation of the factors and forces motivating the needs assessment effort is also essential when determining the type(s) and scope of needs to be assessed. In theory, needs assessments can investigate a range of human needs, constrained only by the limitation that these be addressable through some sort of public or collective action. Although most needs assessments tend to focus on concrete areas of need, it is legitimate to assess a target population's spiritual needs. Clearly, a crucial linkage exists between the choice of the target population and the determination of the nature and scope of needs to be assessed. To pose an example, it would be highly unlikely that anyone would want to invest time and resources in ascertaining the frail elderly's need for job-training services. However, there would clearly be good reason to assess this population's financial needs.

Some needs assessments investigate a range of categories of needs, from transportation to medical care to housing, whereas others are more narrowly focused on just one category of need. A health department or medical facility might want to gather information only about the health care needs of a given target population because these are the only needs such organizations can expect to address. Needs can also be narrowly or broadly defined within a given category, as in the previous example where the state child welfare agency wants to know only about a particular type of social service—parenting education—among its primary clientele. Although a narrow definition of need might seem to simplify the task of framing the research question, it is important to probe the reasons for this narrow definition. Needs assessment often occurs in a context where examining the need for one service implies making at least a tacit comparison with the need for another. It is wise to make this comparison explicit, when possible, lest the resulting data answer the stated research question, but basically miss the point.

Whether to investigate a wide variety of needs or precisely delimit their scope is also conditioned by a number of practical factors, including cost. Given a fixed amount of money, a trade-off might have to be made between examining a more extensive array of needs for a smaller target population or a more restricted range of needs for a larger population. The agency or organization sponsoring the assessment, as well as other stakeholders, usually also carry considerable weight in deciding on both the target population and the scope and nature of the needs to be assessed.

CREATING A MASTER MATRIX FOR THE NEEDS ASSESSMENT

As seen in chapter 1, the most serious conceptual flaws in needs assessment research involve problems with sampling, failing to gather the right information to measure the desired components of need, and using methods inappropriate to justify the conclusions. These weaknesses reflect a basic failure to develop a conceptually coherent, logical, and well-integrated plan for conducting the needs assessment. Methods are used without giving sufficient forethought to whether they will produce the desired information, or if the form and nature of the findings will support the types of conclusions the needs assessment aims to make.

To provide a guiding structure for the needs assessment that can guard against making these types of conceptual mistakes, the next step after developing the research questions is to create a "master matrix" that links the research questions with their associated data elements, data sources, and methods of analysis. The components of the matrix should fit together logically and economically so that, when completed, the matrix furnishes a charter for the design and execution of the project. An example of a master matrix is provided in Table 2.1. This table is discussed here and in chapters 3 and 4.

Because it requires clearly envisioning the interrelations among the various components of the design, developing a matrix effectively forces the hard decisions that have to be made concerning the research design. Putting together the matrix can reveal inconsistencies that might otherwise escape notice. In Table 2.1, the first research question addresses the need for family support services among low-income families with young children in a state. For present purposes, all families in the state at or below 150% of the federal poverty level are defined as low income. Families with young children are families (including adoptive, foster, and extended families) containing one or more parents, foster parents or legal guardians, and one or more children ages 5 and under. Consistent with the definition used in the Omnibus Reconciliation Act of 1993, family support services are community-based services designed to increase the strength and stability of families, increase parents' confidence and competence in their parenting abilities, and afford children a stable and supportive family environment. Examples of such services include: (a) services to improve parenting skills, (b) respite care for children to provide temporary relief for parents and other caregivers, (c) drop-in centers that give families opportunities for informal interaction with other families and with program staff, and (d) information and referral services to afford families access to other community services, including child care, health care, nutrition, adult education and literacy programs, and counseling and mentoring services.

SELECTING DATA ELEMENTS AND DATA SOURCES

After defining the research questions, the next issue raised by the matrix (as shown in Column 2) concerns the kind(s) and level(s) of information required to provide a complete, satisfactory answer to these questions. *Data elements* are those specific pieces of information needed to answer the research question(s). In deciding which data elements will be gathered to answer which questions, it is vital to develop a clear rationale for the choices and ensure a good fit among all the types of data elements in the master matrix. To maximize the persuasiveness of the design, and thus ultimately the results of the needs assessment, it is important to weigh the selection of data elements in terms of their implications for all the interconnected pieces of the overall design.

The data elements are the essential raw materials of analysis. Selecting data elements requires careful, strategic assessment of what constitutes an adequate and appropriate answer to each of the research questions. Following Table 2.1, to assess the extent of need for family support services first requires knowledge of the dimensions of the target population across the state. Thus, as shown, key data elements would be: (a) the number of low-income households with young children in the state, (b) the percentage of all households with young children they represent, and (c) the geographical distribution of these households by urban, suburban, and rural areas.

In addition, information is required on the extent to which the need for family support services is currently being met for the target population, and how this may vary across type of geographical area. Several types of data might provide the desired information. One possibility would be to obtain data on the distribution of agencies providing family support services across the state. A normalized measure, or a measure adjusted to reflect differences in population size from area to area (e.g., a ratio), could be created by assessing the number and distribution of these agencies in relation to the size and geographical distribution of the target population. Such an approach might reveal that the ratio of family support services to target population is 1:10 in urban areas, 1:5 in suburban areas, and 1:50 in rural areas. This could be read as evidence that the need for family support services in the target population is much larger in rural as compared with either urban or suburban areas, and somewhat greater in urban as opposed to suburban areas.

However, limiting the data elements to these pieces of information alone might lead to drawing false conclusions. For example, if facilities are not being used to capacity, can it be assumed that the mere presence of the facility indicates that the need for these services is being met? Moreover, if the need for family support services is much greater in urban as compared with rural areas, then a lower ratio of service facilities to service population would be appropriate, and these data should not necessarily be interpreted as indicating a deficit of services in rural areas.

To address these considerations, additional data might be collected on: (a) variations in level of need for the service across different types of areas in the state, and/or (b) overall rates of utilization, as well as rates of utilization by the target low-income population, across facilities in the three types of areas. Both types of utilization data would be required because high overall utilization rates at these facilities still might not indicate met need for low-income families, who are often subject to access barriers that limit their ability to use services. For example, there might be an abundance of for-pay private facilities

Table 2.1 Master Matrix for Designing Family Support Needs Assessment*

(1) Research Questions	(2) Data Element(s)	(3) Data Source(s)	(4) Analysis Plan(s)
1. What is the overall extent of need for family support services among low-income families with young children in the state?	• Number of low-income families with young children in state • Percentage of all households with young children in the state that are low income • Number and service capacity of agencies delivering different types of family support services in the state	• U.S. census • U.S. census • Existing data from survey of social service facilities	• Calculate statewide ratio(s) of low-income families with young children/number of service facilities • Calculate statewide ratio of low-income families with young children/measures of service capacity of family support service facilities
2. How does the overall level of need for family support services for low-income families with young children vary across rural, suburban, and urban areas?	• Distribution (number and percentage) of low-income families across rural, suburban, and urban areas • Distribution of agencies in rural, suburban, and urban areas • Distribution of service capacity of agencies across rural, suburban, and urban areas	• U.S. census (county-level data) • Existing data (county-level) from survey of social service facilities • Existing data (county-level) from survey of social service facilities	• Develop index of service capacity and apply to rural, suburban, and urban areas • Calculate normalized ratios of low-income families to service capacity for rural, suburban, and urban areas
2.1 Are there significant variations in the overall level of need for family support services in rural, suburban, and urban areas?	• Same as above	• Same as above	• Correlational analyses to detect statistically significant differences in measures of overall need for types of areas

Research Question	Measures	Data Source	Analysis
3. To what extent are existing family support services being utilized by all families in the state? By low-income families in particular?	• Ratio of number of families now served/total number of families that can be served at key service facilities	• Mail survey (sample) of agency personnel	• Calculate and compare overall percentage of utilization across different types of facilities
3.1 How, if at all, does utilization by low-income families vary across rural, suburban, and urban areas?	• Percentage (or estimated percentage) of service population that is low income at different types of facilities across rural, suburban, and urban areas	• Mail survey (sample) of agency personnel	• Compare percentage of low-income clientele in service population with percentage of low-income families in general population for different types of facilities in three types of areas
	• Percentage of all families that are low income across rural, suburban, and urban areas	• U.S. census (see research question #2)	• Construct adjusted measure of low-income utilization for different facilities in three types of areas
3.2 How, if at all, does utilization by low-income families vary across major racial and ethnic groups?	• Percentage of low-income service population that is African American	• Mail survey of agency personnel	• Compare percentage(s) of low-income families on waiting lists for different types of services across rural, suburban, and urban areas with percentages of low-income families in service populations of these areas
	• Percentage of all low-income families that are African American	• U.S. census	
3.3 About what share of low-income families in the state that want key family support services are not now getting them?	• Estimated percentage of low-income families who want, but are not getting, key services –from agency waiting lists –percentage of incomplete or failed referrals for low-income families	• Mail survey (sample) of agency personnel	

Table 2.1 Master Matrix for Designing Family Support Needs Assessment* (*continued*)

(1) Research Questions	(2) Data Element(s)	(3) Data Source(s)	(4) Analysis Plan(s)
4. What are the *patterns* of need for family support services among low-income families across the state?			
4.1 What types of family support services are most needed, and by which type(s) of families?	• Types of family support services perceived as most needed by agency personnel • Types of families (single parent, immigrant, teenage mom) perceived as most needing services	• Telephone survey (sample) of agency personnel • Telephone survey (sample) of agency personnel	• Weighted frequency distributions of types of services most needed for state as a whole, and by rural, suburban, and urban areas • Weighted frequency distributions of types of families most in need of services for state as a whole, and for rural, suburban, and urban areas
4.2 How, if at all, do patterns of need vary across rural, suburban, and urban areas?	• Types of family support services perceived as most needed in rural, suburban, and urban areas	• Telephone survey (sample) of agency personnel	
4.3 How, if at all, do patterns of need vary across racial and ethnic groups?	• Types of family support services perceived as most needed by: –African Americans –Asian Americans –Hispanics –Native Americans –Whites	• Telephone survey (sample) of agency personnel	• Weighted frequency distributions of types of most needed services by specific racial and ethnic groups
4.4 How, if at all, do the needs of different racial and ethnic groups for family support services vary across rural, suburban, and urban areas?			• Cross-tabulations of most needed services for each group by three types of areas (appropriately weighted)

Research Question	Indicator	Data Source	Analysis
5. What types of services do low-income families in the state feel they most need to maintain and strengthen their families? *Why?*	• Services reported as most needed by low-income families, *and why*	• In-person survey of statewide sample of low-income families • *Focus groups with low-income families across state*	• Weighted frequencies of services reported as most needed • *Qualitative analysis of focus group transcript(s) to identify which services are viewed as most needed, and why*
5.1 Which of the services they are currently receiving do low-income families feel they need more of to help maintain and strengthen their families? How does this vary across rural, suburban, and urban areas? *Why?*	• Currently received services families report they need more of, *and why*	• In-person survey of statewide sample of low-income families • *Focus groups with low-income families in rural, suburban, and urban areas*	• Weighted frequency distributions of services that respondents report needing more of, for state as a whole and by rural, urban, and suburban areas • *Qualitative analysis of focus groups' transcripts to identify services that respondents say they need more of, and why*
5.2 Which services *not* currently received do low-income families feel they need? *Why?*	• Services not currently received that families report they need, *and why*	• In-person survey of statewide sample of low-income families • *Focus groups with low-income families*	• Weighted frequencies of services not currently received that respondents report they need • *Qualitative analysis of focus groups' transcripts to identify which new services respondents say they need, and why*

Table 2.1 Master Matrix for Designing Family Support Needs Assessment* *(continued)*

(1) Research Questions	(2) Data Element(s)	(3) Data Source(s)	(4) Analysis Plan(s)
5.3 Which currently received services do families feel have not been particularly useful in helping them to strengthen their families? How does this vary across different racial and ethnic groups? *Why are these services seen as not very helpful?*	• Currently received services that families feel are not helpful in supporting family goals, *and why*	• In-person survey of statewide sample of low-income families • *Intensive interviews with purposive sample of families of different racial and ethnic groups*	• Weighted frequencies of services viewed as not helpful for state as a whole and by major racial and ethnic groups • *Qualitative analysis of intensive interview responses to identify why specific services are seen as not very helpful by different groups*
5.4 Which of the services that low-income families feel they need and/or need more of are considered "family support services" as defined by the service-delivery system? Which are not? *What are the reasons behind any differences?*	• Data elements from 5, 5.1, 5.2, and 5.3	• In-person survey • *Focus groups* • *Intensive interviews (see 5–5.3)*	• Cross-tabulations of specific services families want/ services considered family support, and vice versa • *Qualitative analysis of focus group and intensive interview data to discern reasons underlying differences and discrepancies in views of services*

Question	Indicators	Data Collection Methods	Analysis
6. What are the current barriers to low-income families receiving family support services (e.g., access, transportation, eligibility criteria)? Which are the most important? Why?	• Reported barriers to low-income families receiving services (from service providers, families) • Perceptions of which barriers are most important, *and why* (from service providers, families, key informants)	• Telephone survey of agency personnel • In-person interviews of sample of low-income families • *Focus groups with families* • *Focus groups with interagency personnel*	• Rankings and/or ratings of barriers by agency personnel • Rankings and/or ratings of barriers by families • *Qualitative analysis of focus groups' transcripts to get at perceptions of barriers*
6.1 How, if at all, do these barriers manifest themselves in day-to-day interactions?	• *Observed behavioral barriers*	• *On-site observations of agency interactions*	• *Observational analysis to detect behavioral "signs" of barriers*
6.2 What are the best ways to overcome these barriers?	• *Suggested strategies for overcoming barriers*	• *Focus groups with families, interagency personnel, community leaders, and/or key informant interviews*	• *Qualitative analysis and synthesis of suggested strategies for overcoming barriers and their rationales*

*Italicized phrases indicate questions and methods amenable to qualitative approaches.

in the state that are unavailable to Medicaid recipients and others of limited means. Use of service utilization data alone does not necessarily indicate anything about the relationship between the actual level of need and the observed rate of utilization and therefore may underestimate the influence of poverty or other conditions constraining utilization (Ciarlo, Tweed, Shern, Kirkpatrick, & Sachs-Ericsson, 1992, p. 119). As Harlow (1992) noted, another problem with service utilization statistics is that they do not provide a valid indication of the true level of "felt need" or demand for the service.

This is not to suggest that needs assessment researchers should never make use of service utilization data, only that these or any other secondary data should be critically examined when making inferences about need. One way to guard against being misled by any one type of data is to draw on multiple types of secondary data that can be used to cross-check one another.

As shown in Table 2.1, moving from Research Question 1, which is too broadly framed, to a more precise phrasing as Research Question 2, in terms of levels of variation in need for family support services across the state, entails collecting more and better specified data elements. In addition to the ratio of agencies delivering family support services to the target population in urban, suburban, and rural areas, other needed data elements include: (a) numbers of clients in the target population served per agency and relative to the size of the target population, (b) the service capacity of existing agencies, and (c) rates and patterns of utilization by the low-income target population in urban, suburban, and rural areas.

The previous discussion highlights the dangers of making facile assumptions when selecting data elements for a needs assessment. If it is too difficult or costly to obtain the best possible data to answer each research question, it might be wise either to reduce the number of research questions or concentrate on investigating the need for a few specific types of services, rather than an entire range of services. Another possibility is to accept limitations in some of the data as a strategic trade-off for the larger design. For example, using secondary data on the geographic distribution of agencies might be acceptable if supplemented by detailed primary data collected from a subsample of the larger population. This strategy could yield in-depth information on the need for family support services from a representative subsample that could also be used to test assumptions for estimating need from the agency distribution data.

PRIMARY OR SECONDARY DATA?

Selecting data elements is closely tied to deciding which data sources will be used in the needs assessment, and thus whether to rely on primary data, secondary data, or some combination of the two. *Data sources* supply the needed data elements—data sources might be the U.S. census or a survey of social service providers. Deciding on data sources requires evaluating the conceptual and functional fit between the data elements and analysis plans, as well as the practical feasibility of drawing on different sources for the purposes at hand. Making these judgments requires familiarity with existing secondary data sets as well as the literature on the target population.

In some cases, using secondary data to assess needs is simply out of the question. If the data elements required to answer one or more research questions cannot be obtained from existing secondary data sources, some type of primary data collection is necessary. For example, 9-year-old census data are not helpful in assessing the need for gang prevention services among Southeast Asian Hmong youth who are recent immigrants to a midwestern city.

In other situations, the parameters may be less clear-cut. For example, 7-year-old survey data would be less than ideal as a basis for assessing the need for family support services among low-income families in a state. However, these admittedly somewhat outdated data could still reasonably be employed, with appropriate qualifications, if many of the data elements needed to address the research questions were available in the data set and the state had not experienced major demographic changes in its low-income population during this period. However, if major in-migrations or out-migrations of the target population had occurred during the intervening years, this would more seriously constrain the validity of these data for estimating the current and future needs of the target population.

A variety of analytic considerations should also be weighed when deciding if and how to use secondary data in a needs assessment. In evaluating the viability of employing existing secondary survey data, one important issue concerns how the original sample was drawn. For the data to be usable, the original sample need not have been designed to fit the exact specifications of the current project. Nevertheless, it is important to ascertain whether the original sample includes sufficient data on the specific target population of interest, and how easy it will be to extract these data from the larger data set. It is also vital to know the basis on which the original sample was selected. The goal of the current needs assessment may be to generalize to all low-income families in a state, whereas the original sample may represent the nation as a whole. Under these circumstances, it is critical to determine whether the existing data can be appropriately reweighted to make them amenable to use in the current project. A poorly designed original sample might also argue against using these data at all.

Just as important as the sample is whether the key variables of interest were defined in a manner consistent with the current study's requirements, or can be redefined accordingly. For example, the income categories may not correspond to a proposed definition of low income. The data set may define income in $10,000/year increments, whereas, for present purposes, it is desirable to use a cutoff point in the middle of the range (e.g., $25,000). How easy is it to regroup the data to reflect the desired categorization? Such changes can often be handled quite simply by creating new programming specifications. However, if extensive reworking would be needed to make the data amenable to the needs of the current project, it may be prudent to accept the definitions as given and adjust the research design accordingly. It is easy to neutralize cost savings by spending an inordinate amount of time, money, and effort on making secondary data suitable for current purposes.

In addition to reanalysis of survey data, another type of secondary data analysis frequently employed in needs assessment involves using social indicator data (e.g., percentage of population in poverty, percentage of high school graduates) for a geographic area to characterize the population's overall level of need for specific types of services. Ciarlo et al. (1992) described two basic indirect needs assessment methods often used to estimate service needs from secondary data: (a) social area analysis uses of one or several statistical social indicators (e.g., percentage of the population in poverty, percentage of female-run households) at the area level to characterize the population's overall level of need, and (b) the synthetic estimation model applies individual-level demographic data from previous population surveys (e.g., age- or race-specific rates for certain diseases or mental disorders) to similar subgroups residing in the area for which the need is to be estimated. Then the numbers of cases found in all subgroups are summed to obtain a total figure for the area. Comparing model estimates for subareas of a state with findings from a population-based probability survey of that state, Ciarlo et al. (1992) found that neither model in its original form was very accurate in predicting service needs for alcoholism, drug abuse, and mental health services. However, accuracy improved after adjusting model parameters and more carefully specifying the components or measures of need.

Appropriately applying a social area or synthetic estimation model in any given case requires skill in manipulating data, adjusting models and using various types of computer technology (Basu & Keimig, 1990). Therefore, although potentially useful, a social-indicator or synthetic-estimation method should only be adopted when an analyst with the appropriate skills and experience is available for the project.

Following Table 2.1, using secondary data to answer Research Question 2 might involve combining census data with generalizable findings from a state survey on the numbers, distribution, and service capacities of social service agencies across the state. As a further step, it might also be useful (as shown in column 4 beside Research Question 2) to develop an index of family support service capacity from these data that could be adjusted for rural, suburban, and urban areas in the state.

SUMMARY

Table 2.1 provides a framework for ensuring the conceptual coherence and internal logic of the research design that is used to investigate the needs of the target population. The decision of what information is obtained from which source(s) and, more specifically, whether, when, and how to use secondary data in assessing need hinges on several interrelated considerations, including: (a) the specific data elements needed to answer the research question(s); (b) the amount (and phasing) of money available to conduct the research; (c) the accessibility, adaptability, and accuracy of existing secondary data sources for answering the research questions; and (d) the analytic skills and capabilities of the researcher or research team. The choice involves strategic weighing of all these factors within the specific research context.

Chapters 3 and 4 are designed for readers considering use of quantitative or qualitative primary data collection, whether alone or in combination with secondary data. Chapter 3 discusses the sample survey approach to needs assessment. Chapter 4 addresses the use of qualitative methods and shows how quantitative and qualitative approaches can be appropriately and effectively combined in needs assessment research. Both chapters extend the use of Table 2.1.

3

Taking the Sample Survey Approach

Susan Berkowitz

Searching through existing data sets may reveal that none of the available secondary data sources fail to meet all the data requirements for the needs assessment. Some form of primary data collection is required, either to provide the main source of data for the project or to supplement secondary sources. The issue turns to deciding the type of primary data collection best suited to answering the specific research questions.

The sample survey is almost always the method of choice in quantitative primary data collection for needs assessment. A *sample survey* collects primary data from a probability sample of respondents using a standardized, structured survey instrument. As seen in chapter 1, despite their popularity, sample survey methods have not always been used correctly, or to best advantage, in much needs assessment research. Moreover, just as exclusive reliance on secondary data can be limiting, sample surveys also have their limitations for assessing need. Harlow (1992) noted the dangers of simplistically assuming people can just be asked what they need and then are able to say. People's perceptions of their own and others' needs are necessarily influenced by sociohistorical context, as well as their roles and power in society. Service providers' views of their clients' needs may be filtered through professional ideologies with unrecognized "blind spots" (Ong, Humphris, Annett, & Rifkin, 1991; Solomon & Evans, 1992; Sung, 1992). Similarly, target populations may lack the tools to recognize and name their own needs (McLain,1992). Consequently, in designing survey instruments and analyzing the findings, it is essential to recognize that all perceptions of need have a subjective element.

This chapter

- provides a framework for deciding whether it is advisable and feasible to use survey methods in any given needs assessment project;
- discusses probability sampling for surveys;
- evaluates when to use mail, telephone, and in-person modes of survey administration;
- provides guidelines to follow and procedures to use in designing mail, telephone, and in-person survey instruments; and
- considers appropriate techniques for analyzing the data and presenting the results.

CHOOSING THE SAMPLE SURVEY APPROACH

To return to Table 2.1, suppose available secondary data are too sparse to allow a satisfactory answer to Research Questions 3, 3.1, 3.2, and 3.3 on utilization of family support services by low-income families in rural, suburban, and urban areas of the state. The questions as phrased suggest that the findings should statistically represent the state as a whole to serve as a basis for estimating family support service needs of the target population statewide. Given this, the most viable approach would be to conduct a survey of a probability sample of agencies within the state to collect information on the number and types of agencies that deliver these services, the specific services they deliver, and the numbers and characteristics of low-income clients served.

The respondents for the survey might be representatives of county public child welfare agencies, administrators of community-based organizations involved in delivering family support services, or some combination of the two. This would largely depend on how family support services are delivered in the state. In some counties, these services might be contracted out to private groups or agencies; in others, they might be delivered directly by county social workers. Therefore, before determining who the respondents should be, something should be known about the configurations of service delivery in the state. This information is also useful for designing the probability sample drawn to generalize to all family support agencies in the state.

DESIGNING A PROBABILITY SAMPLE FOR A SURVEY

Poor sample design is the single biggest methodological flaw in past needs assessment research (Harlow & Turner, 1993; Lareau, 1983; Robins, 1982). At least as much careful thought should be devoted to designing the sample as to developing the other components of the research design. A well-designed, efficient sample enables properly addressing the research questions, and provides the necessary support for drawing appropriate conclusions from the results. A poorly designed or haphazard sample can undermine the research.

Sampling is a way to examine a smaller set of items to learn something about the larger class from which the set is drawn. In social science research, sampling is used to look at a subset of individuals (residents of a state), organizations (local health departments), or events (high school football games) within a larger population of the same class or category. Sampling recognizes that it usually is not feasible to examine all persons, organizations, or events in that class. It would be expensive and overwhelmingly difficult to contact every adult resident of a certain state, or every local health department in the United States. When the study population is small enough, a census, or survey of all the individuals or elements in that population, may be all that is required. If hired to carry out a needs assessment of the elderly residents of a 50-bed nursing home, taking a census would probably be the most sensible approach. The type of sample most commonly used in survey research and most social science is a *probability sample.* A probability sample is one in which every element of the population has a known, nonzero chance of being selected (Williamson, Karp, & Dalphin, 1977). Utilizing any type of probability sample enables generalization, within a certain margin of error, from the sample to the larger population from which it was drawn. Selecting a probability sample of social service agencies and/or community-based organizations delivering family support services in a state allows one to make statements about all such agencies in the state without having to actually survey all of them.

Drawing a probability sample requires having reasonably accurate information on the dimensions and boundaries of the populations to be sampled. It depends on obtaining or building comprehensive lists of all the units in the universe to serve as the sampling frame. In the previous example, one would need to develop a list of all social service agencies and community-based organizations delivering family support services in the state. The accuracy and completeness of the sampling frame(s) define the boundaries of the population from which all the sampled elements are taken. Consequently, a systematic flaw in the frame—such as nonrandom exclusion of certain groups—will affect the sample, and thus weaken any analyses based on the sample. For example, using the telephone directory as the sampling frame for a community in which virtually all of the migrant workers lack a phone could seriously bias the sample.

Developing the sampling frame can be relatively straightforward or extremely challenging, depending on the nature of the research questions, characteristics of the target population(s), and required level of precision of the answers. To determine the health care needs of all adults in a relatively affluent county, it would be reasonable to construct a sampling frame from telephone directories, voter registration lists, or a combination of the two. However, building a frame can be far more demanding when all or part of the target population is difficult to delimit, or when existing lists might systematically exclude an important part of the target population.

There are several types of probability samples that might be used in a needs assessment. The most common is a *simple random sample,* in which each element in the population has an equal chance of being included in the sample (Williamson et al., 1977). Every element in the population is numbered, and a table of random numbers is used to select elements corresponding to the numbers in the table until the desired total is reached. A systematic sample is a variant on the simple random sample, in which a random starting point is selected on the list and every "nth" (i.e., every 10th) name or unit is chosen from then on.

Depending on the research questions, other types of probability samples might be used. These might include a *stratified random sample,* in which the population is divided into two or more strata and a simple random or systematic sample is then drawn from each stratum (Williamson et al., 1977). The advantage of stratifying is that selecting strata that are internally homogeneous, but different from one another in relation to the dimension in question, increases the precision of the results. The decision of which variables to use as stratifiers should be informed by differences in the target population that may bear on the results. For example, Research Question 4.2 in Table 2.1 addresses family support service needs in urban, rural, and suburban areas in a state. To obtain the most precise results for each type of area, three sample strata might be created corresponding to this distinction.

Stratifying can be done proportionately, by selecting each element in the stratum in proportion to its percentage in the total population, or disproportionately, by choosing elements on the basis of some other proportion. Disproportionate sampling is used to ensure enough elements in each stratum to support the desired types of statistical analyses. For example, oversampling African Americans may be necessary to ensure enough African-American families in the sample to be able to generalize to all such families in the state.

Cluster sampling is another multistage type of probability sampling, often employed when it is difficult to construct an adequate sampling frame for all elements in the population at the outset. In the first stage, sampling is done from groups of elements or clusters, such as regions or counties. In subsequent stages, a simple random, systematic, or stratified random sample is drawn from each of the clusters. If there were no adequate statewide list of all agencies delivering family support services, a complete list of all counties in the state could be obtained, from which a stratified random sample of counties could then be chosen. Each of the sampled counties could, in turn, provide the information to create lists of all the family support agencies and organizations in their counties. These lists would then serve as the sampling frame of agencies.

SELECTING THE MODE OF SURVEY DATA COLLECTION

Suppose family support agency personnel will be surveyed about the services they provide to their low-income clients with young children. Should the survey be conducted by mail, telephone, or in person? The choice depends on the amount of money available to spend, as well as what types of information are needed, from whom, and in what level of detail.

Mail surveys—the most basic of the three types of surveys—are best suited to collecting relatively straightforward, factual information, as well as specific counts or numbers (e.g, of clients served) or detailed budgetary data. As long as the instrument is short and to the point, conducting mail surveys is a viable and economical choice for surveying family support agency personnel in a state. Although they are the least expensive means of obtaining data, mail surveys usually require one or more rounds of remailings, postcard or telephone reminders, or follow-up telephone interviews to obtain satisfactory response rates. One tactic commonly used to compensate for expected high nonresponse is to draw a sample considerably larger than the total number of responses actually needed.

If the survey instrument begins to seriously probe attitudes, requires that the respondent make professional judgments, or seeks relatively detailed information on service availability and service gaps, a telephone survey would probably be a better choice than a mail survey. As shown in the transition from

Research Question 2 to Research Question 3 in Table 2.1, once the research questions delve into areas of perceived needs of different groups and ask respondents to make professional judgments about the adequacy of existing services, it makes sense to move from a mail to a telephone survey. Compared with mail surveys, telephone surveys introduce an element of human communication that allows for clarification of questions and response patterns, thus reducing the likelihood that the respondent will misconstrue questions. Also, agency personnel, who are usually very busy, may prefer to spend 45 minutes talking to an interviewer, rather than filling out a form.

Because they add the expenses of interviewer time and training, as well as charges for telephone time as compared with postage costs, telephone surveys are usually more expensive to field than mail surveys. However, telephone interviews generally yield higher response rates and better quality answers, which can partially offset the additional follow-up costs associated with mail surveys. Although response rates are rarely as high for mail surveys as they are for telephone surveys across all respondent groups, in general, mail surveys work better with social service and health care agency personnel, teachers, principals, and others accustomed to routinely filling out and returning forms. Obviously, mail surveys should be avoided if any significant portion of respondents is likely to have problems reading and understanding the questions or filling out the survey form.

Another option would be to survey a sample of respondents in person, using trained interviewers who would administer the instrument face to face. Given the increased costs of in-person versus telephone administration, unless it is relevant to explore agency personnel's views on the service delivery system in considerable depth, it would not make sense to use an in-person mode with this respondent group. However, knowing the target population's perspective on its unmet needs for family support services may be extremely important. The major research question, as shown in Table 2.1, Question 5, may be: What types of services do the low-income families with young children in this state believe they most need to maintain and strengthen their families? In theory, there is no reason why these interviews could not be conducted over the telephone. However, telephone interviews may not be the best choice, depending on: (a) who the respondents are, (b) the length of the survey, and (c) the types and depth of questions to be asked.

In general, the more different the respondents from the middle-class mainstream, the longer and more complicated the questionnaire, and the more personal and potentially sensitive the questions, the better suited the situation is to in-person interviewing. Suppose an estimated 20% of the low-income target families in a state have no telephones in their homes. Add to this that many of those who do will be uncomfortable speaking on the telephone with strangers about family needs. In this situation, in-person interviews might be the best way to administer the survey to the target population.

The primary value of conducting in-person surveys is that they enable direct examination of the target population's perceptions of their unmet needs for different services. The overarching research question (Research Question 5, Table 2.1) is phrased to allow for the possibility that the target population might view services other than those "officially" defined as family support services as helping strengthen their families. It does not ask which family support services the target population believes they need, but which services they believe they need to best maintain and strengthen their families. Respondents might consider safer housing in a better neighborhood the most helpful service they could get, yet this would not be defined as a family support service by the service delivery system.

As suggested by the research questions shown below Question 5 in Table 2.1, in-person surveys might approach the target population's unmet service needs in various ways. One way, illustrated in Question 5.1, would be to ask low-income respondents in the state if they believe that receiving more of any of their current services would help them maintain and strengthen their families. Other ways to approach the question are shown in Questions 5.2 and 5.3, which ask respondents about services not currently received that would be potentially helpful, as well as services currently received that respondents do not consider helpful. Question 5.4 directly addresses the degree and areas of overlap or discrepancy between what families say they need and what the current service delivery system defines as family support services. This would be valuable information for policymakers and program planners because it might highlight critical divergences between the system's and the clients' views of different services, which could be used in redesigning services and policies and in developing more "client-friendly" practices.

Despite the many benefits of an in-person approach, it should not be forgotten that successfully carrying out an in-person survey of this target population would be quite challenging and costly. Especially in states with racially and ethnically diverse populations, conducting in-person interviews with an appropriate sample of all low-income families would be no simple matter. Designing and drawing the sample would require care and technical precision. The instrument would need to be (a) developed with skill and cultural sensitivity, (b) translated into several languages, (c) pretested on a range of potential respondents, and (d) administered by well-trained bilingual interviewers. A decision to proceed with this type of interviewing should be based on a careful assessment of the costs and benefits and a realistic appraisal of the tasks and resources that will be needed.

OBTAINING MULTIPLE PERSPECTIVES ON NEED

As shown earlier, several subsidiary research questions can be developed from a single overarching research question, each representing a somewhat distinctive way of getting at answers to the main question. This strengthens the overall design by providing several different, yet overlapping, lines of approach. Similarly, because there is never just one "true" perspective on service needs, an optimal needs assessment should also examine need from more than one relevant group's perspective. Posing the same questions to different groups of survey respondents can reveal interesting similarities as well as telling differences in perceptions of needed services. For example, researchers have found that service providers tend to say their clients need more of the specialized services they provide, whereas the clients often report a need for less specialized services that cut across conventional agency boundaries (Solomon & Evans, 1992; Sung, 1992). Asking only one or the other group what is needed might result in a skewed picture.

Various design strategies can be used to obtain perspectives from different groups. One approach is to survey samples of two or more respondent groups and ask them the same basic question(s) on needs. Following Research Question 6 in Table 2.1, to compare service recipients' and service providers' perceptions of barriers to delivery of family support services to the target population, one possibility would be to conduct a telephone survey of a sample of agency personnel and an in-person survey of a sample of low-income families. The analysis of these data could focus on across-group, as well as within-group, similarities and differences, thus yielding a richer answer concerning perceived barriers to service delivery than could be provided by focusing on one group alone.

Survey Instrument Design

Now that all four columns of the master matrix have been completed, it is time for the critically important step of designing the survey instrument(s). Sampling considerations aside, a sample survey can only be as good as the instrument used to obtain the data. This section first presents general procedures to follow and considerations to keep in mind in developing instruments for any type of needs assessment survey. It then offers guidance specifically tailored to designing mail, telephone, and in-person survey instruments.

GENERAL STEPS TO FOLLOW IN QUESTIONNAIRE DESIGN

The master matrix contains a list of all the important data elements that need to be included in each instrument being developed. For example, as shown in the table, in designing a mail survey instrument to address Research Questions 3, 3.1, and 3.3, column 2 indicates which data elements should be collected in the mail survey. The same holds for the data elements that should be included in the telephone survey of agency personnel, which will address Research Questions 4.1–4.4 concerning patterns of need for family support services across the state. For each instrument, the matrix should be used to cross-walk the research questions in column 1 to the corresponding data elements in column 2. The list should then be reviewed to identify any missing data items.

The next step is to outline a meaningful and effective order for different topical categories of questions in the instrument, and to arrange the corresponding data elements under each major category. The order of topics can differ from one type of instrument to another, but should follow a logical progression that builds as much as possible on the questions that came before.

For example, asking respondents about their satisfaction with program services before ascertaining which services they receive would make little sense.

If the master matrix is the guiding framework, it might seem reasonable to follow the exact order of data elements as they appear in the research questions. Although logical, this might not be the best order in which to present topics to respondents. An order that feels unnatural or requires ranging across different topics will frustrate and tire respondents, and will probably lower the response rate. For telephone and in-person instruments, a useful model might be to parallel the pattern of a normal conversation on the same set of topics.

After the basic order of the topics has been decided, it is time to construct the specific questions or items that will be asked of the respondents. No matter what kind of survey instrument is being developed, unless the project can afford the time and expense of breaking new ground, there is little point in starting from scratch. It is a good idea to contact other researchers who have designed similar types of instruments and consider adapting their questions to the study's requirements. However, before using items from an existing instrument, it is important to ascertain how well the questions worked, and to solicit suggestions on how they could be improved.

Reliability and Validity

Reliability and validity are two central concerns in survey construction. A data collection instrument is reliable when using it will produce the same result when applied to the same object, regardless of when it is applied (instrument reliability) or who applies it (rater reliability). *Reliability* is essentially a matter of consistency. In constructing reliable instruments, it is important to ensure that questions are clear, explicit, and not subject to interpretations that might vary from one instance to another. When questions or items are ambiguous, cases that are actually identical can produce different answer patterns. To achieve high instrument reliability, it is important to avoid depending on respondents' inherent understanding of terms that may vary widely in meaning. Explicit definitions of terms, with concrete referents, should be used wherever possible. Another way to ensure reliability is to use already tested and proven question modules from existing instruments.

Validity refers to the degree to which the instrument successfully measures what it intends to measure. *Content* or *face validity* refers to whether a question or measure appears, "on the face of it," to correspond well to the concept being examined. An instrument can be reliable without being valid, in that it can reliably measure something it is not trying to measure. For example, the questions may be intended to measure family-centeredness when they are really measuring something else.

Although validity is at least as important as reliability, it is unfortunately more difficult to test. In developing questions for an index of family-centeredness of service delivery personnel, it would be important to know if the index is a valid measure of family-centeredness. One test is to ask whether the questions constituting the index cover all relevant dimensions of family-centeredness. Other useful ways to assess validity include: (a) making sure the questions include variables known to be direct measures of the concept or areas being examined, (b) observing whether the questions effectively elicit responses or are confusing to respondents, and (c) seeing if answers are spread over an expected broad response pattern or pile up in only one category. Validity, like reliability, is enhanced by using existing questions that have already been validated in some fashion.

Constructing Questions

Before constructing specific items for the survey, the topical outline and associated data elements should be examined, and specific items from other instruments should be inserted in their appropriate places in the outline. This procedure indicates which data elements still need to be addressed, in whole or in part, to make the instrument complete.

Next, the particular data elements need to be translated into the specific questions to be asked of the respondent. There is rarely a simple, one-to-one relationship between data elements and survey questions. Sometimes a series of questions needs to be asked to obtain the full range of information required. Other times, indirect ways of getting at the needed data elements have to be devised. For example, a whole set of questions may be needed to serve as an index of attitudes toward family-centeredness.

The survey should contain mostly, if not entirely, *close-ended* (or fixed response) questions, or questions that provide the respondent with a fixed set of answers from which to choose. In general, the multiple-choice response categories in close-ended questions should be exhaustive of all the possible choices (e.g., should encompass the full range of possible answers) and mutually exclusive so that the answer fits in only one response category.

In designing basic questions about age, income, or education level, respondents (or interviewers) might be asked to check a box corresponding to their level of education or annual income. In asking about education level, the response categories should encompass the spectrum from grade school dropouts to persons holding several doctorates. How and how finely response categories are defined depends on: (a) the characteristics of the respondent population; (b) how much information is desired and will be used; (c) what the meaningful gradations of response might be, based on theory and the existing literature; and (d) the data needed to perform specific analyses. If all that matters is whether the respondent is at least a high school graduate, a simple "yes–no" question will suffice. If more information is desired, more refined categories are required, such as: not a high school graduate, a high school graduate, some college, a bachelor's degree, a master's degree, or a doctorate or other professional degree beyond the master's level. To perform analyses requiring certain levels of data, questions might instead be asked in terms of the total number of years of education completed, rather than the level of degree(s) attained.

If the stated choices do not represent the full range of possible responses, an "Other (specify)" category can be included. For example, to provide for anomalous or unexpected responses, family support agency personnel might be asked:

What type of agency do you work for? Please check one.

_____ Public/governmental
_____ Private, nonprofit
_____ Private, for-profit
_____ Other (specify)

However, before designing a close-ended question, the likely range of answers should be reasonably well known. The "Other (specify)" category should not be an excuse for poorly thought out response categories.

There are various types of close-ended questions. One type asks respondents to indicate their reaction to a certain idea or viewpoint along a given scale. An example would be:

Please indicate, by checking the appropriate box, the extent to which you agree or disagree with the following statement: "Professionals are in the best position to decide what is best for families."

_____ Strongly agree
_____ Agree somewhat
_____ Neither agree nor disagree
_____ Disagree somewhat
_____ Strongly disagree
_____ Don't know

A "Don't know" category should be included because a respondent might have no opinion on the subject, which is not the same as neither agreeing nor disagreeing. Other types of close-ended questions include (but are not limited to): (a) questions that require "yes–no" or "true–false" responses; (b) questions that ask for a ranking of the relative priority of a set of items ("Please rank the following problems presented by low-income families in relative order of how often they occur, from *most frequent* [1] to *least frequent* [5]"); and (c) questions that ask for a rating of the relative importance of a set of items ("Please rate the following in terms of their importance as barriers to receipt of family support services, on a scale from *very important* [1] to *very unimportant* [5]").

There is no absolute rule on the mix of types of questions to include in a survey instrument. The mix is determined by the fit between the data elements being addressed and the types of questions that best fulfill that function. In general, within a given section of the instrument, the simpler types of questions should come first. Respondents can also become confused if too many types of questions are quickly alternated.

Instructions and Skip Patterns

Once the basic organization of the data collection instrument and questions for each section have been designed, instructions should be developed for completing each survey section and each question. Depending on the type of instrument, these may be instructions to the respondent or the interviewer, including directions for skipping questions or sections of the instrument(s) that are inapplicable to a particular type of case. These skip patterns are important for streamlining the delivery of the instrument and minimizing repetition, and should be carefully reviewed for accuracy and completeness.

Designing a Mail Survey

To return to Table 2.1, suppose the task at hand is to design a mail survey to be sent to a stratified random sample of family support agency personnel in a state. Unlike telephone or in-person instruments, a mail survey cannot rely on verbal persuasion. The respondent's incentive to accurately answer and complete the survey has to be built into the questionnaire. The challenge is to achieve a high response rate by making replying as painless as possible for the respondent(s) while still obtaining the needed information.

This survey is meant to address Research Questions 3, 3.1, 3.2, and 3.3 concerning service utilization by low-income families in the state. Looking at column 2 shows that the needed data elements are almost all quantitative, and will require creating percentages of client families in different categories. The survey might begin with a brief series of background questions on the respondent's agency (e.g., whether it is public, private nonprofit, church-associated; how long it has existed; its central mission) and its role in the service delivery system.

The second section might request data on the types of family support services provided by the respondent agency, and the numbers of all families, and low-income families, currently being served in each of the relevant categories of service. These questions could be presented as a matrix to be completed, with the different categories of services arranged in rows down the left-hand side (including several "Other, specify" categories to allow respondents to indicate additional types of services), and appropriately labeled boxes beside each service category in which the respondent can write in the requested number(s) of families.

When requesting numeric data, to minimize the potential for confusion and thus inaccuracy, the instructions for the question should precisely indicate which pieces of information are desired. A numeric response can be uninterpretable or even misleading in the absence of information on exactly how it was generated and what it means. Requests for the numbers of families and low-income families served in each service category should specify whether the number sought is the number of families served as of a given point in time, the total number served over a defined period (such as a year), or the number of new client families who came into each category of service over a given period. Whether the data are being reported by calendar, federal fiscal, or state fiscal year should also be noted.

Another issue that frequently arises in collecting client data is whether client counts are duplicated or unduplicated. If the counts are duplicated, the same family or individual could be counted once or more in every category of service they receive, and possibly every time they receive the service. Although researchers usually prefer cleaner, unduplicated counts, many service delivery agencies do not keep records in a way that allows them to easily unduplicate. In addition, it may be important to clarify how the agency defines a *case*. Is a case a parent and child unit, an adult individual, or a child? Widely varying definitions of a case could create large divergences in numbers reported by different agencies, which might not reflect actual differences in the numbers of persons served.

Given the many ways that data reporting can vary within and across agencies, the respondents should be asked to provide the necessary qualifications to explain their numbers. One way to do this is to create a checklist built into each question, where the respondent can circle whether the counts are duplicated or unduplicated, represent all cases or only new cases, are for calendar year 1994 or federal fiscal year 1994, and so on. This saves having to track down this information later, before coding and entering the data in the computer.

In any type of survey, but especially in mail surveys, respondents can be asked to provide estimates rather than exact numbers when a more approximate answer will suffice. The data elements for answering Research Question 3.3 include estimated percentages of low-income families on agency waiting lists. If ranges of low-income families on waiting lists (e.g., 25% vs. 50%) are all that are needed, relatively little is lost by asking for a well-informed estimate. Selectively relieving respondent burden in this way may help to enlist the cooperation necessary to ensure that the entire survey is completed.

Designing Telephone Surveys

Telephone surveys are intermediate between mail surveys and in-person instruments in their level of intensity and depth, as well as in the type and degree of human contact involved. In Table 2.1, the plan is to use a telephone survey to address Research Questions 4, 4.1., 4.2, 4.3, and 4.4, which have to do with variations in patterns of need for family support services by areas of the state, types of families, and racial and ethnic groups. This set of research questions focuses exclusively on perceptions of patterns of need. More objective data could also be obtained at a small additional cost by sending the respondents a mail supplement requesting numbers of clients, as previously described for the mail survey.

A telephone instrument should ideally take about 45 minutes to administer (certainly not more than 1 hour). Looking at the data elements that should be included, the following topical outline could be constructed:

- Survey cover sheet, including respondent's name, position, agency, address, and phone number.

- Section 1—Agency Organization and Mission: questions on the respondent agency's mission, organization, functions in delivery of family support services, and relationship to other family support agencies in the community.
- Section 2—Definitions of Services: how the agency defines *family support*; services/restrictions on those definitions; specific family support services provided by the agency; any new types of family support services being planned and impetus for this; sources of referrals and types of referrals made to other agencies; eligibility criteria for service provision; waiting list policies and procedures.
- Section 3—Characteristics of Client Families: characteristics of client families with young children, income categories, family structures, racial and ethnic composition, presenting problems; perceived level of severity of problems; relevant variations across low-income family groups.
- Section 4—Limitations on Availability of Services: availability of a range of services, limitations on availability of these services, and reasons for these limitations; which services of limited availability are most needed, in which area(s), and by which specific target population groups; needed services not currently available, reasons why no such service(s) exist, and any plans to do so in future; agency staffing and other factors limiting capacity to provide needed services.
- Section 5—Highest Need Families: types of low-income client families presenting special challenges and why (including family structure and race and ethnicity); availability of suitable services for these families, and limitations on suitability; current efforts or plans to address these specific needs; new presenting problems in recent years and expected trends in near future.

In telephone surveys, the relationship between needed data elements and survey questions is often less direct than in mail surveys because formulating questions on perceptions of need may require a subtler approach to item construction. For example, in section 4, rather than directly asking agency personnel which types of services are most needed by low-income families with young children, the question could be asked in a matrix format, on a service-by-service basis, as follows: type of service, whether the service is available in the agency's service area, how geographically widespread it is (e.g., only in more urban areas), limitations on availability (e.g., only in English or to certain categories of parents), and reasons for its unavailability (legal or policy barriers, limited resources). Although the data obtained from this question are still based on the respondent's perceptions, posing the question in this manner asks the respondent to make a comprehensive review of service availability, rather than immediately leap into opinions on which services are most needed. Constructing the question in this way helps to guard against the respondent's tendency to answer in terms of what first springs to mind, rather than providing a more balanced assessment of the larger service picture.

Asking questions about unmet needs and needed categories of services in several different ways will allow for determining whether there is a convergence of responses across questions. For example, if responses indicate the existence of linguistic limitations on availability of parenting education services, and these same services are also noted as presenting a special challenge to serving non-English speaking families, this would strengthen the basis for claiming that parenting education services for non-English speaking families are an important area of unmet or partially met need.

A well-designed telephone survey should be like a well-structured conversation, with a clear beginning, middle, and end. One advantage of telephone surveys over mail surveys is that some of the burden of answering can be shifted from the respondent to the interviewer, which means that in developing the instrument close attention should be paid to carefully specifying interviewer instructions and skip patterns. These are actually "the glue" that holds the telephone instrument together.

Designing In-Person Surveys

In-person surveys are probably the most challenging type of survey to design and administer. In-person survey instruments should not be confused with intensive interview guides—a type of qualitative instrument used in face-to-face interviewing that is discussed in chapter 4 on qualitative methods. In-person survey instruments: (a) have a clearly defined structure and a fixed, invariant order and phrasing of questions; (b) are composed of mostly close-ended questions, although there may be a mixture of close- and open-ended items; (c) aim for standardization in both the construction of the questions and how the instrument is delivered to minimize all possible sources of variation; and (d) are administered by interviewers carefully trained in procedures for standard delivery who are not allowed to deviate from a prepared script.

Research Questions 5, 5.1, 5.2, 5.3, and 5.4 in Table 2.1 have to do with the types of family support services that low-income families in the state believe they most need to maintain and strengthen their families. These questions are to be addressed by an in-person survey instrument administered to a population-based stratified random sample of low-income families throughout the state. One of the largest design challenges is to move from the rather abstract research questions and data elements to the actual framing and phrasing of individual questions that are meaningful and understandable to the respondents.

Although service providers understand and speak the language of service delivery, many respondents in the target population will not. It will be important to find appropriate and effective ways to address the concept of "services" in terms that are readily understandable to a low-income population. Other surveys that have successfully translated professional service nomenclature to lay terms for the target population should be used as models, even if their exact subject matter was somewhat different. It would also be a good idea to obtain feedback on survey questions from stakeholders and experts knowledgeable about specific target population groups, especially racial and ethnic minority populations.

One approach to a question about services might be as follows:

Here are some things that might be done to help families with small children keep their families strong. Are you and your family getting any of these types of help right now?

_____ Help finding better housing or a better neighborhood in which to live?

_____ Help with obtaining information on how to get medical care for your child?

_____ Help with learning how to be a better parent?

_____ Help with getting information about things you can do to make sure your child is healthy?

_____ Help with finding child care?

_____ A place you could bring your child for a few hours to give you some time to yourself?

_____ A place you and your child could go to play together and be with other parents and children of the same age?

The question is phrased simply, and relevant categories of family support services are described in easily understandable terms. Defining services as "things that can be done to help families" reduces the potential for misinterpretation and may also reduce negative connotations associated with the word services. The question pattern could then be further developed by asking, for each type of service, "If you are not now getting this kind of help for you and your family, would you like to receive it?" Or, for those who are getting the help, subsequent question sequences could ask how valuable the respondents find this kind of help in keeping their families strong, and whether they would like to receive more of it. The question pattern follows a logical sequence easily accommodated through skip patterns based on whether the respondent is, or is not, receiving the particular type of help. In exploring varied aspects of service receipt and perceptions of services, this sequence also addresses several different research questions at once, which makes for a shorter, more efficient instrument.

Pretesting, important in all three types of sample surveys, is essential for an in-person instrument. During instrument development, applied researchers are usually accountable to a range of stakeholders and simultaneously balancing a variety of substantive and technical considerations. Ultimately, the real question is whether the instrument will work for the target population. Therefore, after completing the survey instrument, it is essential to perform a pretest. *Pretesting* involves administering the instrument to a small number of persons as similar as possible to the proposed respondents, using exactly the same procedures that are used in the full study. Although it may not uncover every minor flaw, pretesting almost certainly detects major problems in structure, pacing, and question wording. At the very least, it helps fine tune the instrument for smoother delivery.

ANALYSIS OF SURVEY DATA

Careful, thoughtful analysis of data from needs assessment surveys is essential for informing program and policy development. The serious work of data analysis begins once the data are collected, coded, cleaned, and entered into the computer. It is important to be selective and strategic in deciding which statistics to present in a report or other presentation. Analyses should be chosen on the basis of their ability to inform the research questions. The audience should not be overwhelmed with a mass of unprocessed numbers or frequency distributions. Statistics are used to organize the large quantities of numeric data collected in a sample survey into comprehensible order. Statistics provide tools for summarizing, describing, examining, and explaining the survey findings about needs. Descriptive statistics summarize and describe the data in a variety of useful, succinct ways, but make no claim to be able to explain what was found. Explanatory statistics provide tools for establishing and examining causal relationships in the data. Because most analyses of needs assessment survey data are descriptive, this brief section covers a few basic descriptive statistical measures. The supplemental suggested reading list found at the end of this book cites a number of sources that can be consulted by those interested in performing more advanced statistical analyses, including causal analysis.

Several types of descriptive statistics may be useful in summarizing needs assessment survey data. The decision of which to use, and in what combination, depends on the data as well as the research questions being addressed.

Frequency distributions are rankings that give information on how the data are distributed in frequency of occurrence, by listing categories of data and their corresponding frequencies. To use an example from Table 2.1, data from the telephone survey of agency personnel might give different counts for different types of services the respondents considered most needed by the target population. Suppose that, of 509 service providers, 236 responded that the service their clients most need is respite programs, 144 answered drop-in centers, and 129 in-home parenting programs. This information could be presented more concisely and understandably in a table, as follows:

Service Most Needed	Respondents
Respite	46.4% (236)
Drop-in centers	28.3% (144)
In-home parenting	25.3% (129)
TOTAL	100% (509)

A bar histogram could also be constructed showing types of needed services (or scores on any measure) along the horizontal axis and their corresponding frequencies (the number of respondents selecting this category) on the vertical axis. Frequencies are the basis for developing ratios, percentages, and proportions, all of which are useful ways to summarize and compare findings.

Measures of central tendency are statistics that provide a single value typical of the data as a whole. The mode is the single score that occurs most often in a set of scores. As the only measure of central tendency appropriate for data that cannot be ranked or measured quantitatively, the mode might be used to describe the modal or most reported category of service needed (i.e., parenting education) or the most commonly reported barrier to service utilization (e.g., eligibility criteria).

The median is the middle value of a set of incrementally ranked scores. For example, if respondents reported their number of years of education as 9, 11, 13, 15, and 17, the median would be 13. The mean is a single value representing a set of data obtained by adding all the values and dividing by the number of values added. In this example, the mean number of years of education would also be 13 (65/5). The median and mean happen to be the same in this instance, but this is not often the case. The mean is generally preferred over the mode because it is more stable, or less subject to being influenced by extreme outlying values. The mean is also used more often in more advanced types of statistical analyses. Another example would be the average or mean number of visits all clients make to their family support service workers in a given year.

Measures of dispersion indicate the degree of variation in a set of values or responses. The range is the difference between the highest and lowest score in a set of values. Because it depends only on the highest and lowest score, it is not a particularly good overall representation of the variation in the data, but may be reported to give a quick sense of the spread of a particular measure (e.g., "respondents ranged in age from 14 to 84").

The standard deviation—a measure of how scores vary around the mean in units of the original data—is a better overall measure of dispersion than the range. If urban dwellers with disabilities report needing help with three to five activities of daily living (ADLs) and rural dwellers report need for assistance with two to eight activities, both groups would require assistance with an average of four activities. However, the two populations are clearly different in that the degree of variation is greater among those living in rural areas. Whereas the mean fails to capture this, the standard deviation would provide a measure of this difference in variability. To effectively plan services, it might be important for agency personnel to know both the mean number of ADL limitations and the degree of variation in ADL limitations in the target populations. The formula for calculating the standard deviation can be found in any basic statistics text, including several referenced in the recommended supplemental reading list.

Analyzing Data Based on a Probability Sample

If survey data are drawn from a probability sample of respondents, use of descriptive statistics alone will tell about the characteristics of the sample, but will not indicate the extent to which this description also applies to the larger population from which the sample was drawn. Inferential statistics allow for making inferences about the characteristics of the whole population based on data from a probability sample of that population. Inferential statistics provide the underpinnings of the ability to generalize to the larger population—one of the cornerstones of the sample survey method. With a large enough sample, the shape of the frequency distribution of responses should resemble a bell with more scores in the center and fewer on either end. This normal curve is the basis for much of statistical inference in probability sampling.

Several issues should be addressed in inferring population characteristics from sample data. All data drawn from samples of a larger population are subject to some degree of sampling error as a result of the sampling process. If the same survey had been administered to a different sample from the same population, the responses would not have been identical. Had another random sample been drawn of service providers in a state, their answers to questions about needed services would not have been exactly the same as those obtained. Sampling error depends on both sample size and heterogeneity in the population being sampled; the larger and more homogeneous the sample, the lower the sampling error.

The standard error measures the variability due to sampling when estimating a statistic from a sample. It indicates the amount of variability in the population of possible estimates of a parameter for a given sample size, and is thus a measure of the results' precision. Standard errors can be used to figure a confidence interval around the sample values. If all possible samples were surveyed under similar conditions, intervals of 1.96 standard errors below to 1.96 standard errors above a particular statistic would include the true population parameter being estimated in about 95% of the samples. This is the 95% confidence interval often reported with sample survey data to indicate the extent to which sample findings reflect the characteristics of the larger population. For example, a 95% confidence interval could be figured for the percentage of service providers in the sample who reported in-home parenting training as the service most needed by their clients. If 26.4% of 509 respondents gave this response, assuming a purely hypothetical standard error of 4, the confidence interval would be 18.6%–34.2%, meaning that, in 95% of the samples, this range would reflect the true percentage of respondents giving this as the most needed service. Many statistical programs compute standard errors, from which confidence intervals are easily calculated. The formula for figuring standard errors is available in any basic statistics text.

Another consideration that may arise in analyzing sample survey data is that the data may need to be reweighted to reflect how the sample was drawn. The sampling section described the possible need to oversample a particular group to guarantee enough cases in a certain stratum. If disproportionate sampling was employed, data from the different sample strata must now be reweighted to correct for different probabilities of selection into the sample (Bailey, 1994). Failure to do this produces inaccurate findings.

Nonresponse bias resulting from any systematic differences between those who did and did not respond to the survey is another issue that may arise in analyzing and reporting sample survey data. Nonresponse bias is a particular problem in surveys with low response rates. One way to anticipate this problem is to draw a larger sample than needed. After the sample has been drawn, another way to handle the issue is to compare characteristics of a small sample of respondents with those of a small sample of nonrespondents as a way to determine the likely kind and direction of bias. When this is impossible, it is important to qualify findings accordingly.

Another kind of response bias that could lead to overestimating the target population's awareness of services occurs when respondents report knowledge of nonexistent agencies. One suggested remedy is to embed one or more fictitious agencies in a list of real agencies, and then either eliminate the scores of those who gave these answers or correct them based on the scores of the other respondents (Calsyn & Klinkenberg, 1995).

The larger point behind this discussion of inferential statistics is that properly analyzing survey data drawn from a probability sample requires knowledge of how to accommodate sampling error, as well as how to appropriately adjust for disproportionate sampling and cope with different kinds of nonresponse bias and other issues that may arise in inferring from sample statistics to the larger population. This is critically important because the power of the survey sample approach rests, in large part, on its ability to support this kind of statistical generalization.

SUMMARY

The sample survey is the most frequently used method in needs assessment research. However, it has not always been applied correctly. Sample surveys are most appropriately employed when there is a need or desire to generalize estimates of need to a larger population. The sample survey approach requires (a) effective and accurate use of probability sampling; (b) development and use of reliable, valid and effective survey instruments; (c) standardized efficient means of administration of the survey, whether by mail, telephone or in person; (d) measures to ensure an acceptable response rate; and (e) use of thoughtful and technically correct techniques of analyzing the data. When these requirements are met and can be supported by available resources and expertise, the sample survey is a powerful tool for documenting and accurately estimating the needs of the target population.

4

Using Qualitative and Mixed-Method Approaches

Susan Berkowitz

Qualitative methods have been employed far less frequently than sample surveys or quantitative secondary data analysis in needs assessment and most types of applied social research. Of the five most common needs assessment methods identified by Lareau (1983), only two—reliance on key informants, and use of group process/public hearings or community forums—might be considered qualitative. However, recent years have witnessed widely expanded interest in qualitative methods in a range of social science disciplines and applied fields, including psychology, sociology, health care, program evaluation, and policy analysis (Miles & Huberman, 1994; Reichardt & Rallis, 1994). This interest is beginning to extend to needs assessment. Applied properly, and with an appropriate recognition of their underlying assumptions, qualitative methods have an important and useful role to play in needs assessment research.

Qualitative methods of primary data collection employ less structured and more open-ended ways of gathering data than quantitative methods. They include intensive interviews, focus groups, and observational methods. Qualitative modes of data analysis provide ways of discerning, examining, comparing, and contrasting meaningful patterns or themes in qualitative data. It is difficult not to define *qualitative methods* in contrast to *quantitative methods*, and thus to emphasize what qualitative methods are not, rather than what they are. Strauss and Corbin (1990) offered a definition that is a bit of both: "By the term qualitative research we mean any kind of research that produces findings not arrived at by means of statistical procedures or other means of quantification. It can refer to research about person's lives, stories, behavior, but also about organizational functioning, social movements, or interactional relationships" (p. 17).

Unfortunately, use of qualitative methods in needs assessment research has too often been motivated by expedience rather than a considered judgment about when these methods are most appropriate. Public hearings are conducted, or key informants are used, when resource limitations make a sample survey impractical. Consequently, researchers have paid too little attention to the function(s) that qualitative methods can legitimately and most effectively fulfill in a research design. Specific qualitative methods, such as focus groups, have been applied without giving systematic thought to sampling or selection

53

of cases. The resulting data are often poorly or reductively analyzed, thus undermining their richness, arguably their greatest potential benefit. To address the tendency to misunderstand, and thus misuse, qualitative methods, this chapter

- evaluates the circumstances in which it is useful, appropriate, and advisable to use qualitative methods in needs assessment research;
- discusses and illustrates the concept of purposive analytic sampling;
- describes particular qualitative methods, especially intensive interviews and focus groups, and demonstrates how they might be used; and
- presents principles for analyzing qualitative needs assessment data.

Table 4.1 presents some key contrasts between qualitative and quantitative research methods to help guide the discussion.

WHEN TO USE QUALITATIVE METHODS IN NEEDS ASSESSMENT

The most salient reason to use qualitative methods in needs assessment is that they offer the opportunity to probe an issue or question in depth, and to explore respondents' views and perspectives in their own terms and framework of understanding. A qualitative approach is especially appropriate for exploring the viewpoints of persons and groups whose assumptions differ from those of the mainstream culture, and who, therefore, have a particular need to speak, and be heard, "in their own voices." Such groups might include street gang members or other youth, immigrants, members of racial and ethnic minorities, and older persons. However, even apparently "unexotic" professionals such as social workers, program administrators, and teachers, may operate with subcultural professional assumptions that need to be better understood. For example, how teachers view their mission and role vis-à-vis their students may strongly influence their ideas of what their students need to make them more successful. Teachers who see their role as primarily imparting information might tend to perceive the issue very differently than those viewing themselves as ministering to the students' socioemotional needs. Qualitative approaches are useful for explicating the kinds of differences in world view that can underlie assessments of what is needed to address a situation or redress an identified problem.

Some research questions are unambiguous in requiring a quantitative answer that allows generalization from a probability sample to a larger population. Other research questions can be approached either quantitatively or qualitatively, depending on the relative emphasis given to different aspects of the question. In Table 2.1, Research Question 5 asks about the types of family support services that low-income families in a state believe they need to maintain and strengthen their families. As seen in chapter 3, one way to address this question would be to conduct a survey with a stratified random sample of low-income families with young children in the state. This would yield results such as: "Thirty-five percent of the families reported needing help with par-

Table 4.1 Salient Contrasts Between Qualitative and Quantitative Methods

Key Points of Contrast in . . .	Qualitative (Words)	Quantitative (Numbers)
Sampling	Purposive, theoretical/conceptual sequential sampling (within-case and across-case)	Probability sampling (e.g., random, random stratified; individuals as units)
Common data collection methods	• Intensive interviews • Participant observation • Focus groups • Documents as texts	• Sample surveys (close-ended) • Structured interviews • Collection of record data
Modes of analysis	• Data reduction, ordered data display, conclusion-drawing and verification • "Constant comparative method" • Configurational synthesis/synoposis	• Descriptive, inferential statistics • Univariate, multivariate, modeling analyses (analysis of variance, multiple regression, logistic regression)
Type(s) of generalization	• Process generalizations • Analytic or theoretical generalizations (generalizability to theoretical propositions)	• Statistical (generalization to wider population)

enting." However, there still might be uncertainty as to what such a statement really means. Did the Hispanic families interpret the question in the same way as the African-American families? What does the phrase "services to help families keep strong" mean to different respondents? Taking the qualitative approach of conducting focus groups or intensive interviews allows respondents to explain in their own terms what these issues mean to them, and why.

However, there is one important caveat to be kept in mind. Qualitative methods do not usually fit with the assumptions or requirements of probability sampling. Unlike sample survey methods, qualitative data collection and data analysis are quite labor-intensive, and usually focus on examining fewer cases in greater depth, rather than collecting data on large numbers of cases or respondents. Thus, compared with a sample survey approach, addressing Research Questions 5, 5.1, 5.2, 5.3, and 5.4 only by conducting focus groups and intensive interviews would likely yield greater depth of understanding of the research questions. However, partly because of the limits it places on the number of interviews that can reasonably be conducted, use of qualitative methods would probably not allow statistical generalization of the responses to the population of all low-income families in the state. In this situation, a decision of whether to pursue a quantitative or qualitative approach might best be based on how much is already known about the target population's perceptions in this area. If little is known, focus groups or intensive interviews might be carried out as a first step in gaining a better and deeper understanding of the issues. The results of the focus groups and intensive interviews could then be used to develop a structured survey instrument for a later study or phase of the study. Conversely, if a plethora of survey responses on the subject already exists, but no one seems to know quite how to interpret them, this would also recommend a qualitative approach.

Research Question 6, which asks about the most important existing barriers to receipt of family support services by low-income families with young children, could also be explored either through a sample survey, with qualitative methods, or both. Suppose existing research indicates that agency personnel and families disagree on which barriers they regard as most important, but the reasons for these differences remain largely unexplored. Rather than undertake yet another survey, it might be more useful to do a more in-depth, qualitative exploration of the reasons underlying these differences.

In a slightly different vein, Question 6.1 asks about behavioral or interactional barriers to receipt of services. Service delivery personnel may unintentionally act in a way that "turns off" families seeking information on available services. Prospective clients may be treated brusquely, impatiently, or in a manner they perceive as disrespectful. Because service delivery personnel may not be aware of these behaviors, this kind of research question cannot be satisfactorily addressed by self-reported survey data, and can be explored only indirectly in focus groups or intensive interviews. As shown in Table 2.1, in-person observations of interactions between service providers and client families would be a good way to detect these often unintentional, but very real, barriers. In addition to registering the overt content of the interaction(s), direct observation can capture subtle behavioral signs and cues in body language, eye contact, and tone of voice.

SELECTION OF CASES

Qualitative research employs purposive (or purposeful) sampling, in which the researcher systematically selects certain groups, individuals, situations, or sites to study on the basis of their relevance to the central research issue. Different premises underlie purposive, as contrasted with probability, sampling. Failure to grasp these differences and their implications is at the root of much of the misunderstanding between quantitative and qualitative researchers.

As Patton (1990) noted, "qualitative inquiry typically focuses in-depth on relatively small samples, even single cases ($n = 1$) . . . the logic and power of purposeful sampling lies in selecting information-rich cases . . . [or] those from which one can learn a great deal about the issues of central importance to the purpose of the research" (p. 169). Patton identified 15 purposeful sampling strategies that can be used in evaluation research, each serving a specific evaluation purpose.

Purposive sampling criteria are defined in relation to the specific needs of a given study. Question 6 from Table 2.1 explores perceptions of the most important barriers to low-income families receiving family support services. A central reason for taking a qualitative approach to answering this question would be to probe the reasons why service providers and families tend to express different views on the subject. Thus, it would be important to include some families and some service providers in the sample. Beyond that, if different kinds of barriers exist for different clusters of services, families and service providers might be further subdivided according to the specific type(s) of services received and delivered.

Purposive sampling criteria should be based on an idea of the categories or distinctions that are likely to prove relevant in analyzing the data. Samples may be selected on the basis of demographic characteristics such as gender or race, but different kinds of distinctions can also figure into choosing a purposive sample. For example, if this would help cast light on the research question, teachers might be chosen based on differences in how they conceive of their mission vis-à-vis their students.

Purposive sampling provides more room for play than probability sampling because it is not subject to constraints on achieving a minimum sample size or drawing a random sample from a comprehensive sampling frame. Further, the sample design does not have to be absolutely fixed at the start. This allows the flexibility to develop more refined sampling criteria as the study progresses. Changing or refining purposive sampling criteria is perfectly legitimate as long as such changes can be justified in relation to an unfolding understanding of the important characteristics or dimensions of the situation. For example, holding a first set of focus groups with low-income families may reveal that families with infants and young toddlers are experiencing different barriers than those with older children. In the next round of focus groups, age of child might serve as another criterion in selecting families.

The number of cases selected is not subject to any fixed rules. It depends on the nature of the research question(s), the available resources and what the various audience(s) to the needs assessment will find credible (Patton, 1990). If focus groups examining barriers to receipt of family support services are to be conducted with families and service providers throughout a state, how many different focus groups should be held? The research questions indicate that rural, suburban, and urban areas of the state might present different types or patterns of barriers to receipt of services. This would suggest holding at least one set of focus groups (one focus group each with families and service providers) in each of these three types of areas, which would translate into a minimum of six focus groups.

If categories of families and service providers were to be further subdivided as described earlier, this would double the number of groups to be held in each type of geographic area, requiring a minimum of 12 focus groups. To build continuity and develop themes from previous sessions, it might be useful to conduct multiple focus group sessions with the same sets of people. Holding two such sessions for each group would raise the number to 24 focus group sessions.

Although in theory the possibilities are infinitely expandable, at some point practical considerations of time, money, logistics, and personnel inevitably intrude. In addition, the task of analyzing this many focus groups' transcripts could easily become unwieldy, and might ultimately result in diffusing the analytic focus of the study. The point is not to pile on cases, but to have enough internal diversity in the sample to amply explore the questions of interest. As Patton (1990) put it: "The validity, meaningfulness and insights generated from qualitative inquiry have more to do with the information-richness of the cases selected and the observational/analytic capabilities of the researcher than with sample size" (p. 185).

FOCUS GROUPS AND INTENSIVE INTERVIEWS

Both focus groups and intensive interviews are in-person qualitative interviewing methods that pose questions to people in a way designed to ascertain and explore their views on a given subject in their own terms and framework of understanding. Both methods involve the use of unstructured or open-ended instruments that concentrate on clearly defined subjects or sets of interrelated topics. The central difference between them is that intensive interviews are typically conducted in one-on-one interview situations, whereas focus groups pose a question or series of questions for discussion to a group of people.

Unlike structured, close-ended in-person surveys, intensive interviews pursue in-depth exploration of a subject or set of subjects and typically take the form of a patterned dialogue or conversation. In sharp contrast to survey instruments, intensive interviews are designed to encourage interchange, leaving room for give and take between the interviewer and the respondent. Although usually following a general outline of topics to be covered, the actual pattern of questioning in intensive interviews is built up "naturally" from the progression of responses.

Because of their discursive or "conversational" format, intensive interviews are best suited to situations in which the interviewer is trying to develop a working understanding of the respondent's views in the respondent's own terms, and in relation to how the respondent integrates these views into an overall perspective. Intensive interviews are also suited to probing topics in depth and in a variety of ways. The interview becomes more than a means of data collection; it is also an opportunity for the respondent to elaborate on, crystallize, and perhaps clarify his or her perspective while engaging in a focused dialogue with the interviewer.

The qualities needed for conducting intensive interviews are quite different than those required for administering a close-ended survey instrument. In-person survey interviewers are trained in standardized delivery, keeping interviewer-to-interviewer variation to the barest minimum. In intensive interviewing, the role of the interviewer is much more active: The interviewer guides the dialogue, draws out the respondent, and clarifies and makes sense of the respondent's answers. When conducting intensive interviews, interviewers need to be able to assimilate and interpret the material in process, as the interview proceeds. They must be prepared to probe on the spot to ensure they have accurately understood what the respondent said and how it connects to something else he or she might have said earlier. Similarly, because the interview guide serves only as a rough "roadmap" to the topics to be covered, to orchestrate the flow of the dialogue, the interviewer must be ready to adapt to the specific situation by changing the order or altering the specific phrasing of the questions. Intensive interviewers should also be sufficiently conversant with the subject matter at hand to "speak the same language" as the respondent, and so be able to probe intelligently.

These central contrasts between in-person surveys and intensive interviews illustrate several important differences between quantitative and qualitative methods of data collection. Qualitative methods are not "context-free" in the same way that quantitative methods are. In sample surveys, interviewers can be trained to administer an instrument on a subject about which they know very little. The expertise rests in the instrument's design, not the delivery. In intensive interviewing, the interviewer in a sense becomes the instrument. The same interview guide can be more or less effective in the hands of different interviewers with varying levels of skill and knowledge. One important implication of these differences is that intensive interviews should be conducted by people who are both well trained in the method and knowledgeable about the subject matter.

Reliability is a major issue in survey design. The central aim is to avoid a situation in which the same question(s) might be interpreted differently at different times. In qualitative interviewing, because the intent of the two methods is so different, concerns about reliability are not the same. If an intensive interviewer were to consistently ask exactly the same questions in precisely the same way of all respondents, it would be a sure sign that he or she was missing the point—it would be as if a psychiatrist always said exactly the same thing to all patients regardless of their individual circumstances. The intent of qualitative interviewing is to explore ideas and perceptions, stimulate further discussion, and encourage mutual clarification. The process is inherently interactive.

Nevertheless, it is important to have some assurance that intensive interviewers are not leading respondents by even unintentionally directing them to say certain things. The opposite danger is allowing respondents to digress on subjects unrelated to the central focus of the interview. As seen in chapter 3, reliability and validity are paramount concerns in survey research. The analogous concern in qualitative research might be called *fidelity*—understood in the sense of remaining true to the goals of the interview and the sense of what the respondent is saying. The key elements needed to ensure the fidelity of the intensive interview situation are: (a) training and practice in the use of the specific interview guide, (b) experience in this type of interviewing, (c) a good understanding of the substance and goals of the interview, and (d) an ability to critically reflect on the interview situation and use these insights in subsequent interviews and in analysis of the data.

Focus groups are a type of in-depth qualitative group interview that bring together a small number of preselected persons to explore a set of topics or issues. Focus groups differ from intensive interviews and other types of group interviews in their emphasis on interaction within the group (Morgan, 1988; Stewart & Shamdasani, 1990). The focus group format is specifically designed to promote verbal interchange among participants. What emerges from a focus group session is a group-generated response—presumably something different than the sum of what the participants would have said if each had been interviewed separately.

Focus groups usually bring together 8–12 participants who have been chosen on the basis of certain characteristics making them particularly suitable for discussing the subject at hand. Focus groups are generally led by one or more moderators, working from a protocol of open-ended questions. The moderator's role is to guide the discussion, ensure participation by all, and periodically summarize the sense of the group on a given issue. The moderator should be knowledgeable about the characteristics and culture of the focus group participants and the subject under discussion, skilled in group facilitation techniques, and able to adapt to the particular circumstances as needed. Another individual may act as an observer who takes notes on the group context and interactions.

What should determine whether focus groups or intensive interviews should be selected as the qualitative method of choice? The central criterion should be a judgment of whether the research question is better addressed in an individual or group setting. Looking at Research Question 5, Table 2.1 indicates a plan to conduct focus groups to explore the reasons why low-income families in the state identify certain family support services as more needed than others. Holding focus groups makes sense, first, because this topic is impersonal enough to be posed to a group. Second, an added benefit might be derived from hearing the issue discussed in a group setting. The moderator and observer might be able to observe an interesting group dynamic in how participants develop their ideas while talking to one another about needed services.

In contrast, Table 2.1 suggests using intensive interviews to address Research Question 5.3—on why respondents from different racial and ethnic groups feel that certain services have not been particularly helpful to them and their families. In this case, the subject is personal enough so that, even in a focus session composed entirely of members of the same racial and ethnic group, respondents might be reluctant to talk about what has not helped their families with specific problems. Fuller and more honest responses might be elicited in a one-on-one setting. Also, in exploring why a particular service is not seen as helpful, it may be desirable to have the freedom to pursue potentially fruitful individual lines of questioning in greater depth than would be possible in focus groups.

There are no absolute rules on when to use intensive interviews rather than focus groups. Although focus groups are less expensive on a per capita basis, they also limit how and how much individual responses can be probed. Cost considerations should be secondary to a judgment as to which approach is better able to address the research questions.

DESIGNING INTENSIVE INTERVIEW GUIDES

An interview guide is an open-ended instrument used to help direct the dialogue during intensive interviews. Like other needs assessment instruments, guides are designed to address specific research questions organized around definite themes or sets of interrelated subjects and ordered in a logical and developmental topical or chronological sequence.

Interview guides are unstructured in the sense of not asking an identical, standardized schedule of questions to all respondents. Most guides are exclusively, or almost exclusively, composed of open-ended questions that ask respondents to formulate responses in their own terms, rather than in preestablished categories. An example of an open-ended question to a service provider might be: "What do you think of your agency's new first-come, first-served policy in providing family support services, and why?"

There is an art to designing effective open-ended questions for interview guides. Three basic rules follow:

1. Design questions that lend themselves to thoughtful exploration. Just because a question ends in a question mark and provides no preestablished response categories does not make it open-ended. Questions that pose an issue in a categorical, or "yes–no," fashion should be avoided. For example, the following question is not phrased in a way that invites discussion: "Were you or were you not satisfied with how your first appointment for services was made?" Although a talkative respondent might expand on what he or she thought, someone else might answer with a simple "Yes" or "No." To

capture the target population's first impressions of agency staff and how that affected subsequent interactions, questioning might begin with: "Can you recall how you felt the very first time you walked into the agency?" From there, a series of questions could be developed based on a chronological sequence of events and how these were perceived by the respondent.

2. Questions should be framed broadly enough to encourage discussion, but not so broadly or generically that the respondent has no idea of what the question is trying to get at. An example of the latter would be to start an intensive interview with: "Tell me about x agency." This question leaves respondents with no guidance as to which aspects of the agency, or their interactions with it, are of interest. A better way to approach this would be to create a sequence of questions concerning various aspects of the respondent's experience with the agency staff. This sequence might end with: "Overall, all things considered, how would you characterize your interactions with the staff of the x agency? Has that changed since you first began receiving services from them?"

3. Probing should be used as a way to clarify a response or establish the meaning of a respondent's answer. Questions or probes that lead the respondent toward a desired answer are just as taboo in open-ended as in close-ended instruments. Researchers may have ideas about what responses they would expect to hear, or entertain hypotheses about possible connections between different phenomena. These assumptions should never slip into the wording of the open-ended questions. For example, a tentative hypothesis may have been developed that language barriers are the single most important impediment to Hispanic families' receipt of needed family support services. This does not mean that the question should ask: "Don't you agree that not speaking the same language is the biggest problem you have with the agency staff?" This fails to clarify respondents' views, and forces them to resist a strong pressure to agree. A better approach would be to ask: "So far, what do you think has been the most important reason why you have not been able to get all the services you need?" If the respondent does not provide a clear answer, further probing might suggest language difficulties as one of a number of other possibilities. For example: "What about problems with agency staff not speaking Spanish? with transportation? with rules in the agency?" Phrased this way, probes offer respondents suggestions they can weigh and then accept or reject.

Development of intensive interview guides, like intensive interviewing itself, is a skill honed over the years. If this is a maiden attempt at creating a guide, the draft should be reviewed by someone with more experience in qualitative instrument design.

DESIGNING FOCUS GROUP PROTOCOLS

A focus group protocol is a list of topics or open-ended questions to be covered in a focus group session that is used to guide the group discussion.

The focus group protocol serves the same function in the focus group setting as the interview guide does in the intensive interview situation. Like the interview guide, the protocol is open-ended and unstructured, and not intended as a fixed script to be strictly followed under all circumstances (Morgan, 1988).

The primary difference between focus group protocols and intensive interview guides is that the former are meant to promote verbal exchange among participants rather than dialogue between the moderator and individual participants. The protocol should: (a) cover topics in a logical, developmental order, building on one another, with a different protocol for each focus group session; (b) raise open-ended issues that are engaging and relevant to the participants and that invite the group to make a collective response; and (c) carve out manageable "chunks" of topics to be examined one at a time in a delimited period.

Suppose the goal is to design a protocol to address Research Question 6 in Table 2.1. To simplify the task, assume the participants will all be low-income African-American women with young children receiving some type of family support service. Sessions will be held in rural, suburban, and urban areas of the state to explore participants' perceptions of the most important barriers they have faced in obtaining needed services and (see Question 6.1) their ideas on the best ways to overcome these barriers.

The protocol outline for a 2-hour session might be as follows:

1. Introduction—greetings; explain purpose of the session; fill out name cards; introduce observers, ground rules, and how focus group works. (10 minutes)
2. Participant introductions—give names (first names only), where participants live, age of child or children, which family support services are received and for how long, and other services participants receive. (10 minutes)
3. Introduce idea of barriers to services, and ask participants for their views on what have been most important barriers to receipt of family support services (probe, if necessary, on factors such as transportation, treatment by agency personnel, regulations, waiting lists)—have they discontinued any services or been unable to get ones they want? (30 minutes)
4. Probe the reasons behind their choices of most important barriers. (20 minutes)
5. Ask for ideas on what could be done to overcome barriers in the future—what would make it or would have made it easier to enter and remain in service loop. (30 minutes)
6. Debrief and wrap up—moderator summary, clarifications, and additional comments or questions. (10 minutes)

As seen next, considerable material for analysis might be generated by such a seemingly simple approach.

ANALYZING QUALITATIVE DATA

In contrast to quantitative approaches, in which numbers and what they represent are the material of analysis, qualitative analysis deals primarily in words, and rests on the ability to systematically identify and interpret meaningful patterns of response and interrelationships in what is said by and/or observed about respondents. *Meaningfulness* is defined in terms of the goals and objectives of the project at hand. Although qualitative analysis is guided by fewer agreed on rules and standard procedures than statistical analysis, the past 10 years have witnessed considerable progress in systematizing a description of how to carry out qualitative analysis.

At the simplest level, qualitative analysis in needs assessment involves examining the data to determine how they respond to the research question(s) at hand. Researchers have identified some basic commonalities in the process of making sense of qualitative data. First, there is the need to meaningfully reduce the large volume of data. After holding 10 focus group sessions or conducting 20 intensive interviews, the sheer volume of transcripts may seem forbidding. Miles and Huberman (1994) described this first of three elements of qualitative data analysis as *data reduction:* "Data reduction refers to the process of selecting, focusing, simplifying, abstracting, and transforming the data that appear in written up field notes or transcriptions" (p. 10). Not only do the data need to be reduced for the sake of manageability, but, to use Wolcott's (1994) term, they have to be "transformed" so they can be made intelligible in terms of the issues being addressed. Data reduction is not a one-time occurrence, but happens continuously throughout the life of a research project (Miles & Huberman, 1994; Patton, 1990; Wolcott, 1994).

Miles and Huberman (1994) pointed out that the process of data reduction involves making sometimes painful analytic choices—some aspects of the data are highlighted, others minimized, and still others discarded altogether. It is hard not to get attached to qualitative data because the words represent real people, places, and events far more concretely than the numbers in quantitative analysis. Especially for beginners, it is difficult not to get lost in the welter of detail and lose the "story line." Qualitative analysis demands the discipline to step back and carefully select those elements most critical for answering the research question.

Data display represents the second element or level of analysis in Miles and Huberman's model. Data display goes a step beyond data reduction to provide "an organized, compressed assembly of information that permits conclusion drawing and action" (p. 11). A display could be an extended piece of text, but other forms of data display—such as diagrams, charts, or matrices—can also provide powerful ways to present and think about the data. Data displays facilitate an additional distancing from the data to discern systematic patterns and interrelationships. Wolcott (1994) called this the *analysis component* of transforming qualitative data. Analysis "addresses the identification of essential features and the systematic description of interrelationships among them . . . (analysis) may also be employed . . . to address questions of why a system is not working or how it might be made to work 'better'" (Wolcott, 1994, p. 12).

Conclusion drawing and *verification* constitute Miles and Huberman's third element of qualitative analysis. This involves deciding what the data mean—what their implications are for the questions at hand--and simultaneously going back into the data to cross-check or verify these conclusions. "The meanings emerging from the data have to be tested for their plausibility, their sturdiness, their 'confirmability'—that is, their validity" (Miles & Huberman, 1994, p. 11). In this process, the analyst should document and demonstrate the basis on which he or she is drawing these conclusions, however tentative or conditional. Other people must be "walked through" the process so they can decide for themselves whether the conclusions make sense. Qualitative analysts "have an obligation to monitor and report their own analytic procedures and processes as fully and truthfully as possible" (Patton, 1990, p. 372).

Timing works very differently in qualitative than in quantitative research. Quantitative research is more easily divided into discrete stages of research design, instrument design, data collection, data processing, and data analysis. By contrast, in qualitative research, data collection and data analysis are not discrete stages: As soon as the first pieces of data are collected, the researcher begins the process of making sense of the information. Moreover, the three components of qualitative analysis—data reduction, data display, and conclusion drawing/verification—overlap in time: All three occur both during and after the data collection period and interact in a variety of nonlinear ways (Miles & Huberman, 1994). Part of what distinguishes qualitative analysis is a "looplike" quality of multiple rounds of revisiting the data as additional questions emerge, new connections are unearthed, and more complex formulations develop along with deepening understanding of the material.

ANALYZING FOCUS GROUP DATA: AN ILLUSTRATIVE EXAMPLE

To give a more concrete feel for what is involved in qualitative data analysis, a brief illustration is provided of a strategy that might be applied in analyzing the data collected in focus groups with low-income African-American women with young children receiving family support services in a state.

Analysis of focus group data differs from other types of qualitative analysis in that the group, rather than the individual, is the primary unit of analysis. To provide a context for interpreting what was said, the material for each focus session should include a brief account of the setting and a description of the group interactions that occurred during the session. Such an account might also incorporate the observations of the moderator, or a trained observer who witnessed the session, concerning ways in which the group dynamics might have influenced what occurred and what was said.

Two basic forms of qualitative analysis are used to analyze these hypothetical data: intra- and cross-case analysis. A *case* may be differently defined for different analytic purposes. Depending on the situation, a case could be a single individual or a program site. In this example, a case is a single focus group session. Thus, intracase analysis examines what happens in a single focus group session, and cross-case analysis systematically compares and contrasts across sessions.

The first step in intracase analysis is to examine the transcript of the session for each major question that was asked, in an effort to identify key themes and factors that emerged (e.g., what the participants said about what they perceived as the single most important barrier to receiving family support services might be examined). What did they say, how did they say it, and on what bases did they make their statements? How much difference of opinion existed within the group, and what seemed to lie behind these differences?

Analytically relevant themes and factors emerge from systematic examination and reexamination of the data; these themes cannot be predetermined. Much of the value of qualitative analysis rests on its potential to produce fresh insights. Interesting, yet unexpected, patterns or connections may emerge. For example, participants may view as most important the barriers that came at "critical times" or moments in their family's life, rather than those they experienced most often. In examining the data, the analyst should be open to perceiving such unexpected patterns or themes in the data.

To help ensure that some potentially important themes or factors are not missed, and to provide cross-checking across analysts, it is useful to have two or three people—who are familiar with the topic, the types of participants, and the goals of the needs assessment project—independently examine the data and then compare and discuss their results. The product of this exercise is a list of identified themes for each question.

Once having agreed on key themes and factors for individual questions, a second conceptual "sorting" of the data would occur to systematically compare responses and identified themes and factors across questions. For example, a possible analytic concern at this "sorting" would be to see whether there is any relationship between why people identify certain barriers as most important and what they think would need to be done to overcome them. Again, it is helpful if more than one person is involved in this part of the analysis.

Because the group is the most appropriate unit of analysis for focus group data, these data quite naturally lend themselves to cross-case analyses, in which the transcripts and materials from one group are systematically compared and contrasted with those from another. This should occur after the intra-case analyses for individual focus groups have been completed. Racial and ethnic factors have been "controlled for" by limiting the groups to low-income African-American women in the three types of areas. Thus, the overarching question driving the comparison among the groups of service recipients would be differences across the rural, urban, and suburban areas of the state. What are the factors, if any, that differentiate the views of service recipients in these three types of areas? How might these differences relate to differences in the service delivery system?

The process of analyzing the data across the three cases is much like that for the intracase analysis. The first step would be to compare the key themes and factors identified for each focus question across the groups to see to what extent they overlap or are different. If some themes or factors emerge uniformly or almost uniformly in one group and not the others, this would clearly be very telling. For example, if almost all the participants in the rural area mentioned not knowing what services were available as an important barrier, but no one in either of the other two groups even referred to this, it would point to a problem with effective dissemination of information about services to African-American families in the rural area. It is more likely that some factors or themes, or some combinations of factors and themes, will be expressed more often, more intensely, or perhaps somewhat differently in one group than in the others. The analysis will have to be correspondingly more refined to reflect this.

The final step in the across-group comparison parallels the second step in the within-group comparison. Now that the responses of the three groups have been compared and contrasted for each of the focus questions, the same is done with responses across questions. The issue is: do the same or similar patterns of connection seem to emerge within groups, or are there differences? For example, if participants in two groups both name the same barrier as most important (e.g., "they make you jump through too many hoops"), do they also give the same reasons for picking it? If not, why not?

The different analytic paths that might be pursued just for three focus group sessions with reasonably homogeneous groups are already quite rich and varied. Imagine how much more challenging the task would be if other dimensions of comparison were added (e.g., if focus groups were also conducted with service providers or with families from other racial and ethnic groups in these same areas). In this regard, it does well to remember Patton's (1990) dictum that it is the information-richness of the cases and the skills of the analyst that make for good qualitative analysis. What should drive the analytic process, above all else, is the need to answer the research questions in as much relevant depth as possible.

QUASI-QUALITATIVE APPROACHES TO NEEDS ASSESSMENT

This section briefly describes several techniques used in recent needs assessment studies that are "qualitative" in initially approaching the process of identifying needs in an open-ended fashion. However, they are closer to quantitative than to qualitative modes of analysis in their use of ranking and rating procedures to categorize, reduce, and analyze the data (Ong et al., 1991; Pruitt, 1992; Twible, 1992).

The nominal group technique (NGT) derives from research on group decision making. NGT involves asking individuals in a group to write down their responses to a given question. All responses are listed on a board by a group leader or facilitator. Individual participants are then asked to choose some number of these responses (e.g., 5 or 10) they consider most important, and to rank them on a numeric scale from most to least important. The leader collects the individual rating sheets and calculates the average group score.

The items receiving the highest scores represent the issues seen as most important (Twible, 1992).

Delphi techniques are similar to NGT in that they involve structuring a group process to allow individuals to focus on a common problem or set of issues. Delphi techniques were originally developed for use with expert panels, and were designed to avoid the "distractions" of an open discussion. They typically take place in several rounds, in which individuals on a panel are separately posed open-ended questions (e.g., concerning needed services, barriers to services, and what it would take to remove these barriers; Pruitt, 1992). In the second round, the researcher combines and groups the first-round responses and asks panelists to individually rank the importance of the reduced list of items. A third round enables panelists to review, reconsider, and, if desired, change their responses to the second round, based on comparing their individual ranking with the mean group ranking for that item.

Rapid appraisal is another "quasi-qualitative" approach used in needs assessment that covers a variety of techniques with the following common elements: (a) greater speed than conventional methods; (b) working in the field; (c) an emphasis on learning directly from local inhabitants; (d) a semistructured, multidisciplinary approach allowing for flexibility and innovation; and (e) an open-ended emphasis on gaining insights and developing tentative hypotheses (Ong et al., 1991).

All these techniques have been used to assess needs, and, in many cases, have uncovered aspects or dimensions of the situation that might not have been discovered using more formal, structured approaches. NGT, applied in planning a health promotion campaign for veterans, revealed an important overriding theme—that respondents associated increased age with an inherent, inevitable decline in health and vitality (Twible, 1992). This finding provided the basis of all subsequent efforts to plan health interventions for this population. Ong et al. (1991) used rapid appraisal techniques to define the nature and magnitude of health and social needs of a deprived urban community in England. Key informants included professionals who worked in the community (e.g., social workers or health workers), "grassroots" community leaders (e.g., leaders of self-help groups and voluntary associations), and people centrally placed due to the nature of their work or social role (e.g., a corner shopkeeper, postman, or bookie). Interviews with key informants produced a list of five priority problem areas and associated problems. Once problem areas were categorized, the research team returned to the community and asked the key informants to rank these items. The priorities set by the community became the point of departure for formulating a series of action plans, with the professionals serving as facilitators rather than deciding priorities and strategies for the community. Interestingly, the priorities established by the community differed from those chosen by the professionals as well as the professionals' appraisal of what the community would have selected (Ong et al., 1991).

NGT, Delphi techniques, and rapid appraisal are less labor-intensive and time-consuming than "strictly" qualitative methods such as intensive interviews and focus groups. As such, they sacrifice some of the richness and depth of the findings. Before these quasi-qualitative techniques can be used to best advantage, however, their practitioners need to pay more attention to technical issues of sampling and data analysis.

COMBINING QUANTITATIVE AND QUALITATIVE APPROACHES

This chapter and the two preceding it demonstrate the working principles of good research design for a needs assessment. They argue for the advantages of combining secondary and primary data; addressing the same research question in multiple, overlapping ways; and obtaining multiple perspectives on need from different groups of respondents. This brief concluding section discusses the distinctive value of combining quantitative and qualitative approaches in designing and executing a needs assessment.

One major advantage of mixing methods in any research project comes from triangulation—or employing several different, independent approaches to addressing the research questions. Quantitative and qualitative methods, although based on different premises, are ultimately compatible. They can be used together successfully, but only with an understanding of their differences and within a well-reasoned framework in which the approach follows from the research questions being addressed. Triangulation, achieved through the use of different data sources, researchers, theoretical perspectives, or methods, strengthens the basis for drawing conclusions from a study.

Wiley, Huelsman, and Hilgemann (1994) put triangulation to the test, obtaining convergent results when they used both qualitative intensive interviews and a quantitative concept mapping technique to identify agency and client needs of a nonprofit mental health agency. They pointed to three methodological advantages of combining qualitative and quantitative approaches in needs assessment: (a) qualitative methods can be used in the same study both to prepare for the use of quantitative methods and to collect independent evidence on need, (b) using the two approaches simultaneously offers the possibility of convergence across maximally different methods, and (c) qualitative analysis complemented concept mapping by providing valuable information about the context in which the mapping occurs (Wiener, Wiley, Huelsman, & Hilgemann, 1994).

Combining qualitative and quantitative approaches in the same study simultaneously benefits from the respective advantages of depth and breadth, understanding and generalizability, and closeness to context, as well as standardization across settings (see Table 4.1). Research Question 5 addresses the types of services that low-income families with young children believe they most need to maintain and strengthen their families. As the matrix suggests, a powerful approach would be to conduct an in-person survey of a statewide probability sample of low-income families combined with focus groups of purposively chosen families. The in-person survey would indicate the services families throughout the state reported as most needed; its advantage would rest in breadth and statistical generalizability. The focus group findings, although not statistically generalizable, would give meaning and context to the survey results by illuminating the reasons for the choices. Although taking a combined approach would be more expensive than pursuing either method alone, holding only a relatively few focus groups would add considerable value, in understanding, to the research design.

SUMMARY

In the end, research design is both science and art. The design must be formulated precisely enough to accurately answer the research questions, but flexibly enough to capture the distinctive "spirit" of the research questions and the particulars of the specific situation. Deciding on the right combination of methods, approaches, and personnel to use in conducting a needs assessment is a challenging, but rewarding, enterprise that requires creativity and fore-thought. It is vital to consider and weigh in advance the multiple implications of taking one or another approach to assessing needs in light of what this will yield. The components of the design should fit together, both conceptually and operationally, like pieces of a puzzle. As an ideal, the overall design should strive to achieve a "synergy" among its various components, in which the whole becomes more than the sum of its parts. This is where the art comes in.

5

Planning a Needs Assessment

Rebecca Reviere
Carolyn C. Carter

Thorough and thoughtful planning is essential to a successful needs assessment. In this chapter, planning is separated into two distinct phases: (a) strategic planning—the identification and monitoring of relevant external and internal factors that can potentially impact the needs assessment, and (b) project planning—the specific steps, procedures, and resources required to conduct a needs assessment. Together the strategic planning emphasis on the broad context and the project planning emphasis on detail lay the groundwork for a successful needs assessment.

STRATEGIC PLANNING

Elements both outside and inside the agency or sponsoring organization may influence the course of a needs assessment. Circumstances may change while conducting a needs assessment and may continue to change as the results are disseminated. Strategic planning acknowledges and accommodates forces beyond the scope of the project that may have an impact on the needs assessment. Each needs assessment is unique in that a specific set of conditions comes to the fore. There are three aspects of strategic planning: (a) the identification of relevant external factors, (b) the identification of relevant internal factors, and (c) the monitoring of the likelihood and impact of these factors.

IDENTIFICATION OF EXTERNAL FACTORS

External forces are those outside the immediate system of the needs assessment and include conditions of and changes in: public sentiment, regulations and legislation, the economy, technology, and population. These forces can have an influence on the local or neighborhood level or, more broadly, on the regional, state, national, or even international level. Planners often ignore external factors because they are perceived to be unrelated to a specific needs assessment, but outside factors and trends can influence the timing, methods, and dissemination of the needs assessment's results. Developing an overview of external factors can help pinpoint opportunities to conduct a relatively smooth, successful needs assessment, or to identify threats that, if ignored or not addressed, can abort the project.

Public Sentiment

Public sentiment refers to the zeitgeist of the times—the beliefs, feelings, and values that, in part, can determine the popularity and acceptability of investigating needs and implementing programs for a particular group. This sentiment both reflects and is reflected in actions of elected officials as they write policies or reorder priorities. For example, policy discussions surrounding welfare reform could impact approaches to and importance of needs assessments for the welfare population. A needs assessment of that group would look very different depending on the definition of and feelings toward the target population.

Public sentiment is also related to attitudes and expectations and the manner in which they change over time in a particular area. For example, issues of teen sexuality would be approached differently depending on prevailing religious and cultural norms in a community. These issues can best be addressed by incorporating a sensitivity and a responsiveness to relevant public sentiment from early stages of planning.

Regulatory and Legislative Changes

A needs assessment that could result in changing policy should be based on knowledge of local, state, and federal laws and regulations, as well as pending legislation. For example, states generally regulate the amount of health care provided in various types of adult care residences. Policymakers must attempt to determine where subsidies are most crucial: adult care residences where the overall health care cost is lower, or nursing homes where both level of health care and costs are higher. Assessment of needs and implementation of procedures aimed at individuals living in these situations would change, depending on their policy decisions.

There are a multitude of resources that can be used to research legislative and regulatory activity. Congressional delegates' or senators' staff may have or know where to find pertinent information. The *Congressional Quarterly* (a weekly publication devoted to the ins and outs of Washington politics) and the *Federal Register* are available (both in print and online) in many libraries and other public and university settings. National coalitions and trade associations may be helpful in locating appropriate information; federal regulatory agencies may have updates and written guidelines for a given area. At the state level, municipal leagues and state associations might provide useful material. Members of a state's general assembly should be able to locate relevant or draft legislation.

Information on existing and pending laws and regulations might influence the choice of stakeholders, the target population, method, and implementation strategies. Any successful and enduring needs assessment must be well grounded in knowledge of relevant regulations and legislation.

Economic Conditions

Economic conditions refer here to the larger economic picture that can impact the funding available to the agency to conduct and implement the needs assessment. Regulatory and legislative changes at a local, state, or national level can have consequences for the economic environment in which the needs assessment is being conducted (e.g., research conducted with federal money will be terminated if the funds supporting that research are reapportioned). The money available to an agency or sponsoring organization may influence a project by determining if: (a) the cost and scope are sustainable, (b) timing is appropriate, (c) the affordable effort is acceptable to the stakeholders, and (d) implementation of findings is feasible. Cost and scope may be a function of the climate for soliciting revenue, and may depend on whether contributions are public or private and whether they are from sources such as government, the private sector, foundations, or benefactors. If government funding is unavailable, private foundations may offer an alternative source of funds to conduct the needs assessment or to implement the findings later. Writing a grant is usually a major part of obtaining outside funding to underwrite a needs assessment. Sources that discuss grant writing in detail are included in Suggested Additional Readings.

Cutbacks in funding can impact the timing of the needs assessment. Cutbacks may simply mean a delay in the timetable of the project until resources become available. The reverse, however, may also be true. One reason for conducting a needs assessment may be to justify need when economic times are tough, resulting in populations, services, or programs competing for the same funds. Under these conditions, a needs assessment may have a positive impact on receiving scarce resources because needs have been documented.

If resources are limited, fewer approaches to conducting the needs assessment may be viable. However, less expensive approaches may elicit valid, reliable, useful information. For example, if funding is not available to do a random sample survey of the needs of the physically disabled population, discussions in focus groups held with individuals with disabilities might give valuable and valid information.

Further, economic factors ultimately affect the feasibility of implementing recommendations. This is further discussed in chapter 9.

Technological Changes

Technology is equipment and the knowledge required to use that equipment. Technological forces may, on the surface, appear irrelevant to a needs assessment; however, it is critical to consider the importance of technology to the very people and issues being assessed. For example, as industries rely less on manual labor and more on automation, employment and training issues, and their ripple effects on the population, may become part of the equation for the assessment of need.

Technological opportunities can facilitate many stages of a needs assessment project, from communication during planning to disseminating results and implementation strategies. Computer networks, such as e-mail, are valuable options in communicating with stakeholders and sending information to others. Changes in available technology may also increase options for creative solutions to found needs. In considering implementation of possible housing developments, for example, manufactured housing may be a technological option acceptable under the local zoning ordinance. Creative use of technology may provide a wide array of alternatives during the project, and social scientists should stay attuned to new and relevant advances.

Population Dynamics

Demographic (population) composition and change is often the easiest external factor to document, but the hardest to control. Unlike legislative or economic changes where creative solutions may arise (e.g., introducing legislation, reducing costs), demographic changes persist regardless of stakeholders' interest or involvement. Changes (i.e., age, income, marital status, living arrangements) in the existing population and changes due to immigration or out-migration may determine the "who, what, and where" of the target population and needs assessment. Although the development of a population profile of the target population is often a first step in assessing need, the target population should be seen in the context of the larger demographic picture of the area. Documenting the relative size, proportion, mobility, and composition of the target population highlights the salience and timeliness of the project.

A study of community service needs of elderly developmentally disabled persons in a rural area illustrated the importance of demographic comparisons (See, Ellis, Spellman, & Cress, 1990). The researchers compared the characteristics of their target population to national statistics on individuals with developmental disabilities. By contrasting the needs of the rural population with their more urban counterparts, the researchers concluded that, in a rural setting, a lower incidence of developmental disability, greater distance between those with service needs and site of service provision, and diversity in rural and urban lifestyle would make service delivery based on a more urban model problematic.

Chapter 7 on maternal and child health presents another example of the importance of examining the demographic landscape. Terrie discusses geographic variability in infant mortality rates as a determinant of where risk is greatest and how interventions should be targeted.

IDENTIFICATION OF INTERNAL FACTORS

Internal factors are within the system of the needs assessment and include: the administrative role of the agency or sponsoring organization, the purview and background of the existing organization, relationships with comparable organizations, and resource availability. These factors are often more apparent than external factors in their impact on the project and are generally more amenable to influence or change.

Administrative Role

Recognizing the key role of the administration of a sponsoring organization and obtaining their cooperation and support is critical to the success of most needs assessments. The more the administrators know about and backs the project, the more likely they are to cooperate in supplying necessary resources. This cooperation is most likely when communication throughout the process is open and straightforward. The importance of the administrative position is discussed again later.

Existing Organization

One early step is to review the programs, policies, and past efforts of the sponsoring organization or agency. Planning for future projects should be based on a realistic appraisal of the organization's past and present successes, failures, strengths, and weaknesses. Funders often look to this type of "self-study" to determine if the organization requesting money has a realistic grasp of organizational capability. This overview should include a review of several questions: What sorts of problems is the agency already addressing or capable of addressing? What sorts of problems would be completely impossible? What relevant strengths does the organization have in approaching a needs assessment? What difficulties is the organization experiencing? Further, have any units within the agency conducted a needs assessment of any type? For example, one unit in a health department may have investigated childhood immunization needs. Despite the limited scope, those procedures and findings might be useful for other health department personnel.

Comparable Organizations

Public and private organizations that share similar concerns or serve the same target population in another capacity are also part of the needs assessment system. These agencies may have done an earlier needs assessment, which could be used as a model or for comparison. Collaboration across agencies can also strengthen the base of support for a needs assessment. Cooperating with other organizations, especially involving them early in the planning stages of needs assessment, may reduce their fears of competition and produce a team effort. For example, during a meeting to discuss the longitudinal needs assessment of the elderly discussed in chapter 8, a woman from an agency dealing with substance abuse asked that questions on patterns of drug and alcohol use be included in the assessment. As a result, her agency did not carry out their own assessment, but lent support to the project already underway.

By identifying possible benefits that other organizations would receive from the completed needs assessments and inviting them to have input into the process, it may be possible to receive their support in various ways. Staff from other agencies might have relevant research expertise. An organization might be willing to share a meeting room or help with printing or graphics for the final report. By identifying and including other organizations throughout planning and implementation, all may benefit from the expanded pool of experience, expertise, resources, and, eventually, the study findings.

Resource Availability

Many types of resources—from personnel to computer equipment—are necessary to complete a needs assessment. The strategic planning level is the opportunity to examine the available resources and determine if the sponsoring organization is in the position to directly support the project in its various stages. If it is not, this is the time to explore other avenues for resources, such as using stakeholders to provide personnel, funding, in-kind contributions (space, phone, paper costs), or volunteer services. If meeting deadlines for the completion of a needs assessment is difficult or impossible with existing resources, a reordering of other agency/organization priorities yielding more resources toward the project may facilitate timely completion. Finally, look for ways that others have mobilized different resources and approaches in garnering resources if available internal resources are not adequate to complete a useful needs assessment.

MONITORING EXTERNAL AND INTERNAL FORCES

After relevant external and internal factors have been identified, monitoring those forces becomes an ongoing task throughout the needs assessment. Monitoring involves observing significant external and internal forces, determining the chance that they will occur, and, if they do, weighing their possible impact on the project.

For example, suppose the target population is migrant workers and their families, and the agency is interested in improving education for migrant children. Demographic characteristics and changes (numbers and mobility of migrant families and ages of their children) and legislative factors (regulations designed to reduce immigration and assistance to immigrants) would clearly be issues of top priority throughout planning, conducting, and implementing the needs assessment.

Sorkin, Ferris, and Hudak (1985) recommended constructing a matrix of germane external and internal factors to record and evaluate the probability and likely impact of those factors that are most relevant and compelling. Figure 5.1 is an example of an external factor matrix developed for a hypothetical assessment of need for child day care. (Note that factors may overlap two or more categories.) Increases in the number of dual-income families and changes in birth rates are both probable demographic events, but with differential impact on the needs assessment. In contrast, legislation such as the enactment of federal and state day care regulations is unlikely to occur, and, if it did, would have low impact on the study. Telecommuting, a technological advance in this example, although unlikely, would have high impact if developed. Economic factors, such as stability of source of funding, are very possible and have

Need for Child Day Care

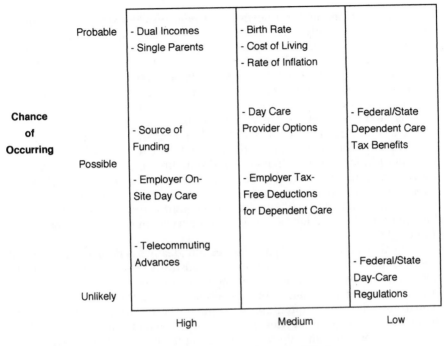

Figure 5.1. Matrix of external forces.

high impact. Such a matrix can be as detailed or broad as necessary and useful. It should be modified when and if additional factors or changes in existing factors develop.

Monitoring also includes reviewing other information and research related to the target or similar population. Findings may influence decisions by increasing understanding and insights about the target group. This review of the literature should be standard fare for all needs assessment projects because both similarities and differences in other findings are likely to be instructive.

Ongoing monitoring of relevant factors is a crucial part of preparing for and implementing the various stages of a needs assessment. A periodic review of the strategic plan should be an integral part of all subsequent phases of the project. Necessary adaptations are easier when forces surrounding the needs assessment are routinely considered, rather than ignored until a crisis arises.

PROJECT PLANNING

Thoughtful planning for a needs assessment provides structure and allows for flexibility. Certainly, plans are made to be changed, time lines are constructed to be modified, and budgets are developed to be recalculated. However, it is easier to make adjustments to a plan that is already in place than to start from scratch each time the unexpected happens (which is to be expected). Planning for a needs assessment is a multistage process. It is impossible to carry out an involved project with only one planning session, and planning sessions should be built into the process from the beginning.

Notes summarizing discussion and highlighting follow-up steps should be standard parts of the planning process. Details can be easily forgotten; a division of labor can be "slighted," and time lines can be overlooked. Further, a complete record of the process can be useful if a follow-up is planned, if someone else is planning a needs assessment, or if certain decisions need to be retrospectively justified. As Posavac and Carey (1989) pointed out, documentation is needed not from lack of trust, but to ensure simple accountability.

A practical and successful planning session ideally has both a facilitator and a note-taker. The agency director and administrative assistant may automatically fill these roles, but, if not, someone needs to take responsibility for these tasks. Recording information on newsprint or a chalkboard in a size large enough for all to see is often useful. Type and distribute this information to the group—these notes may serve as the institutional memory for the project, allow latecomers to catch up on what has happened, and help in writing the final report.

Three considerations should guide planning: (a) the initial reason for undertaking the needs assessment, (b) the methodological design, and (c) the intended uses of the information. First, the motivation for undertaking the needs assessment should provide a frame of reference for the study. As discussed, the process will evolve differently if the motivation is for additional program development, increased funding, or justification for a grant proposal. Second, the choice of research method will also direct planning. Different methods have different requirements for time, expertise, and supplies. Some approaches will require fewer planning steps, and some will require more. The use of a matrix, as discussed in earlier chapters (see Table 2.1), can clarify planning for each methodological approach. The third consideration is the intended use of the findings. The interests of the primary audience and the primary purpose of the needs assessment shape the final products of a needs assessment. These should be clear, at least in part, during the early stages of the project.

What follows is a brief review of steps necessary to begin a needs assessment. Each research team customizes the following points to fit the specific and unique demands of the situation.

DEVELOPING A RESEARCH TEAM

The persons responsible for the implementation of the needs assessment are referred to as the researchers; those working with them constitute the research team. Some agencies hire outside consultants to serve as researchers, and others utilize available staff. Each choice has it strengths and weaknesses. An outside person has no preconceived expectations of the organizational culture, and this fresh view can allow for a constructive new approach. However, because of that lack of knowledge, an outside consultant must learn about the organizational context and sometimes the subject itself (AIDS, aging, etc.) before beginning, or while conducting, the needs assessment. Additionally, extra funds are usually required to pay for an outside researcher. An insider has the advantage of already being familiar with the facilities, personnel, and style of the organization. However, this familiarity can lead to a fixed perception of what is right, wrong, and amenable to change. As insiders are already on the payroll, they usually do not require additional funds, but it is unrealistic to expect an individual to carry out a large-scale needs assessment while continuing his or her other responsibilities.

Whether from inside or outside the organization, the roles of the researcher and research team must be clear. There are many stages to a needs assessment; conducting the actual research is only one. Although researchers are committed to planning, collecting, and analyzing data, they may be less prepared to organize and lead meetings with stakeholders. If the researcher is expected to take the leadership role during these meetings, this individual needs both the knowledge of group dynamics and the skills to facilitate meetings with diverse audiences. If the members of the research team are not comfortable with the task of leading meetings, another person knowledgeable of the project must take that job. In addition, as an applied researcher, the individual is generally expected to utilize findings once the data are collected. Clearly defining expectations and roles for the researchers, and all members of the project, expedites task completion and facilitates transitions because different individuals begin and end their work on the needs assessment.

The assumption here is that a needs assessment is done in an organizational setting with an organizational chart. A "chain of command" implies that someone in administration is directly or indirectly responsible for the assessment and its impact. An existing organizational chart makes planning the needs assessment easier because it clarifies position and responsibility. If such a chart is unavailable, it might be useful to consider lines of authority within the parent organization so as to work within the existing structure as closely as possible. Similarly, an early planning task is producing an organizational chart specifically for the needs assessment project if many people are involved. If researchers must cross traditional hierarchical lines of authority during the project, the agency director should communicate that information to the rest of the staff. If outside consultants or staff are brought in, they need to know their place in the organizational structure. Although this may seem petty, confusion and disagreement over issues of responsibility can seriously impede the project.

Central to developing a research team is determining what tasks, skills, and knowledge are necessary and knowing who is potentially available to participate, such as agency staff, organizational volunteers, interns, and other stakeholders. Delegating responsibility to capable workers is an efficient way to balance the workload, and communicating clear instructions and deadlines allows personnel to avoid wasting time wondering what they should do. However, researchers can only communicate specific guidelines and responsibilities to others if they know themselves what has to be done.

Developing a research team continues throughout the project, as one person finishes a job and another begins. New tasks and new personnel requirements arise routinely. Stakeholder involvement varies from task to task. The transition is easier if there is a clear, cohesive, well-documented plan, and personnel can be recruited in advance.

Whether the actual director of the sponsoring organization is involved in the early stages of planning, projects are most successful if information circulates freely and often across the ranks of those involved. The agency director, or whoever is ultimately responsible for the needs assessment, should always be informed of what is going on, even if only in the form of intermittent progress reports or memos. The following issues should be considered:

Research Team Checklist

Who has primary responsibility for the needs assessment?

_____ Is this person from inside or outside the agency?
_____ If from the outside, what is the funding source?
_____ Who else will make up the research team?
_____ Are the lines of authority clearly communicated?
_____ Are all stages of the project sketched out?
_____ Do individuals on the research team have a clear idea of their responsibilities?
_____ What are the plans for organizational communication?

Working with Stakeholders

Practically speaking, the identification of stakeholders should be an early priority in project planning because stakeholders should be involved as soon and as often as possible. In some cases, the range of stakeholders is mandated by the funding agency. For example, in chapter 7, Terrie describes infant health care coalitions composed of health care providers, governmental representatives, and consumers of family planning services (the formation of which was dictated by law). In other cases, identification of stakeholders starts from a network already in place. For example, Area Agencies on Aging must have an advisory group composed of a majority of elderly citizens, and communities have Parent–Teacher Associations (PTAs). Existing advisory, advocacy, or community groups are natural starting places because they usually have considerable interest in furthering the well-being of their constituencies. These existing groups can serve as a window into the larger stakeholder community.

In other more difficult cases, however, the research team must start with no organization in place. In the most extreme instances (e.g., substance abusers), individuals in need are unlikely to readily step forward, even if they have been identified, recognize help is needed, and are given incentives. If a group feels victimized by the system, its members are not likely to be willing participants in a process they see as inherently flawed due to its place in that system. There are no easy paths to winning the trust of a group. Ideally, the research team should be able to identify one or more key players—individuals who are inside the stakeholding group to some extent and who are willing to straddle the boundaries among the target population, stakeholders and research team. The chapter on needs assessment of the elderly (chapter 8) describes this scenario. Often caseworkers, community activists, or concerned family members can provide a clue to such individuals. It is unwise, however, to have only one person to negotiate the boundary. The more stakeholders involved, the more vigorous and reliable the process, especially in the early stages of decision making. Every person who can "touch" the process, even in anger, should be heard.

In the early stages of planning, it might be useful to have several fairly large meetings at different places and times to accommodate various schedules. Announcements should be posted in well-visited locales, such as churches or recreation centers. If possible, invited stakeholders should be called and sent follow-up notes. In addition, members of the research team might ask to be included in scheduled meetings that are being held in the community of interest. These meetings can be used as forums for the research team to explain what they are trying to accomplish, to allow interested stakeholders to express themselves on the issues, and to solicit assistance. The research team should bring printed material in appropriate translations. At a minimum, a brief outline of the project and several telephone numbers should be provided for follow-up information.

For other groups, a one-on-one approach may work better. Researchers should be prepared to communicate with stakeholders in ways that best reach that particular group. Elected officials and members of the business community may not come to planning meetings but still want to be part of the process and respond to calls, letters, or e-mail. All communication should be clear and concise. Stakeholders should be told what they need to know about the project, what they could do, and what they will receive in return.

If stakeholders belong to distinct cultural or ethnic groups, awareness and sensitivity to specific norms and values are important issues. At a minimum, language skills or good translators are often required. One translator without a good feel for colloquial usage translated "meals on wheels" as "food on tires." In addition, cultural norms should be researched. Symbols convey different meanings to different populations. For example, a research team once put a picture of an owl on materials discussing health resources without knowing that owls represented death to the group being addressed.

Stakeholders can be involved in various ways throughout the project. Each situation is unique in its design to incorporate and utilize stakeholders. For example, stakeholders may have input on questionnaire development, sample selection, data interpretation, and program implementation strategies. An important contribution of service consumers as stakeholders is to present their views of reality. Because service providers talk primarily among themselves (Hobbs, 1987), they often perceive a different world than those inside the consumer circle, who may give a very unexpected view.

The key to successful integration of stakeholders into the needs assessment is to ensure their active involvement during key parts of the process. It is not always easy to accommodate the differing viewpoints and approaches that a large spectrum of participants bring to the planning process. This was illustrated well in a project dealing with services for pregnant teens in Canada. In the report, the author stated that, although dialogue was qualitatively different when teenagers were involved, it was also more "reality-based" (Kerr, 1989).

The type of stakeholder involvement expected should be made clear. If the team needs individuals who speak Vietnamese to make phone calls, or individuals to help develop a questionnaire or plan dissemination strategies, early meetings are an excellent time to ask. Individuals respond much more quickly to requests for fairly small, readily defined tasks than to vague requests for help. From these various venues, a group of dedicated stakeholders is likely to emerge. If the group becomes too large, break into smaller groups. If the group is too small, develop supports to avoid overworking those who are available.

Although the research team may believe that the process is straightforward and unbiased, stakeholders may feel differently. The research team should be ready to deal with conflict and anger that can erupt at meetings. Coping with hostility may require compromise, negotiation, open discussion, and patience. It may be useful to reiterate the overall goal of the project as a reminder to all that there is a shared vision, although it may look very different from different perspectives. Clearly, these situations are the exception, but it is useful to give thought to the contingency. Discussing possible sources of conflict and/or role playing various scenarios before meetings might prove useful. For extreme circumstances, a paid or volunteer facilitator may become necessary to conduct mediation or reconciliation. Introducing a new dynamic into meetings may have positive or negative consequences, and the research team should carefully consider alternatives. Sometimes handling conflicts within the group has important team-building implications; at other times, outside help is more practical and efficacious.

On a more positive note, there is the consideration of how (or if) stakeholders will benefit from their participation. They may feel good about their part in a project that is intended to better conditions for a group to which they have an attachment, but are there other rewards for their involvement? Stakeholders or volunteers of any kind need to feel that they are valued and their efforts appreciated. Common courtesy and respect are mandatory and minimal expectations. Including the names of workers in newsletters or reports is a common technique for acknowledging participation. In this case, spell names correctly, and print them only with permission. Stakeholders would probably prefer actual payment, but letters of recognition, plaques, or small presents can be thoughtful remembrances. Simple thank you notes and refreshments at meetings are always appreciated. However, it is important not to "tokenize" the efforts of stakeholders (Kerr, 1989), especially those who are unaccustomed to a formal meeting process. A sincere handshake and acknowledgment after a meeting add a personal touch and may help less "professional" stakeholders feel that they are integral parts of the project. Consider the following:

Checklist for Developing a Stakeholder Group

How are groups and individuals relevant to the process identified?

_____ Phone book?
_____ Agency referrals (sponsoring and others)?
_____ Asking groups or individuals previously identified to refer?
_____ Churches, temples, other places of worship?
_____ School system?
_____ Charitable organizations (e.g., Red Cross)?
_____ Chamber of Commerce?
_____ Elected officials?

How will communication and involvement be structured?

_____ Meetings arranged by the research team?
_____ Meetings scheduled by other groups?
_____ Phone calls?
_____ Individual meetings?

Are there cultural norms to consider?

_____ Are translations necessary?
_____ Are interpreters needed for meetings?
_____ Who will translate written material?
_____ Can volunteers be used?

Are expectations and requirements of stakeholders clear?
Have possible conflicts and potential solutions been discussed?

_____ What are the incentives for stakeholders to cooperate?
_____ Who is responsible for providing "thank yous"?

SETTING GOALS AND OBJECTIVES

According to Hobbs (1987), no consideration is more important to the success of a project than having a clear statement of its purpose and goals.

Two aspects of goals are included here: (a) the overall philosophy of the organization sponsoring the needs assessment, and (b) the specific end desired from the research project. Reviewing the overall philosophy and mission statement of the sponsoring agency helps focus participants and remind them of the larger purpose that frames the project. A review of the guiding assumptions of the agency or supporting organization will put everyone on the same path and focus the discussion as researchers and stakeholders begin to detail the goals of the project. In the absence of agency or organizational mission statements, or if the agency is not the sponsor of the project, the mission of the funding entity needs to be highlighted and periodically revisited.

The second aspect of goal elaboration is the determination of the goals and objectives aimed at the project's intended outcome. Goals and objectives are established at various points in the needs assessment process such as planning for data collection, dissemination, and implementation of policies resulting from the findings.

Goals and objectives are distinct. *Goals* are abstract and general statements of desired outcomes; they are not meant to be directly measurable (Chambers, 1993). For example, if a needs assessment found that community members were uninformed on the problem of domestic violence in the area, one goal might be to increase community awareness of domestic violence. This goal is vague about the specific outcome, although it points in a general direction. *Objectives* are specific, empirical, operational statements about a desired observable outcome; they are concrete in that it is clear when they have been attained (Chambers, 1993). Using the goal of increasing awareness of domestic violence, a clear objective would be to cooperate with local community college faculty to present two forums on wife abuse during the upcoming academic year.

Goals and objectives should be short- and long-term and should be set throughout the project. As they guide the project, goals and objectives should be discussed in the first project planning meeting and reviewed at the beginning of each subsequent meeting. Measuring progress toward goals and objectives is an excellent evaluation device during and after the project because it gives a standard against which to measure actual achievement (Chambers, 1993).

Setting goals and objectives remains very important once the research has been completed in the implementation and dissemination stages of the project. Needs of the target population become clear as the data are collected and analyzed. At that point, careful articulation and prioritization of goals and objectives helps to ensure that the most pressing needs are addressed first. The following questions should be considered:

Goal Checklist

   _____ What is the goal or mission of the sponsoring organization?
   _____ What are the overall goal(s) of the project?
      _____ Planning goals
      _____ Implementation goals

_____ What are the objectives for each goal?
_____ Are objectives:
_____ Achievable?
_____ Measurable, observable?
_____ Do objectives include:
_____ Time frame?
_____ Desired outcome?
_____ Target population?
_____ Person or group responsible?

ESTABLISHING A TIME LINE

Administrators of the sponsoring organization, funders, stakeholders, and researchers should agree on a broad time frame for conducting the needs assessment and disseminating the findings. Once the overall time parameters are set, the timing of individual tasks can be allocated accordingly. Early in the process, construct a time line with specific names next to specific tasks and subtasks. Schedules can be modified, but most individuals work better with deadlines. Gantt and Pert charts* are useful conceptual devices for scheduling time and tasks.

The schedule should include time lines for: (a) planning and conceptualization, (b) data collection, (c) data analysis, and (d) report writing and revision. It should also include time for making recommendations and disseminating findings, although the time frame for these may be vague in the early planning stages. Some deadlines are imposed from outside, as when reports are due to state agencies. Otherwise, it should be decided when the project should be finished, and then everyone works backward. If stakeholders from outside the agency are involved, it may be impossible to have more than two planning meetings a month and more than 2 productive hours per meeting. If meetings start on time, less time is lost and the project feels more on task. As many planning meetings as necessary should be set, but the meeting should not become the end in itself. At some point, everyone has had their say, and will say it again and again if there is time (and if there is a weak facilitator). Redundancy should be avoided. The time and place of the next planning meeting should be set or announced at the beginning and end of each meeting.

Interruptions to the schedule should be anticipated. For example, December is a difficult month for scheduling meetings or completing interviews. If the assessment deals with educational issues, summer activities may be impractical. Religious and ethnic holidays also should be taken into consideration when scheduling.

*Gantt charts plot activities associated with a project over time. Pert charts trace the path through the various steps that must be completed to accomplish the final goal of a needs assessment.

SUPPLYING RESOURCES

Different approaches require different resources, and each project has unique requirements. This section discusses details of supplies, equipment, and space that must be considered. Funding issues were discussed earlier.

Supplies and Equipment

Necessary supplies such as paper, computer discs, writing utensils, and staples, should be listed. Equipment needs may include computers, copiers, fax machines, and printers. These are just a few examples of indirect costs that have to be covered. If the sponsoring agency is well supplied and equipped, this may not be an important issue. But if supplies and/or equipment must be purchased or requisitioned, a careful inventory of materials needed throughout the project must be prepared and often justified.

This is an area where contributions are popular. Donating funds or providing or loaning of supplies are practical alternatives; the donor may have a surplus, or may be interested in the tax break for a contribution.

Early in the project, it is hard to plan for all necessary supplies and equipment, but visualizing each step of the process is helpful. For example, the use of in-person interviewers may require pencils, typed questionnaires, microrecorders, bus passes, and identification badges. Writing the final report might require special statistical software.

Space

Another important resource is space for meetings and work areas to store supplies and house the project. The sponsoring organization usually supplies much, if not all, of the necessary offices and storage, but community meetings may require locating and requesting rooms and equipment, sometimes weeks in advance.

A consideration of the location is availability and affordability of transportation because stakeholders may or may not have access to cars. Try to arrange meetings in sites accessible to public transportation, or try to ensure that transportation is provided in other ways. Decisions on choice of location and transportation invoke safety issues. Researchers and stakeholders should feel comfortable traveling to and from meeting sites, entering and exiting meeting facilities, and working alone in offices. Stakeholders also feel more comfortable in locations with which they are familiar.

The following list details items to be addressed in planning for meeting space.

Checklist for Space Requirements

_____ What are the space requirements?
_____ Where will planning meetings be held?

_____ Is setup necessary?
 _____ Tables and chairs?
 _____ Dry marker board or chalkboard?
 _____ Temperature and lighting?
 _____ Refreshments?
 _____ Restrooms?
_____ Do offices have adequate privacy and access to supplies?
_____ Are there facilities for secure storage?
_____ Is there extra space for other personnel, such as interns or volunteers?
_____ Is transportation an issue?
_____ Have safety issues been addressed?

MANAGING PUBLICITY

Publicity is useful in two ways: It encourages the public to cooperate and it enhances the visibility of the agency (Neuber, Atkins, Jacobson, & Reuterman, 1980). If community involvement is desirable, community members must be aware of the project, and there are many avenues to reach them. First, all groups to inform (including target population and other stakeholders) should be identified, and the best ways to reach them should be strategized. The purpose of publicity should also be considered to solicit participation or to increase awareness of the project. A public awareness campaign should focus on the media the stakeholders are most likely to access, such as Spanish-speaking radio, local and public access television, or church bulletins; and gathering places, such as places or worship, recreation centers, or libraries. One Area Agency on Aging published articles in its monthly newspaper to alert their constituency to the upcoming assessment. One organization paid to have a message—"Call in your opinions"—on the side of city buses. There are also less expensive alternatives to separate mailings: information inserted in an upcoming mailing, newsletters from other organizations, or postcards. The media should be informed of stakeholder meetings. A key social psychological concept—the "mere exposure effect" (Zajonc, 1968)—holds that the more one is exposed to something, the more one comes to accept it. It is probably impossible to get too much positive exposure for a needs assessment; however, care should be taken to ensure that the publicity is accurate and favorable. The following issues should be addressed when managing publicity:

Publicity Checklist

_____ Who should know about the project?
_____ Why should they be informed?
_____ How will information be publicized?
 _____ Local media?
 _____ Newspapers?
 _____ Special interest publications?

_____ Free papers?
_____ Radio?
_____ Television?
_____ Local access cable?
_____ Local news program?
_____ Agency publications?
_____ Monthly or annual reports?
_____ Bulletin boards of relevant agencies or locations frequented by stakeholders?
_____ Newsletters?
_____ Mailings?
_____ Online bulletin boards?
_____ Presentations?
_____ Funders?
_____ Boards?
_____ Luncheon clubs?
_____ Local service organizations?
_____ Professional organizations?

EVALUATING THE PROCESS

Each stage of planning, conducting, and implementing a needs assessment should include evaluation. Each time the research team meets, a few minutes at the beginning should be reserved for reviewing the time line, goals, and objectives; considering and troubleshooting any problems; and dealing with unforeseen circumstances. This is the time to make adjustments to the schedule or plans if necessary. The sooner a difficulty can be corrected, the less impact it has on the overall project. The evaluator (Feuz, 1989) for the British Columbia teen pregnancy project found that the most successful projects were those in which a formal outside evaluation was conducted in the first 6 months. The outside attention served to keep the project on course.

Evaluation is also crucial after the project is over. Many funders require that evaluation be built into a grant proposal. Hindsight does not eliminate problems that have already occurred, but may prevent a repetition of those same problems in future efforts. Further, the advantages, disadvantages, strengths, and weaknesses of the project should be discussed in the final report and whenever the findings are presented. The following questions should be considered:

Evaluation Checklist

_____ Is there a brief informal evaluation each time the research team meets?
_____ Is there an opportunity for formal outside evaluation?

_____ Is there a scheduled thorough evaluation of the entire project when it is completed?
    _____ Have the strengths and advantages of the project been evaluated?
    _____ Have the weaknesses and disadvantages of the project been evaluated?

SUMMARY

Planning continues throughout the entire needs assessment. A good plan eliminates many obstacles; two crucial aspects of planning include anticipating barriers and interruptions and devising coping strategies. When unexpected or difficult circumstances do arise, there are no substitutes for flexibility and creativity. Researchers must simultaneously adhere as closely as possible to the developed plan, yet be willing to modify it as necessary. Social scientists doing needs assessments have more freedom to conduct research and implement findings when a comprehensive and cohesive plan is in place.

II

CASE STUDIES: VARIOUS APPROACHES

The following three chapters present examples of four needs assessments focusing on three very different substantive areas and using varied methodological approaches. The first (chapter 6) is a case study of an assessment of the AIDS-related needs of women living in a housing project in New York City. The assessment was conducted by the staff of a community-based organization under the sponsorship of the Centers for Disease Control and Prevention (CDC) using the services of a part-time researcher as a consultant. The second case study (chapter 7) describes a state-mandated assessment of child and maternal health needs of residents of a county in northwest Florida. This project, carried out by a group of researchers, employed innovative techniques for presenting and analyzing secondary data from vital statistics registers and a state-developed screening instrument. The target population and methods to be used were clearly specified from the start by the terms of the legislative mandate. The third case study (chapter 8) discusses two very different projects both investigating needs of elderly residents of suburban counties in metropolitan Northern Virginia: a longitudinal survey of the general elderly population, and a qualitative assessment of the unmet service needs of homebound African-American, Hispanic, and Vietnamese elders. Both assessments were conducted for county government agencies by outside researchers under the auspices of a special postdoctoral fellowship program in applied gerontology.

The case studies illustrate, singly and in combination, the concrete range of issues, approaches, resources, and outcomes integral to a needs assessment effort. They are presented less for their substantive content (although that is also of interest) than as examples demonstrating how specific approaches and strategies can be applied to different types of needs of target populations in diverse contexts focused at different levels. Most articles on needs assessment focus on methods and findings without presenting much meaningful contextual background or thoughtful consideration of the process. In contrast, as integrated accounts of what happened and why, the case studies tell the story of these different needs assessment efforts, including why the assessment was conducted, in what context, by whom, how the research was carried out, and what happened to the findings. The authors also present their thoughts on the strengths and weaknesses of their respective approaches to needs assessment and their views of what might have been done differently, and why. This is a more productive way to understand the bases and processes of needs assessment, and to illustrate the points made in other chapters, without losing sight of the specific content involved. Each case study chapter provides some or all of the following elements:

- a brief description of the demographic and geographic setting of the needs assessment, the political and administrative environment in which it was initiated and carried out, and the central motivation or impetus for the project;
- a discussion of the method(s) used for conducting the needs assessment including the reasons for selecting the specific target population and methodological approach, a step-by-step description of the procedures employed to gather and analyze the data, and a presentation of salient findings and conclusions; a look at the practical implications and applications of the study findings, how and to whom the results were disseminated, which groups did and did not "buy into" the findings and why, and any ongoing or future plans to use the assessment's processes or findings; and
- an overview of the strengths and weaknesses of the project and thoughts on what might have been done better or differently to improve any or all aspects of the needs assessment. This section should be particularly useful in planning and conducting a needs assessment.

In reading the case studies, the following questions should be kept in mind:

- How, if at all, were different groups of stakeholders involved in the various stages of the needs assessment? What impact did their involvement (or noninvolvement) have on the effort?
- How much and what types of planning occurred, and with what effects?
- What methods were used to ascertain need, and why? Could other methods, or combinations of methods, have worked as well or better?
- How were the findings presented, disseminated, and used to recommend or make changes in policy or practice?
- What unanticipated factors or events developed during the course of the needs assessment and how effectively were they addressed?

6

Assessing the AIDS-Related Needs of Women in an Urban Housing Development

Robin L. Miller
Elizabeth E. Solomon

This chapter concerns an experience implementing an iterative, multiple-method needs assessment of women living in a Brooklyn community. The needs assessment was conducted with a small AIDS-related community-based organization in New York City and evolved from a primary prevention grant received from the Centers for Disease Control and Prevention (CDC). Throughout the description, particular attention is paid to how organizational and stakeholder politics affected the development and execution of the study. Among the central issues discussed are how dependence on untrained staff and organizational upheaval influenced the research design and its complexity.

The objectives in conducting the needs assessment were threefold: to specify the nature of the problem, to facilitate the organization's selecting a well-defined target population, and to ensure the organization had adequate knowledge about the target population ultimately selected. These objectives were to be achieved through a series of simple steps, which the organization could execute with minimal assistance. These steps included: (a) identifying important community resources, (b) compiling existing community and health indicator data, (c) engaging program recipients and stakeholders, and (d) identifying factors that impeded or facilitated women's ability to change AIDS-related risk behaviors. Background information on the organization and its target population is presented first.

AIDS SERVICE ORGANIZATIONS

Throughout the United States, community-based AIDS service organizations (ASOs) are the primary providers of AIDS-related education and services. The majority of ASOs grew out of the failure by government, social

The needs assessment activities described in this chapter were funded by a grant from the Centers for Disease Control and Prevention.

The authors gratefully acknowledge the assistance of Marie Lucie Brutus, the late Cathy D. Ewan, Daveth Forbes, Margaret Gerard, and Beverly Greene in collecting needs assessment data, and Susan Berkowitz, J. Brian Cassel, Yvonne Chambers, Jennifer Kaplan, Terence Kiernan, Rebecca Reviere, and David Knapp Whittier for their helpful remarks on this chapter.

service, and health service institutions to adequately address the needs and concerns of local constituents (Altman, 1994). For example, the first ASO in the United States was founded in New York City in 1981 by six gay males who were disturbed by the unexplained deaths of many of their friends. Later, a multitude of organizations were founded to serve various populations affected by HIV. These organizations typically receive the majority of their financial support from city, state, and federal grants, principally through money managed by the CDC and several other federal agencies.

Funding organizations have become increasingly concerned that the funds they provide contribute to successful programs (Peterson, Card, Eisen, & Sherman-Williams, 1994). AIDS funding organizations are no exception to this general trend. In the late 1980s and early 1990s, funding organizations began to require that ASOs engage in needs assessment and program evaluation activities as a condition of funding. However, few of the organizations funded under these initiatives have the capacity to conduct evaluation research (National Community AIDS Partnership, 1993). Additionally, funding organizations rarely provide financial support for evaluation activities at a level necessary to produce more than documentation of service units delivered. ASOs are struggling to gather useful information to meet their own needs and to provide high-quality program evaluation data to funding organizations without the personnel and financial resources to perform either task well.

Simultaneously, ASO staff have become increasingly aware how complex the challenge of successful HIV prevention is. The informational seminars provided by ASOs in the early years of the epidemic, although necessary, are insufficient to affect the variety of factors that influence HIV-related risk-taking behavior. ASO staff are anxious for needs assessment data that could assist them to plan effective interventions.

HIV AND WOMEN

African-American and Latina women constitute the majority of female AIDS cases in the United States, despite that they constitute less than 20% of women in the United States. Nationally, African-American and Latina women most often become HIV infected through unprotected heterosexual sex with a "man at risk" and through injection drug use with tainted equipment (Centers for Disease Control, 1994). Women of low socioeconomic status (SES) are at greater risk of HIV infection. In New York City, African-American women constitute 52% and Latinas constitute 31% of all AIDS cases among women. Consistent with national data, injection drug use is the primary mode of transmission among New York City Latina and African-American women, followed by heterosexual contact (New York City Department of Health, 1994; New York State Department of Health, 1994a).

The community where the needs assessment ultimately took place exceeds citywide norms in percentage of uninsured residents, percentage of low birth weight infants, adult and infant mortality rates, unemployment rate, and other vital statistics that describe community well-being (New York State Department of Health, 1994b; United Hospital Fund of New York, 1994). The percentage of households in poverty also exceeds the citywide value. About 25% of the community's residents are on public assistance. In 1990, 70% of births in the community were to unmarried women. Low birth weight infants were 12% of all births, and 20% of infants born in the community received no prenatal care. The infant mortality rate was 14%. The case rate for gonorrhea was 654.7 per 100,000 women (compared with a national average of 172 cases per 100,000 people), and the case rate for AIDS was 323.5. The community has the second largest HIV prevalence rate among women in Brooklyn and the third largest in New York City. AIDS was the fourth leading cause of death among women in the community in 1990. African-American women constitute 86% of all women residing in the community.

THE BROOKLYN WOMEN'S PROJECT

The ASO that developed the Brooklyn Women's Project was founded in 1987 by a group of woman of diverse ethnic backgrounds to serve the AIDS-related needs of women, especially women of color, in New York City. The organization was originally a volunteer, grassroots effort supervised by a voluntary board. At the time of this needs assessment project, the organization was staffed entirely by African-American, Caribbean, and Latina women, and it provided educational and support services throughout New York City and in several women's prison wards.

The Brooklyn Women's Project was funded by the CDC in 1990. The original grant was co-authored by the project director and the executive director who left the organization shortly after the grant was awarded. Prior to her resignation, the executive director had provided the majority of the organization's expertise in program development, program implementation, and grant administration. The new executive director had little experience in the implementation of prevention programs. The subsequent lack of organizational expertise in program planning, program development, and government grant administration, coupled with a major transition in organizational leadership, put the organization in a difficult position for the successful implementation of the grant.

The original grant proposal to the CDC targeted a variety of women, including former drug users, female partners of current and former drug users, and adolescent women in three communities severely affected by HIV. The program was to address HIV-related skills, attitudes, and knowledge to increase women's ability to practice safer sex. Specific objectives included increasing HIV-related knowledge through community involvement and outreach, encouraging accurate risk assessment and behavior change through a curriculum, and diffusing behavior change through community involvement in the program. The actual program plan, however, was vague. In the first months of the grant, a community advisory panel was to assist in the development of curriculum and program evaluation tools. In the second half of the first year, the program evaluation, curriculum, and outreach activities were to be implemented. Implicit in the grant was the notion that staff would monitor the efficacy of activities to refine recruitment and program-delivery strategies. As described in the grant, outreach strategies comprised a variety of efforts to recruit women to participate in the curriculum-based small-group program. The grant included funding for two full-time outreach workers and the project director and was later modified to include a part-time interviewer.

During the first year of the grant, the organization met few of its stated objectives. A community advisory board was established, but could not agree on the strategies for implementing the program. The organization's board, the community advisory board, the staff, and the CDC's project officer each had different (and not always compatible) visions for the effort. The project director and outreach workers spent the first 12 months of the grant providing basic AIDS education seminars at a variety of invited speaking engagements. Other activities conducted in the first year of the project are inadequately documented. By the 12th month of the project, the CDC's project officer was concerned about the organization's ability to execute the grant's objectives successfully. Although it was not part of the original grant proposal, he requested that the organization develop a needs assessment to focus the project more carefully, and hire a consultant to help in its design and execution. He also told the organization that renewal funding for the grant might be jeopardized if the organization could not demonstrate significant progress toward the grant's objectives.

The project director was reluctant to engage a consultant to assist with the design and implementation of a needs assessment. She felt adequate skills were already available, and therefore presented the job to potential consultants as merely conducting data analyses rather than assisting the organization to develop and implement a needs assessment. A consultant was hired without realizing the full extent of assistance required by the ASO.

In addition to advising the project director on needs assessment activities, the executive director wanted some assistance monitoring project employees' performance. The CDC project officer wanted assistance assessing the organization's capacity to execute the grant and clarifying the amount of time staff spent on grant-related activities. Amidst the various needs of the stakeholders, it was not certain the project staff wanted a needs assessment or understood how it might be used.

The CDC project officer convened a meeting with the executive director, the project staff, and the consultant to discuss two primary goals. The first was to make clear to the organization that he was dissatisfied with its performance. He wanted the project's staff to accept his and the consultant's roles in structuring a needs assessment that would be meaningful and that the organization could execute on its own. His second goal was to stimulate a more careful specification of the target population to be served.

DEFINING THE TARGET POPULATION

The first step in planning an intervention is to specify the target population. The organization had broadly framed its target as women living in several Brooklyn communities, but it did not have the resources to target such a large and geographically dispersed population. More important, framing a target population so broadly did not facilitate the development of interventions that would succeed for the variety of women living in these neighborhoods. The organization's staff did not have enough information about the communities to make reasonable decisions about targeting the project. Several activities were designed to gather information to assist staff in selecting a specific target population of at-risk women in the community. Concurrent activities included nonparticipant community observation, key informant interviews with community service providers, collection of information from the local police precincts regarding neighborhood activities, and interviews with tenant, block, and neighborhood associations. Staff were also to work on the development of an interview protocol for women and to be trained as interviewers while these other data collection activities were conducted.

Community Observation

In discussions of why community women were at risk for HIV infection, staff hypothesized that drug use and prostitution activities might be prevalent, but were unclear regarding the extent of these activities, where these activities occurred, and who engaged in these activities. Staff could not describe life in the communities in much detail because few had spent much time in the target communities. The CDC project officer suggested that the staff needed to gather information systematically to confirm their ideas.

The CDC project officer decided that staff would focus on women of child-bearing age in one neighborhood and suggested a series of community observations to determine general patterns of daily living, with a specific focus on settings where women were believed to spend time. Observations were to yield a picture of the activities and people in the neighborhood and to confirm when and where drug and prostitution activities occurred (because these activities could be the focus of an intervention).

The CDC project officer briefly presented how to conduct observations. Subsequent to the meeting, the three project staff members were provided with articles on conducting nonparticipant observations and taking field notes and samples of completed observations, which they reviewed with the consultant. A schedule was developed of locations and times at which 2-hour observations would occur. A standard observation protocol was developed in which staff were asked to record the date and time of the observation, location of the observation, a description of what was observed, and notes about what was observed.

Facsimiles of the observations completed in the first week were sent to the CDC project officer and consultant for review. The first set of observations lacked detail and focus. For example, the activities spanning a 5-minute period of time on a central neighborhood street were described as "a fire engine went by." The notes did not provide a sense of the street, who was on the street, and what those individuals were doing at the time the fire engine passed. Nor was it clear why a fire engine's passing might be a salient event to describe.

This was not surprising because the staff had never collected research data before.

The consultant arranged to meet with staff weekly to review activities and provide guidance. She also arranged for practice observations, in which two staff members would simultaneously make observations and then discuss and compare their notes. Staff notes did not substantially improve over time, however; they continued to lack focus, detail, and rigor.

Discussions with staff revealed several obstacles to conducting observations. First, outreach staff expressed considerable discomfort with the task and perceived observation as intrusive. Second, staff were unclear regarding what to observe in order to describe community life. Third, staff were ambivalent about being in high-risk areas and were concerned about their own safety. Fourth, staff were under pressure to maintain a schedule of speaking engagements, regardless of whether they were related to the project. Fifth, staff remained unclear why they should focus on a narrowly defined subset of women living in the neighborhood, which influenced them to make general observations about everyone rather than specific observations about women of child-bearing age. Sixth, the project director had become increasingly open about her frustration at having to spend so much time collecting data rather than providing HIV-prevention workshops.

Measures were taken to address each of these challenges. Regarding concerns about intruding on people's privacy, staff revealed that they did not know how to respond to inquiries about what they were doing in the neighborhood and what they were writing down. The consultant and staff spent several hours together brainstorming and role playing how to handle situations in the field. The consultant and staff also discussed the role of personal appearance in making sure that they did not stand out as strangers and the potential benefits of engaging people as community informants. Regarding personal safety, in addition to developing safety tips when in the field, the observation schedule was modified so that two observers were always somewhat near one another or near a store or similar venue at all times.

Assisting staff to better understand the task and its relevance was more difficult. None of the staff had ever been part of a research effort or developed a prevention program. The consultant had staff regularly discuss issues of understanding communities and how programs are developed. Staff were also provided with a guide to HIV-related program planning and development written for racial minority community-based organizations (Thomas, So'Brien van Putten, & Chen, 1991).

To document that staff did spend all of their time on the grant, staff were asked to keep a diary of their activities and observations. For each seminar or presentation, staff were to document participant characteristics (e.g., gender, race, zip code) and the presentation's location to assess whether the presentation was delivered to the target audience. In addition to providing the ASO with basic documentation of program activities, these data revealed that staff did not spend all of their time on project-related activities.

It was clear that the project director did not accept the goals and objectives of the needs assessment. The project director enjoyed making presentations and community contacts and was frustrated with the project's direction and demands. Concurrently, the project officer had requested that the staff produce documentation of the community contacts made over the prior year. When that documentation proved inadequate, the consultant suggested the organization conduct key informant interviews to fulfill the CDC's request. The consultant hoped the key informant interviews would provide the project director with a task she could control and enjoy, thereby encouraging her more enthusiastic participation with the needs assessment.

Interviews with Local Police and Tenant and Neighborhood Associations

Community observations did not produce data to verify or challenge staff's assertions that drug use and prostitution activities were widespread in the neighborhood. The consultant hoped police arrest and complaint data for neighborhood drug and prostitution activities would identify social intersections for high-risk behavior, and would confirm whether prostitution was, in fact, a prevalent risk behavior in the community. The consultant also wanted to gain insight into the extent to which women were principals in these activities. Staff contacted the local police precinct to find out how they could obtain police data. After a 1-month series of phone calls to various police representatives, staff determined that the organization must write to police headquarters to request permission to obtain data. The organization did not receive permission to access the data of interest. Therefore, the consultant advised staff to interview the community affairs officers in the local housing police precinct.

The housing police proved to be a useful source of information and assistance. The community affairs officer was knowledgeable of the many housing developments in the community, the leaders of neighborhood and tenant associations, and the associations that were active, and was able to clearly describe challenges faced by the community. He took a staff member on a daylong neighborhood tour. He was also willing to assist the organization to develop AIDS programs in the community by helping it access tenant groups.

Key Informant Interviews

Because service providers and organizations already working in the community could provide staff with valuable information about existing prevention services and experiences with women in the community, a key informant survey was planned. New York City is divided into community districts that correspond to community health districts and sets of zip code zones. The community district supervisor for the neighborhood was contacted and asked for a list of all local health and social service providers, community organizations, and churches. This list was supplemented by the ASO's list of contacts and the phone book. A list of about 100 potential informant organizations was developed from these sources.

The key informant survey instrument was based on a protocol developed by the CDC. Respondents were asked to answer questions about their experiences with the community, to identify the various groups of women living in the community, and to identify the greatest needs and barriers to using services among women in the community. Respondents were also asked to identify other knowledgeable individuals who should be interviewed. Because the list of key informants was primarily composed of organizations, not individuals, staff were instructed only to administer the protocol to people who showed themselves to have "specific, valuable information regarding the target population." That is, when an organization was called, staff attempted to identify the most appropriate informant(s) in the organization.

Prior to the interviews, procedural steps for managing the interviews were reviewed with the project director. These steps included assigning staff members specific interviews to complete, monitoring the status of interviews, verifying the accuracy of the phone list, and establishing procedures for handling phone calls returned to the organization about the interviews. The project director did not develop these procedures prior to starting the interviews. Thus, there was some inconsistency in the quality of the early interviews and confusion among staff regarding which organizations had and had not been called. Although it was their primary work task, the three staff members had only completed thirty-three 15-minute interviews over a 1-month period. It was at about this time that the project director submitted her resignation. Fortunately, the part-time interviewer, who had joined the project shortly before these interviews began, took the initiative to oversee the implementation of these interviews until a new project director could be appointed.

Staff conducted the majority of key informant interviews by telephone. Some individuals were more easily interviewed in person, so staff accommodated these informants. Staff also interviewed people who were knowledgeable about the community (e.g., the community district manager) and who would know informative respondents in the community. Interviews were conducted until no new information or names for other contacts were elicited.

Each staff person coded and tabulated responses to one of the protocol's questions across the entire set of 60 completed interviews. Staff were also asked to code a common question across all of the interviews they had completed. Staff then presented their coding schemes and summaries of the findings at a staff meeting. Discrepancies and clarifications were discussed. The consultant and staff agreed on a final coding scheme, the classification of ambiguous items, and interpretations of the findings. The new project director summarized the staff's work into a final document.

The results of the key informant interviews indicate that there was a diverse population of women in the community in need of HIV education services. The groups of women most frequently mentioned were African-American women and female substance abusers. These responses were consistent with the epidemiological profile of AIDS cases available from the New York City Department of Health. Prostitutes were mentioned by 2% of the respondents. Service providers also identified women who were in socially marginal positions (e.g., homeless or impoverished women) as prevalent in the community and in need of HIV-related services.

Service providers did not see a difference in the HIV-related needs of women in general versus women who were involved with drugs or prostitution. Fifty-two percent of the providers indicated that education was one of the three greatest needs in the community. Jobs and housing were also seen as significant needs. Other needs identified included empowerment, information, programs, support groups, and health care facilities.

Twenty percent of the informants identified lack of awareness as a major barrier to effective HIV-prevention education. Some service providers felt that information was simply not available for the women they served. Others felt that information was available, but that other barriers—such as transportation, language, and literacy skills—prevented women from accessing it. Some service providers felt that information was often provided above the educational level of the target audience. Many respondents also identified denial and fear as barriers.

Review of Epidemiological and Community Data

The consultant wanted staff to develop an epidemiological profile of the community and to collect any other data they could regarding challenges the community faced. The new project director received census tract data for the district and the district needs statement from the community district manager. The consultant supplemented this with later census data for the district and health profile data from the city's Department of Health and the United Hospital Fund.

Preparing to Assess Residents' Needs

The new project director was receptive to the idea of the needs assessment. She had no significant experience in the implementation of a prevention project, and she had a positive view of the needs assessment as a tool for the development of the program. However, she recognized that staff members were not receptive to the needs assessment, and that their views must change to ensure their use of the information collected. The new project director undertook an evaluation of the project activities to date and a reevaluation of project goals. Although the organization had done no formal needs assessments in the past, the new project director believed staff had significant anecdotal information regarding levels of knowledge and HIV-related attitudes among women who had participated in the organization's educational and counseling programs. She compiled this information through staff interviews and examination of program documents. She was particularly interested in eliciting ideas the project staff had regarding gaps in the ASO's current prevention program.

The anecdotal information indicated that women utilizing agency services had a relatively high level of knowledge regarding HIV transmission and risk-reduction strategies, but did not see themselves as being personally at risk. The staff hypothesized that the women's lack of perceived susceptibility would lead to low utilization of known risk-reduction strategies for HIV infection.

Through these discussions, the staff became interested in whether the results of the needs assessment would confirm or contradict the anecdotal information they had acquired.

The new project director searched city resources in an attempt to locate any existing needs assessments or research about the HIV-related knowledge, attitudes, and behaviors of New York City women. Her search revealed very little completed research. However, she located a fairly recent borough-wide survey of 1,850 women ages 15–44 conducted by the New York City Department of Health (Fordyce, Balanon, Stoneburner, & Rautenberg, 1989), which corroborated the anecdotal evidence accumulated by staff. One of the survey's findings was that most of the respondents had a high level of knowledge regarding HIV transmission (90% of the women correctly identified all primary means of HIV transmission), but had low perceived risk and engaged in few risk-reduction behaviors.

Integrating staff into the needs assessment process. The project staff perceived the needs assessment as additional and unnecessary work imposed on them by the funding agency. The new project director used the borough-wide study report to help increase staff awareness of the utility of undertaking a needs assessment. Staff developed a more positive attitude toward the needs assessment when they discovered that the borough-wide survey corroborated their individual experiences and observations. The new project director presented the ongoing needs assessment as a tool for developing a program that incorporated community input. The staff were then able to accept the needs assessment process as a valuable component of program planning, development, and implementation for addressing the needs of community women.

Population Selection

The new project director reviewed the data from the housing police, key informants, and the epidemiological profile. The community had several zip code zones. The new project director identified a single zip code zone with the highest health and HIV-related risk indices for women of childbearing age. She then examined information from census tracts that corresponded to that zip code zone and about functioning tenant and neighborhood associations and drug-related activity in the zip code zone. The new project director also reviewed what key informants had told the staff about the challenges to providing HIV-related risk-reduction programs to women in the community (e.g., lack of transportation to programs, mistrust of providers). Based on these data, the new project director and staff agreed to focus their effort on a single housing development. Upon review of information from the housing police and the community district about the 13 housing developments in the zip code zone, a housing development was selected: It contained 1,394 female residents of childbearing age (25% of the housing development's total population), had an active tenant association, and reported a high incidence of drug-selling activity.

ASSESSING RESIDENTS' NEEDS

The next steps were to assess housing development residents' needs, and to verify whether the information received from key informants was consistent with women's experiences. The head of the tenant association in the housing development had invited the new project director and staff to attend the association's meetings. By attending the meetings, the new project director and staff were able to get a sense of residents' concerns and life in the complex. They were also able to introduce the project to tenants, secure tenants' collaboration, and get tenants' advice about how best to approach surveying women residents' needs.

Community Input

The development of a new community advisory board was initiated to elicit direct community input into the program. Identification of interested individuals took place primarily through the tenant association. Membership in the advisory board was self-selected. Because the ASO staff members were new to the housing development, the people they were initially able to contact and invite to the meetings tended to be individuals in high-profile positions. The ultimate composition of the community advisory board consisted of the manager of the housing development, the president of the tenant association, the manager of the tenant patrol, the manager of the senior citizen center, and two active members of the tenant association.

All members of the board were actively involved in the day-to-day activities of the housing development, and all had a strong commitment to improving the quality of life in the development. The community advisory board met at least once a month for 6 months and irregularly after that. Meetings were informal and were utilized to disseminate information regarding the progress of the needs assessment and the program, to elicit advice and guidance regarding the needs of the community, and to brainstorm regarding the practical logistics of the needs assessment and program development processes.

Staff also queried project residents about their interest in HIV education programs during regularly scheduled HIV information distribution at tabling events on the project grounds. Information and opinions were also solicited from the staff of the regional social service office of the Housing Authority, the on-site day care center, and the city Department of Health station.

Measure Selection and Development

The consultant and new project director decided that an anonymous interview was the most appropriate means to gather information from women. Anonymity was essential to secure women's cooperation and trust, but a written self-report measure would discourage women with lower literacy skills from responding. Additionally, the consultant was aware of other research projects in New York City housing developments that had been unsuccessful in collecting data through written self-report measures.

To develop a needs assessment interview, the consultant and new project director reviewed several AIDS-related needs assessment interview protocols that had been used with urban inner-city women. The first protocol was the Brief Street Intercept developed by the CDC. This interview was designed to assess sexual and injection risk-taking behavior in the immediate past, and to place respondents into one of Prochaska's stages of change (Prochaska, Redding, Harlow, Rossi, & Velicer, 1994). The second protocol was developed by Joanne Mantell and colleagues as part of their Cultural Network Project with inner-city women in New York City. The latter interview was designed to assess respondents' concerns, social networks, and normative influences on AIDS-related behaviors, including help-seeking. The project's needs assessment interview combined the two protocols. The final protocol assessed basic demographic characteristics of participants; participants' concerns; participants' involvement in social networks, neighborhood organizations, and activities; and AIDS-specific concerns and behaviors. Both closed- and open-ended responses were elicited. As part of the interviewer training, the measure was pilot tested on women working in other offices in the building where the organization was located, as well as on staff's friends.

Interviewers

Initially, the interviewers included the part-time interviewer, the two outreach workers, and the new project director. The part-time interviewer, who had participated in much of the earlier data collection activities, was hired, in part, because she was from the neighborhood, a former drug user, and openly HIV-positive. Prior to actual data collection, one of the outreach workers resigned and was replaced by the part-time interviewer. Thus, the interviews were conducted by the three remaining full-time project staff members.

Interviewer training comprised a variety of activities, including role playing. For role playing, staff interviewed one another in a group setting, with one of the interviewers observing. After each section in the practice interview, the interviewer would talk about what she thought she did well, what she might have done differently, and what was uncomfortable for her in conducting the practice interview. Similarly, the interviewee would discuss her experience of being interviewed and how she felt at particular points in the interview. The observer would then add any comments about what she might have done if she were conducting the same interview. Staff would then change roles so that eventually each woman had the opportunity to be the interviewer, interviewee, and observer. The point of each question and adequate responses were also discussed. Staff were also asked to practice with one another in pairs, to read the measures aloud to themselves in front of a mirror, and to tape-record themselves conducting the interview. (The organization lacked the resources for videotaped practice.) Interviewers also received interviewer training materials developed by the Health Research Programs of the Wagner School of Public Service at New York University, which included an interviewer manual and several chapters on interviewing techniques and ethics in conducting interviews.

Sample and Procedure

The sample was composed of women ages 18 years or older who were on the housing development premises on selected days. (Although there was interest in adolescents, they could not be sampled without parental consent. Women over the age of 44 were included because they might be normative referents for younger women.) The sample was self-selected and one of convenience. Interviews were conducted inside and outside the complex. Interviewers approached women, explained the purpose of the study, and offered information pertinent to the protection of participants' identities and rights as research participants. Women were also told that they would receive a coupon worth $15 at the local grocery store if they completed the entire interview. Two hundred fifty women were approached to participate in interviews. Of those, five were ineligible (less than 18 years old) and 33 refused to participate. Interviews were conducted with the 212 eligible women who agreed to participate, with a response rate of about 85%. Most interviews lasted 15–20 minutes.

Initial quality control procedures proved inadequate. When the consultant reviewed the first set of interviews, inconsistency among interviewers was observed for several series of questions. The most typical problems were not following skip patterns accurately and not probing adequately. The new project director reviewed these problems with the interviewers. The new project director also began to review completed interviews on a more regular basis and increased opportunities for discussion among the staff about how the interviews were going and problems encountered in the field. However, some inconsistencies among interviewers remained. Some of these inconsistencies could be corrected through coding and data analysis. Wherever possible, the most specific categories of response were used.

Data Analyses

Because the data included both open and closed responses, data analyses combined qualitative and quantitative methods. All of the analyses were performed by the consultant. All open-ended responses were hand coded by key words. For example, items asking women to identify who had been supportive and nonsupportive regarding AIDS-related behavior change were coded by relationship type. Data were then entered into a database and cleaned case by case. Finally, the database file was translated into a file that could be read by statistical software. Analyses were descriptive and primarily included computation of frequency distributions, means, and correlations.

Summary of Findings

Respondent characteristics. The median age among respondents was 34 years (range = 18–83 years; mean = 37). About 86% of respondents were

African American, about 8% were Latina, and about 4% were American Indian. About 84% of respondents reported that they lived in the housing development. Most others lived within a six-block radius of the housing development. The average length of time women had lived in the complex was 16 years and 7 months (range = 2 days to 35 years).

Transculturation. Degree of acculturation has been cited as a critical factor in understanding the AIDS-related beliefs and behaviors of people of color (Marin & Marin, 1990). Transculturation was measured with language dependence, birth place, and parents' birth places. About 94% of women were born in the United States. Of these, about 68% were from New York. The majority of respondents' parents were born in the United States. About 14% of women reported use of a language other than English, typically Spanish. Of those, 17% reported they spoke their parent language most of the time, 41% reported equal use of English and the parent language, and 38% reported they spoke English most of the time.

Household composition. About 88% of women had at least one child. The number of children reported ranged from 1 to 12, with an average of 3. About 80% of these women reported their children lived with them. Respondents were asked to name all members of their household, and to describe their relationship to each individual. Households contained an average of four people (range = 1–11). Twenty-nine women reported their husbands lived with them. Several women indicated their husbands were in jail. Women were not asked whether they were divorced, widowed, or separated.

One hundred forty-seven women reported they had a main partner, and 150 women described specific, current sexual relationships. Ninety women reported they had a boyfriend, 41 women reported they had a husband, and 19 described some other relationship that included sex. About 98% of these sexual partners were reported to be male.

Educational attainment and employment status. The average level of educational attainment among women in the sample was slightly less than high school graduate. About 43% of the women reported less than a 12th-grade education, and about 41% had a high school diploma or an equivalency diploma. Although about 11% reported some college, only two women reported a college degree and seven women reported a graduate degree. About 30% of women reported they were employed. About 41% reported that someone else in the household had a job or received some income. The majority of women in the sample lived in households that received some form of public assistance.

Current concerns. Women were asked to what degree they had thought about a list of concerns. The top three concerns expressed were the health and well-being of their children, their own health and well-being, and crime and violence. Concern about protecting themselves from AIDS ranked eighth. Women added concerns about their children's environment, moving out of the housing development, money, keeping in touch with family members, cleanliness of the housing development, and being able to have a healthy baby.

Organizational participation. The extent of engagement in formal and informal institutions was assessed to identify community venues appropriate for intervention.

Volunteer work. Fifty-seven women reported they volunteered for a community institution. Of those, the majority were involved in the tenant association. Other settings in which women were involved were in some way related to children: Head Start, Girl Scouts, and activities at a local school or day care center.

Self-help and personal education. Eighty-eight women reported they participated in educational or self-help groups. Thirty-nine women used the PTA as a source of personal education. Four women were in self-help addiction recovery groups, and three were in counseling. Fourteen women listed other educational activities, including workshops, religious education, life skills training, and athletic classes.

Recreational activities. About 52% of women reported engaging in organized activities for fun. These included organized bus trips, sports, Girl Scouts or Four-H Club, activities organized by the senior center, and church functions (most women were involved in a church). About 29% mentioned activities like picnics, amusement parks, trips, movies, dances, and school-based events.

Informal recreational and social activities. About 70% of respondents reported being part of a group of friends. One hundred twenty-four women reported there were places they went regularly. These places included parks, churches, clubs or bars, and people's homes.

Help-seeking. Seventy-three women reported that they went to a professional for advice. About 12% mentioned doctors; about 11% mentioned social workers, counselors, or therapists; and about 7% mentioned a member of the clergy. About 39% of women reported that there was someone to go to in the community for general advice. Resources in the community for advice included mothers, friends, the tenant association/patrol, neighbors, and clergy.

AIDS-related advice. About 66% said there was someone in the community to give advice on health or AIDS issues. Women mentioned friends, mothers, children, sisters, doctors, boyfriends, and co-workers. For both general and AIDS-specific advice, women reported they relied mainly on nonprofessional assistance—in particular, mothers and friends.

AIDS risk-reduction interactions. About a third of respondents reported that they knew someone who had made a change in behavior because of AIDS. Friends, sisters, and cousins were most frequently reported to have changed. Less frequently mentioned were brothers, sons, daughters, partners, and other family members. The most common adaptations were fewer partners and condom use. Abstinence, education, and quitting drugs were also listed. Eight respondents reported someone they knew had died of HIV illness.

About 53% of women reported people in their lives who helped them to protect themselves from HIV. These included mothers, partners, friends, sisters, and counselors or social workers. These individuals were reported to help women by talking about HIV, giving advice, using or giving them condoms, and providing written materials.

About 20% of women reported that there were people who got upset because they wanted the respondent to be more careful about AIDS. Mothers (43%), fathers (12%), friends (10%), partners (10%), and sisters (9%) were mentioned. The chief means of showing upset were giving advice and showing concern. Women also mentioned being beaten and yelled at.

Twenty women reported that there was someone in their lives who encouraged them to do risky things. Half identified partners, and one quarter identified friends. Women reported they were encouraged to have unprotected intercourse, use drugs, and have multiple sexual partners. About 6% of women reported that someone made it harder for them to protect themselves. Nearly all of these stated this was their partner. Ten women stated their partner refused to use condoms, and two women stated partners were unfaithful. Drugs were mentioned by two women.

Overall, only about one third of the women reported that someone in their acquaintance had changed their behavior in response to AIDS. Although about half the women reported that someone helped them protect themselves, a much smaller percentage reported that there was someone who was upset because they wanted the respondent to be more careful. Some women reported unhelpful behaviors on the part of their sexual partners. Helpful behaviors were most often talking, giving advice, and using or giving condoms.

Sexual history. Half of the women reported that they were sexually active in the 30 days prior to the assessment. Two women reported that they had traded sex for money or drugs in the past 30 days. Each woman reported she had done so less than 10 times. No one reported having sex with a partner who had ever shot drugs or had sex with a man. It is unclear whether women underreported involvement with at-risk partners or whether they did not know if partners had high-risk behavioral profiles.

Drug use and needle sharing. Cigarettes, alcohol, and marijuana were the most commonly reported drugs among these women. More than half the women who ever smoked reported they smoked daily in the prior month. A small number of women reported recent crack use, and one woman reported recent use of cocaine and heroin. Use of injection drugs was not widely reported. No one in the sample reported ever sharing needles or works.

Risk-reduction efficacy expectations. Women were asked how likely they were to engage in a number of acts that would reduce their risk of HIV infection. Women were most likely to say they would be able to refuse drugs and least likely to report they would be able to use condoms or other latex contraceptives.

Barriers. Women described numerous barriers to getting information about AIDS. Among those reporting barriers, about 30% mentioned disinterest in HIV and 25% said fear was a barrier to getting information. Ignorance, not caring about oneself, laziness, shame, perceptions of invulnerability, and denial were also mentioned. Barriers mentioned by small numbers of women included lack of information and resources in the community, monogamy, being needy of relationships, substance use, partners, and poor communication skills.

Implications of Findings

Although it is unclear how representative the women sampled are of all women in the housing development, the data had important implications for the shape of prevention programs targeted to women in the complex. The majority of women sampled were parents, and many lived with their children. Outside of church, many of the settings in which women were involved were related to their having children in day care or school. Both of these settings emerged as potential venues for reaching women. In fact, although women were not involved in a great variety of activities, they were intensely involved in the settings they most often mentioned: the church, the PTA, and other school-based groups. It is important to consider, however, that the women who were most involved in organizations and institutions may be those who are at lower risk because they have the skills and social resources to access information and support.

A majority of the women received some type of income assistance, and a minority were employed. The educational attainment level of most respondents was high school or less. Therefore, any materials developed for these women would have to be written for an audience with lower literacy skills to be accessible. Nearly a quarter of the women lived in households of five or more people. More than two thirds of the women had a partner, most often a male, and, unless he was a husband, it was rare that he lived with the respondent. Many women cited friends, neighbors, and family as resources for general and AIDS-specific advice. Women reported they regularly socialized in church, local parks, and people's homes. These household and family networks appeared to be more frequently used than professional organizations or individuals for information and support. Therefore, programs developed to capitalize on family, neighborhood, and friendship networks might be successful. Programming through homes, local parks, and the tenant association held promise for accessing women through their normal information channels and enhancing their existing relationships.

Women were concerned about AIDS, but it did not rank among their chief worries. Women's primary concerns were more immediate: their own and their children's welfare, crime, violence, and paying their bills. AIDS did not appear to be part of their day-to-day concerns, and was not linked to their overall concept of well-being. Developing ways to integrate HIV into women's concept of well-being might be an important goal of the program.

Women reported that role models to encourage effective risk-reduction behavior were available, although not all of the measures implemented by these individuals were effective for HIV prevention. These individuals were most often friends and relatives. A majority of women reported informal encouragement of AIDS risk-reduction behaviors, mostly among friends and family. Peer role models might be able to offer other women strategies for overcoming obstacles set in place by partners and others who are barriers to risk reduction. These social resources might also be useful for the small number of women who reported that their partners or other individuals were obstacles to implementing risk-reduction behaviors.

The major barriers to AIDS education were disinterest and fear. Other barriers were mentioned (e.g., denial, ignorance, laziness, and perceptions of invulnerability). The nature of women's fear of HIV merits further exploration. Information regarding specific fears might help develop strategies to overcome those fears. Women suggested that advice, condoms, and talking assist them to protect themselves. Increasing accurate advice-giving among friends, family, and neighbors might provide a natural way to encourage risk reduction.

UTILIZATION OF FINDINGS

Applying the Needs Assessment Results

Redefining project goals. Using the organization's anecdotal information, the results of the survey conducted by the Department of Health, the results of the key informant service provider survey, and the interviews with women, staff were able to see how prior programmatic activities were inadequate to address the community's needs for HIV education. All of the data collected suggested that levels of knowledge about transmission and risk-reduction behaviors were not necessarily associated with the actual practice of risk-reduction behaviors. Staff concluded that educational interventions that stressed increasing knowledge would probably not be effective in eliciting behavior change. The lack of a clear relationship between knowledge and behavior suggested the need to modify the original program design, which consisted primarily of one-time workshops and presentations on risk-reduction behaviors.

The interview results suggest that the program needed to use the established information-sharing mechanisms in its design. As stated earlier, the results of the interviews indicate that women in the housing development relied on friends, neighbors, and family members for information and advice regarding HIV. Additionally, contact with supportive family and friends was associated with increased efficacy expectations about condoms. The staff decided that the program should be centered on women sharing and talking with other women.

The interviews suggested that a program focusing solely on HIV and run by professional health educators would probably not be successful, given the stated concerns and social interactions of the women surveyed. The interviews also indicated that women in the housing development had day-to-day concerns that they considered more significant than HIV and that major barriers to AIDS education were disinterest and fear. Staff believed that any program should be flexible enough to consider other life concerns besides HIV, while seeking to help women understand how HIV affected their own and their children's well-being. Creating a program that dealt with women's non-AIDS-related concerns might bridge disinterest in HIV.

Members of the community advisory board, as well as other community residents, expressed concern regarding the exclusivity of the target population. Although residents saw the need to focus on women, most felt strongly that project residents of both genders and of all ages could benefit from AIDS education services. There was concern among both male and female project residents that men needed to be included in the program. The staff recognized the importance of designing activities that would address male and female residents.

The staff determined that women need programs that provide: (a) accurate information to reinforce current knowledge, evaluate relative individual risk, dispel myths regarding HIV infection, and lessen fear; (b) increased self-esteem, self-efficacy, and individual empowerment to prepare women for the challenges associated with behavior change; (c) social skills to increase proficiency in communication, sexual negotiation, and assertiveness; and (d) practical skills in the use of latex barriers, reducing drug use, and alternatives to penetrative sex.

Designing the program. Once clear programmatic goals were established, the staff utilized the results of the interviews and key informant survey and the advice from the community advisory board to develop a program that addressed the specific needs of the women in the housing development. The preliminary program had three primary components: (a) small-group sessions of 8–12 women meeting weekly to discuss health and community concerns, including HIV; (b) peer educators who would perform outreach and education to women and families; and (c) forums and educational interventions open to all project residents on various issues related to HIV.

The staff designed a small-group, intensive, educational risk-reduction intervention program to provide information, support, and skills to female residents of the housing development. The overall goal of the program was to foster changes in HIV-related sexual and drug use risk-taking behaviors. Staff believed that it was important to provide a multisession program in which the same individuals were seen over a period of time. Given that behavior change is a long and involved process, the most that a one-time interaction could be expected to accomplish was to influence knowledge and attitudes. Additionally, the staff believed the needs assessment indicated the need for a long-term, supportive educational program, in which participants could obtain input and reinforcement from their peers while establishing new normative networks. Women suggested that advice and talking were likely to help them to protect themselves from HIV. Thus, staff believed that small groups—in which women would be able to share perspectives and information—were appropriate for providing support, disseminating information, developing skills, and addressing barriers to behavior change.

The staff felt strongly that an exclusive emphasis on AIDS would be counterproductive because the needs assessment indicated women had multiple concerns. Therefore, group interactions would include a broad array of health and community issues. Because professionals were not viewed as a primary resource among women in the community, groups were designed to be managed by a project staff member who facilitated conversation among the women on issues of their choice. Groups were also designed to incorporate diverse women within the housing development, including women from outside the target population, to represent a variety of views. In the needs assessment, staff had learned that women who lived in the surrounding neighborhood were part of the social networks contained in the housing development, therefore women from the neighborhood were allowed to participate. Staff tried to recruit older women into the groups because, in the informal interviews, many women in the target population identified long-term project residents over 50 years of age as primary sources of advice, information, and support. In the interviews, mothers, aunts, and other older relatives were often cited as important resources to women.

The cultivation of peer educators was designed to take advantage of the established support and information-sharing mechanisms in the housing development. Because primary interactions regarding support and advice occurred in networks of family, neighbors, and friends, staff would train a number of influential women in HIV transmission, risk-reduction, and practical and social skills. Staff hoped that these women would diffuse risk-reduction messages to other women throughout the housing development.

Forums and educational interventions open to the entire community were added to the program design as a direct response to community input. The community advisory board and individual women interested in the program felt quite strongly that there was a need to include the entire community in the program. There was particular concern that some mechanism be devised to include men. Although staff recognized that the primary programmatic efforts needed to concentrate on the target population, they felt that periodic community-wide educational interventions, such as tabling and workshops, would both add to the efficacy of the program and address the concerns of the community.

Implementing the Program

Programmatic activities began with the initiation of small-group meetings. Before the formal groups commenced, staff initiated four informational meetings. These meetings served to formally introduce the program to project residents, disseminate the preliminary results of the interviews, and elicit information from women who were interested in participating in program activities. Although these meetings were not organized as formal focus groups, one of their main purposes was to solicit feedback on the preliminary program design. Twenty-one women attended the informational sessions.

The vast majority of women who participated in the informational meetings indicated great interest in participating in ongoing groups. The women were asked for input about what they would like to discuss or see happen as a result of the groups. Although AIDS was mentioned by more than half of the participants, there was an overwhelming desire to address other health issues, such as other sexually transmitted diseases, diabetes, weight control, and children's health issues. Many of the participants were concerned about communication difficulties with their children. Women's feedback confirmed the needs assessment data and community input—that a comprehensive, integrated approach was better suited to residents' needs than a narrow, AIDS-focused approach.

Participants saw a peer-training program as potentially useful. However, no participant expressed a personal interest in becoming a peer educator. Some women indicated that they might be interested in the training after they had participated in the groups. All of the participants wanted to know if the organization was having a program for men and saw a concurrent men's program as very important.

The results of these informational meetings generally confirm the validity of the initial program design. Staff decided to initiate the small-group meetings and the community-wide educational interventions immediately. Peer training was postponed until the staff could cultivate peer leaders from the groups. Because program modifications were made and implemented at nearly the end of the funding cycle, planned program evaluation activities were not implemented.

LESSONS LEARNED: REFLECTING ON
STRENGTHS AND WEAKNESSES

Although the implementation of the needs assessment was a challenge for the ASO, the results facilitated the development of programmatic strategies that addressed the needs of the community and the target population. However, project staff had to overcome a number of challenges that threatened to impede the successful execution of both the needs assessment and the program. The choices made in conducting the needs assessment, along with situational constraints, simultaneously strengthened and weakened the needs assessment.

Organizational Upheaval

Staffing changes at the organizational, project, and funding level were constant. The resignation of the organization's founding executive director at program startup left the program without staff experienced in program development and implementation. An acting executive director was in place for several months. A new executive director was brought to the ASO for her extensive management experience. She was dependent on the original project director to guide the development and implementation of the program, yet the original project director and her staff did not have substantial experience in these areas. The program lost the original project director after 19 months of a 36-month program, and the CDC project director who initiated the needs assessment was replaced before the needs assessment was completed.

Change in an organization is difficult even under the best of circumstances. The strategy had to be flexible and simple enough to accommodate an ever-changing set of organizational players, while not sacrificing clarity of purpose. Throughout the process, there were two main focal points: the needs assessment objectives of defining a target population, understanding its needs, and developing the organization's capacity to develop programs logically; and the organizational objective of demonstrating to the CDC that the ASO had the capacity to develop and implement a sound HIV-prevention program. As the organization's and CDC's staff changed, there remained a willingness to ask new questions or ask questions differently, as long as the broader set of objectives was not compromised. The researcher's role as the project's memory was taken seriously, ensuring that, as the players changed, the project's history was not forgotten.

Project Design

A developmental, iterative approach to designing the needs assessment accommodated the organization as it became more focused and developed new informational needs. A strength of the approach was its flexibility. As the organization changed and the project staff's thinking evolved, strategies were developed for gathering additional information. Rather than rigidly adhering to a predetermined plan, information-gathering plans were fluid and responsive to the organization's current concerns.

However, taking a flexible approach did not preclude an overall plan. Lacking a plan a priori was a weakness, although there were dates by which the CDC expected the organization to have completed certain programmatic tasks. The absence of a general plan linked to the programmatic tasks and overarching questions sometimes meant that staff were not adequately prepared for each phase of data collection. A complete plan to which everyone had agreed might have made it easier to renegotiate deadlines with the CDC when problems arose. Additionally, staff might have accepted the needs assessment earlier if they had been presented with an overall plan and could see how it was related to program planning and data collection activities. Lacking the big picture of how each data collection activity was linked to other data collection activities, and ultimately to the program, staff perceived the research as a series of unrelated events that distracted them from providing services to women.

An understanding of adequate science had to be informed by political and resource considerations. The needs assessment was a device to get the ASO to engage in a logical program planning process. The CDC viewed the needs assessment as the organization's last opportunity to demonstrate that it could develop a sound program, but was more interested in observing the process than the results. Some of the change at the organizational level was intended to increase internal accountability and performance, and staff were scrutinized by the new executive director in that regard. It was unclear which staff would pass this new level of organizational scrutiny, and planning had to assume that staffing might not be stable. Efforts had to be tailored to the staff's skills while trying to remain true to the goals and objectives. Values about good science had to be flexible and negotiated along with everything else.

Multiple Methods of Data Collection

Another important strength of the approach was the use of as many different methods of data collection as possible within the resource constraints of the organization. Combining various data collection techniques and sources produced convergent information across methodologies with different advantages and disadvantages. For example, although key informant surveys require minimal time and resources, they are impressionistic. Citizen surveys, by contrast, are expensive, but provide the target populations' view of their own needs and can clarify information obtained from other sources. For instance, the key informants and the women agreed on many of the barriers to HIV prevention, but the women placed greater emphasis than the service providers on psychological barriers (e.g., disinterest).

Although the information gathered from various sources can corroborate one another, as well as identify important issues that might not be discovered if only a single method were used (e.g., learning that residents believed men should be included in the program), a multiple-method approach also has its weaknesses. Combining multiple methods can be expensive. In the context of limited resources, executing a single method may well be of greater benefit than executing multiple methods poorly. Also, multiple methods should only be used when they are a necessary part of answering the questions under investigation. Some of the methods used here (e.g., observation) required substantial personnel resources and did not add to the information gained through other activities. A better approach would have been to plan how each method used would add to the needs assessment a priori.

Collaboration

Working collaboratively with the staff and involving them in the determination of what questions to ask, the generation of ideas about how to obtain answers to those questions, the collection of information, and the analysis and interpretation of the data provided multiple advantages. Staff's expertise and anecdotal information enriched the needs assessment. As the project progressed, the needs assessment was modified to respond to what staff learned in the field, increasing the relevance and timeliness of the needs assessment activities and the data collected.

A collaborative approach was necessary to successfully address the various challenges inherent in the project. The prevention project underwent significant changes in focus more than halfway through its funding cycle. What started as 1- to 2-hour informational workshops for women throughout Brooklyn became a research project followed by a narrowly focused effort targeted to a single housing development. None of the staff was hired for a research project or a housing development prevention program. Assisting staff to make the transition from their former mode of working to an entirely new one had to become part of the job if the results of the needs assessment were to be useful and used.

The majority of the staff had little, if any, formal training in program planning, education, adult learning, human sexuality, or other areas that might have prepared them to conduct HIV-prevention work or to use the needs assessment findings. As in many ASOs, staff were young, dedicated, concerned citizens whose philosophical commitment to the organization's mission was considered by the organization to be more important than prior experience. Part of the job was to expand the staff's skills and provide support and reassurance throughout programmatic changes. The dramatic changes in the program made the most sense to staff when they had been involved as partners in discussions about the needs assessment and its implications. The staff were more invested in their work with the needs assessment when their ideas were reflected in it. Needs assessments came to be understood as organizational learning processes, as much as processes through which organizations learn about target populations.

Using Untrained Staff

The quality of information collected varied more than was desirable. The fact that the staff members were selected as outreach workers, not researchers, and that the consultant was only on-site 2–4 hours a week contributed to the difficulty of collecting high-quality data. There was no reason to expect that competent outreach workers would necessarily be competent data collectors. Those who did not master data collection skills even after extensive training could not be dismissed, as might be the case in a traditional research setting. Outreach staff were hired to provide services, not collect data.

The outreach staff had to be used wisely, with complete knowledge of their limitations. The CDC, the executive director, and the staff also had to be aware of the limitations of the research and the staff's skills. If it had been the intention of the CDC or ASO to publish the needs assessment or use it for purposes other than the ASO's internal planning process, the needs assessment activities should have been conducted by skilled research personnel, and the funding available to conduct the needs assessment activities should have been increased. Because the needs assessment was, in large part, a training exercise, it was decided to teach the staff how to gather information systematically. In retrospect, however, more thorough systems for monitoring the quality of the data should have been developed, and the availability of free or inexpensive training opportunities for the staff should have been explored.

Organization, Funder, and Consultant Conflict

Unfortunately, the initial mandate for the needs assessment was perceived by project staff as an imposition by the funding agency and a direct challenge of the staff's ability to implement the program. Initially, project staff were unable to see the potential usefulness of the needs assessment, and thus were resistant to its implementation. Project staff often felt they had relinquished control of the project and were unable to influence its direction. For example, it was the CDC project officer who decided on a geographic focus and target population when the project staff were unable or unwilling to do so. The fact that the CDC project officer made major decisions about the program on his own resulted in the project staff having little sense of the utility of the needs assessment and not believing it would address questions of serious concern to them. Additionally, because most of the stakeholders agreed that a needs assessment would be used to settle disputes about the program, but were not all equally involved in determining what questions to ask, there was no assurance of how the organization would utilize the findings.

Earlier collaboration between the project staff, CDC project officer, and consultant would have resulted in a better planned and smoother assessment. This would have required a less adversarial approach to the needs assessment and greater clarity for all the stakeholders about how the needs assessment would be used.

Roles and expectations should have been openly negotiated at several points in the process. Initially, the CDC project officer made all of the decisions about what would occur. The consultant's role was to perform data analyses. The consultant's role later expanded to advising the staff on how to execute the needs assessment activities requested by the CDC. Although it was not formally discussed, at some point the consultant's role further shifted from consultative to directive. Unfortunately, it took too long for the consultant to recognize this shift, to realize that she could challenge the CDC project officer about whether activities like observation were feasible and productive, and to take a proactive role in designing needs assessment strategies and training staff.

The new project director viewed the primary objective of the needs assessment as developing a sound program. The project director was more than satisfied with the amount and quality of the information collected in the needs assessment. The consultant, however, understood that part of her role was to ensure that the data would be credible, and thus was consistently concerned about its scientific rigor. The fact that differing expectations of the consultant's role and of the quality of the research did not lead to conflict was simply a matter of luck. Open discussion throughout the process about what could be expected from untrained data collection staff, what the expectations were about the rigor of the research, and what roles people were expected to play might have substantially reduced tension and confusion among the organization, the CDC, and the consultant.

Community Input

People who live in a community are a rich information resource about the needs, perspectives, and values of community members. Community members might contribute questions to a needs assessment that outsiders might overlook; they also might provide insight about the implementation of the needs assessment and utilization of the findings. In addition, when the community is involved, it is more likely that the program can survive on its own after the initiating agency withdraws its resources from the setting.

The manner in which a needs assessment is conducted can influence the receptiveness of a community to subsequent research and programs. Therefore, it is important to conduct a needs assessment that actively and visibly incorporates the knowledge, perceptions, values, and expertise of the community. The validation of community knowledge and expertise helps to build a positive relationship with the community and facilitates the integration of new programs into community life.

With the exception of the part-time interviewer, who eventually became a full-time staff member, women living in the community became involved too late. Although there was some input from a variety of stakeholder voices in early needs assessment and program planning processes, greater involvement of potential consumers might have added more breadth and depth to the efforts. Although several data-gathering techniques encouraged staff to participate in a dialogue with community members, the community members were most often research participants, rather than collaborators.

When the community became involved in the project, it facilitated access to community members, information, and community resources. The ASO had greater credibility with the target population once the ASO had received the endorsement and cooperation of key community residents. Early involvement of community residents in the needs assessment might have further facilitated the community's acceptance of the data and the program.

Sampling

The sampling strategy was one of convenience. Use of nonrandom sampling procedures makes it impossible to generalize findings to the women who resided in the housing development at the time of the study. In addition, women who did not actually live in the building were eligible if they were spending time there, making the desired sampling frame and the actual sampling frame discrepant. Analyses were also not conducted to determine adequate sample size. Finally, because data were collected in public spaces in the housing development during the daytime, they may not reflect the needs and concerns of women who are homebound, fully employed, or in school.

Several facts increase confidence in the survey results, however. First, the sample generally reflected local demographics, including race, ethnicity, and parenthood. Second, the rate of agreement to participate was quite acceptable, modestly reducing concern about self-selection biases. Third, much of the collected data were corroborated in other data sets and through community input. Thus, the findings may meaningfully reflect the women in the housing development. Nonetheless, issues of sampling should be considered more carefully in future projects.

SUMMARY

There were many challenges to the successful implementation of the needs assessment. However, program staff learned a great deal about how to plan programs, seek community input, and think about assessing community needs. The overall approach provided the organization with a simple guide to program planning. The basic formula is easily adapted to many situations and social problems:

1. Identify key community resources. Extract as much knowledge as possible about the community from those who might know it best. Present sources of information included the community district manager, the police community affairs officer, tenant and neighborhood associations, and neigh-

borhood service providers and institutions, such as churches, hospitals, clinics, and schools. A list of contacts was developed from a variety of sources, including the phone book and local guides to AIDS-related service providers. Had the observations been more successful, important residents who were not necessarily participants in formal settings might also have been identified.

2. Review epidemiological and other available community health indicator data. It was critical to understand the health-related issues facing women in the community and what services were available to them. Information from the census, the CDC, the New York City Department of Health, the community district manager's office, and other available sources was used to develop a health profile.

3. Engage the program's intended recipients and stakeholders. The best information about how to work with women in the community was thought to come from organized community entities and from women themselves. Hence, resources like the police and building superintendents identified tenant, block, and neighborhood associations. Understanding the community and obtaining advice about seeking information from women was facilitated by relationships with the associations identified.

4. Identify factors that can be influenced and are related to the target's attitudes and behaviors, and identify settings where the target normally obtains information and advice. The survey provided information about HIV-related factors identified in the AIDS literature and by key informants, and about how women related to informal and formal social networks and settings.

A reasonably sound strategy was developed that a small, resource-poor organization could implement with minimal expert assistance. Program planning staff were trained in basic information gathering and analyses. This was accomplished within a context of internal organizational tension and tension between the funder and organization. Incorporating the fundamental values of flexibility, collaboration, and organizational development helped to overcome obstacles and produce a profile of AIDS-related needs that could guide a prevention program.

7

Assessing Child and Maternal Health: The First Step in the Design of Community-Based Interventions

E. Walter Terrie

Chapter 383.216 of the Florida Statutes, adopted in 1991, provides for the establishment of community-based prenatal and infant health care coalitions that are composed of health care providers, representatives of state and local government, community alliances, maternal and child health organizations, and consumers of family planning, prenatal care, and primary care services. This legislation was one of a series of measures intended to improve pregnancy and birth outcomes within the state, collectively referred to as the *Healthy Start Initiative*. This initiative was the result of concerns with the human, social, and economic costs associated with unfavorable birth outcomes, such as mortality, developmental delay, and disability. These concerns are, of course, not merely limited to Florida, but are national in scope (Public Health Service, 1986). Community-based intervention models were posited to be cost-effective solutions to the problem that would result in substantial savings later in the health, education, and social services arenas (Public Health Service, 1991).

By the time these initiatives were being formulated, substantial progress had begun to be made with respect to infant mortality, which is the death rate for children from birth to age 1, fetal deaths, which are stillbirths occurring at 20 weeks or more gestation, and maternal health. However, wide disparities remained in race- and county-specific rates of these vital events. Florida's total infant and fetal mortality rates were consistently higher than for the United States as a whole throughout the 1980s, and rates for non-White children were roughly twice those of White children. Progress has been made and total rates of both infant and fetal mortality have declined by almost 30% over the decade. Considerable geographic variability also exists. Between 1989 and 1991, the 3-year infant mortality rate ranged from a high of 17.3 in Union County, Florida to a low of 3.9 per 1,000 in Glades County, Florida.

Maternal death rates fluctuated throughout the decade, primarily due to their low incidence (around 20 deaths per year), but rates for non-White women were about three times that for White women. Between October 1989 and September 1990, there were 19,510 hospitalizations for antepartum complications, which were 9.9% of births during the period. During the following year, there were 16,463 (8.3%) such hospitalizations (Grimm & Parker, 1992).

Another key pregnancy outcome and child development indicator is birth weight. In Florida, rates for low birth weight (LBW), less than 2,500 grams, and very low birth weight (VLBW), less than 1,500 grams, remained relatively constant over the decade—at 75 per 1,000 for LBW and 14 per 1,000 for VLBW. The LBW rates for non-Whites are about twice those for Whites and 2.5 times as great for VLBW. Considerable variability in the incidence of LBW babies by county of residence also exists within the state ranging from a high of 132 per 1,000 to a low of 46 per 1,000.

The law authorizing the healthy start coalitions recognized these geographic and temporal variations in maternal and infant health and specified that each Healthy Start Coalition would:

Perform community assessments, using the Planned Approach to Community Health (PATCH) process, to identify the local need for comprehensive preventive and primary prenatal and infant health care. [According to this law, these assessments shall be used to:]

1. Determine the priority target groups for receipt of care.
2. Determine outcome performance objectives jointly with the department.
3. Identify potential local providers of services.
4. Determine the type of services required to serve the identified priority target groups.
5. Identify the unmet need for services for the identified priority target groups. [Florida Statutes (1991) 383.216(2)(a) 1–5.]

The PATCH program was developed by the Center for Chronic Disease Control and was designed to help communities plan, implement, and evaluate health promotion and education programs (Kreuter, 1992).

Throughout the state, infant advocacy and service groups joined together to form Healthy Start Coalitions—30 coalitions have been formed. Each coalition serves one or more counties. Currently, every county within the state belongs to a coalition. As of mid-1995, 24 coalitions had submitted their needs assessment and service delivery plans and had received Health and Rehabilitative Services (HRS) departmental approval.

One of the first tasks required of each coalition is that it conduct a needs assessment within its service delivery area. The minimum requirements for this assessment were specified by the Department of Health and Rehabilitative Services, State Health Program Office through rules promulgated in Chapter 10-D 113 of the Administrative Code. Specifically, these rules required each coalition to perform an assessment that included:

(a) A demographic and economic profile of the service delivery area that describes the population in terms of age, race, ethnicity, sex, income level, educational level, type of occupation and any other locally relevant characteristics.

(b) An estimate of the number of women who will get pregnant each year in the service delivery area and an estimate of the number of these women who will have insufficient financial means to cover prenatal, labor and delivery, postpartum, and infant care.

(c) A determination of the geographic locations by use of census tracts or zip codes of target population groups that may be at risk of adverse pregnancy outcomes due to medical, socioeconomic conditions, or past experience.

(d) An evaluation of outcomes in facilities within the coalition's service area. (Florida Administrative Code, pp. 6–8.)

Several coalitions that formed within the "Big Bend" region of Florida sought assistance from the Florida State University's Center for Prevention and Early Intervention to conduct their needs assessment. All of these coalitions served relatively sparsely populated, nonmetropolitan areas that present special challenges and problems relative to more populous areas. The remainder of this chapter focuses on the assessment that was performed for Gadsden Citizens for Healthy Babies, Inc. It describes the sources of information and methods used to conduct this assessment, and discusses choices and compromises that had to be made. Some alternatives and potential improvement to what was accomplished are also described.

Gadsden County, Florida is a small, primarily rural, majority African-American county located in north Florida immediately adjacent to Alabama and Georgia. In 1993 the population was 42,589 of which 58.8% were non-White. The 1989 poverty rate was 28%, which is more than twice the rate for the state as a whole, and was the highest in the state at the time of the census. The unemployment rate (6.9%) was lower than the state's, due primarily to the availability of employment in the adjacent and much larger Leon County—site of the City of Tallahassee, which is the state capital. Population density is 82 persons per square mile, which is quite low compared with Florida's density of 248 persons per square mile, and there are six relatively small towns with the county seat, Quincy being the largest with a 1990 population of 7,444.

Considerable improvement in infant mortality, fetal deaths, and prenatal care has occurred during the past decade, although the county still falls short of most of Florida's infant health care goals. There has also been improvement in the proportion of women receiving prenatal care before the third trimester (97.4% compared with 93.3%), due to specific programs, primarily initiated through the County Health Department, designed to ensure the delivery of prenatal care to all women.

PLANNING THE ASSESSMENT

Every needs assessment begins with certain general questions such as who is to be served, how will they be found, what are their specific needs, and how can services be most efficiently and effectively delivered? There are also specific questions concerning what researchers seek to know about the population. Many assessments require substantial efforts during the planning phase in answering these questions of who, what, why, and how.

This type of legally based assessment is somewhat different from ones with less formalized requirements, in that precisely who must be studied and what must be included is spelled out by administrative rules. Legislation requires that pre- and postnatal services are to be provided to targeted groups of pregnant women and infants who reside within a coalition's service area. This is the "who" question. The rules also spell out certain questions that must be answered by the assessment, such as an estimated number of women who will become pregnant each year and the number of them with insufficient financial means to cover the associated expenses. These are the "what" questions. A general statement of "how" is given because the legislation specifies that the assessments are to be performed using PATCH.

PATCH

The PATCH program, as mentioned earlier, was an outgrowth of the PRE-CEDE model developed at Johns Hopkins University beginning in the 1970s (Green & Kreuter, 1992). This analytic framework for health planning and evaluation grew out of a body of accruing evidence that:

> ". . . a health education intervention would likely succeed if the program planners and practitioners
> (1) began from a base of community ownership of problems and solutions,
> (2) planned thoroughly,
> (3) based program decisions on relevant theory, data, and local experience
> (4) knew what types of interventions were most acceptable and feasible
> (5) had an organizational and advocacy plan to orchestrate multiple intervention strategies into a complementary, cohesive program, and
> (6) obtained feedback and progress evaluation as the problem proceeded. (Green & Kreuter, 1992, p. 140)

Essentially, PATCH is a framework for coordinating and securing cooperation among and between diverse public health agencies and interest groups at the federal, state, and local levels. Acting in partnership, these entities identify a problem and then devise, implement, and evaluate intervention activities (Hutsell, Meltzer, Lindsay, & McClain, 1992). Kreuter (1992) pointed out that the gathering and analysis of data are usually the most demanding parts of the process. He also stated that, ironically, "this turns out to be the primary source of local empowerment" (p. 137). Empowering or not, local health agencies may frequently lack the staff, expertise, time, or other resources required to adequately perform these assessments, and therefore look to professional survey researchers, demographers, statisticians, and other specialists for assistance with these critical tasks. This was most often the case with respect to the Healthy Start Coalitions.

SOCIAL, ECONOMIC, AND DEMOGRAPHIC PROFILES

Some of what is needed in most assessments and was required by regulation for the Healthy Start Coalition, is quite straightforward, such as demographic and economic profiles of the service delivery area. These types of profiles are basically "snapshots" of conditions in the service area reflective of current conditions, and are generally descriptive rather than analytic in nature. These kinds of demographic and economic materials are collected by other statistical agencies, such as the Bureau of the Census, Bureau of Labor Statistics or a vital statistics agency, that are concerned with monitoring and reporting social, economic, and demographic trends. One difficulty is that not all this material is collected monthly or even annually, and some of these data may be several years old at the time of the assessment, and are often for different dates, making comparison difficult.

Basic demographic information about a group or community is essential to the development of programs intended to serve them. Examples of this type of information include population size and composition, and measures of economic well-being. These are frequently supplemented with information on the larger "community," such as the state or nation, so that unique features of the locale being studied can be noted. Often, persons in a community are unaware of their particular uniqueness compared with a larger group.

Much of the needed material for the county assessment was collected as part of the decennial U.S. Census of Population and Housing and other censuses such as the Census of Agriculture. In Florida, the University of Florida's Bureau of Economic and Business Research publishes an annual *Florida Statistical Abstract*. Most of the material needed for the demographic and economic profiles is contained in this publication. Another important source of information is the annual publication, *Florida County Comparisons*. Although it contains some of the same material as the *Statistical Abstract, Florida County Comparisons* also contains economic information from trade associations and Florida government agencies. Perhaps the most important resources for developing a profile is a good reference librarian and a library containing relevant government documents.

Most of this section is drawn, with only minor editing, from the county needs assessment. It illustrates basic demographic and economic profiles of a largely rural county (Zervigon-Hakes, Byers, Terrie, Harris, & Sanderson, 1994). The actual assessment included many charts, figures, and tables, as well as a textual description of the material.

Population

The size of the county's population has remained remarkably stable over the past 15 years. During the 1980s, a decade of rapid growth in the state's population, the composition of the county's population changed far more rapidly than did its size. During the 1980s, the number of people who left the county exceeded the number moving in and the population shrank by about 600 people—to 41,105. By 1992, however, the county's population had grown to an estimated 42,466. Over one third (35%) of the growth is attributable to the movement of new residents into the county, many of whom commute to work. The county is one of a few in the state with a majority of African-American residents (57.9%); non-Latin Whites make up 39.9% of the population, and Hispanics constitute the majority of the remaining 2.2%. Overall, 18.1% of births are to teenage mothers. Among African Americans, 22.9% of newborns have a teenage mother.

The newborn population in the county is different from the state's population as a whole. It demonstrates a higher fertility rate among the county's Hispanic and African-American population. African Americans, who constitute 58% of the county population, represented 67% of all births between 1990 and 1992. Similarly, Hispanics are 2.2% of the population, but 6.4% of recent births. The county's uniqueness gives maternal and infant health care providers an opportunity to design services to meet their consumers' special needs.

Economy

Cotton and tobacco, historically the foundations of the strong local economy in Gadsden County, have not been replaced. Service industries employ the largest segment (42.6%) of the labor force. Tomato and mushroom cultivation, light manufacturing, and mining provide some employment, but the county economy depends more than most on external sources of income. In 1990, 42.2% of employed residents traveled outside the county to work (U.S. Bureau of the Census, 1990). This trend, and the accompanying change in the composition of the county's workforce, is reflected in the 237% increase in per capita income between 1980 and 1990 (Florida Department of Commerce, 1993). Still, because the majority of workers occupy low-skill, low-wage positions, the 1990 per capita income of $12,896 in the county was less than 70% of the state average.

Poverty

The economic well-being of individuals and families in this county reflects the county's economic conditions. The median household income is often used to assess family economics and their effective buying income (rather than the per capita income). The 1990 median household income in the county ($19,817) was less than three fourths (72.7%) of the state median $28,297; (Florida Department of Commerce, 1993), and the poverty rate was the highest in the state at the time of the census.

Maternal and Child Poverty

Poverty is one of the most important correlates of poor maternal and child health and educational outcomes. Poverty, by itself, is not a cause of, but contributes to, a population's inability to provide or access fundamental services and goods, such as food, housing, health care, and educational opportunities. Poor nutrition can severely affect fetal growth and infant development (Institute of Medicine, 1985, 1989). The highest rates of poverty exist for families with children under the age of 5. In 1989, 28% of all residents and 22% of families were living below the federal poverty level in the county. In the same year, 37.6% of children under age 5 and well over half (61.3%) of children under age 5 who live in female-headed households in Gadsden County were poor.

ASSESSING PREGNANCY OUTCOMES

Pregnancy outcomes were the principal demographic information assessed. The primary source for these data is the state's vital statistics. In the United States, each state has the legal authority and responsibility for collecting and disseminating information on vital events (e.g., births, deaths, fetal deaths, marriages, and divorces). Laws vary from state to state in terms of exactly what information is collected and especially with respect to issues of confidentiality. The state efforts are encouraged and coordinated by the National Center for Health Statistics. Uniformity between states is ensured as much as possible by a federal–state cooperative system known as the Public Health Conference on Records and Statistics (Shryock & Siegel, 1973).

In Florida, statistics on births and deaths have been collected and reported since 1917. These data have been reported annually in a series of published volumes titled *Florida Vital Statistics*. Data are reported separately for each county, and selected information is also available by incorporated place of residence. Vital events are normally recorded in two ways. The first is by place of occurrence, and the other is by place of usual residence. Vital events tabulated by place of residence should normally be used when conducting a community needs assessment. What is happening to the residents of the community is more interesting than where it is happening. For instance, a child may be born or die in a hospital in another county. The place of occurrence of that vital event is the county in which the hospital is located. Most of the relevant factors associated with the outcome are more properly attributed to the usual county of residence. Therefore, the appropriate vital statistics are births and deaths by place of residence.

Another consideration is the appropriate time period to use. Vital statistics are reported separately for each year. Because events like infant and fetal mortality are relatively rare, there may be few or even no such events in a single year in a small county or town. Therefore, the following year an increase of two or three infant deaths would produce a large change in the rate. Consider a county with 200 births and two infant deaths for each of 2 successive years. That county's infant mortality rate (number of infant deaths—1,000/number of live births) would be 10 per 1,000 live births in each of those years, which is a fairly typical number in the United States. Suppose that in the following year there were also 200 births, but four infant deaths. The rate would double to 20 per 1,000, and would be considered an extremely high rate. Small changes in numbers of events can lead to large changes in rates. The solution to this statistical anomaly is to pool or combine these data into a single rate covering all 3 years. In this example, there would be 600 births and eight deaths, or 13.3 deaths per 1,000 live births for the 3-year period, which is likely more representative of the actual level of infant mortality within that county.

In entire states, large counties, and large cities, rates of vital events by individual year may be stable enough to use by themselves. The downside of using 3-, 4-, or even 5-year rates is that it makes real change harder to detect. A steady increase in the number of deaths over the interval would, for example, be hidden by a multiyear rate.

This is a small county in which multiyear rates are appropriate. It is all the more so because subcounty rates are also required to pinpoint geographic areas with the greatest need for services. The published volumes, however, were not sufficient for all the requirements of this needs assessment. Normally, a great deal more information is collected on birth and death certificates than is published. Also, most publications lack subcounty detail. In Florida, the Office of Vital Statistics makes available public use files of vital data. Confidentiality requirements do, however, severely restrict their usefulness for detailed subcounty analysis. Basically, zip codes are the only subcounty area that can be identified on these files. When a governmental or quasigovernmental agency is conducting the needs assessment, greater geographic specificity is attainable because uncensored records containing complete addresses may be available. One key resource is a linked file of births and any associated infant death certificate. From this file, birth outcomes, such as birth weight or delivery complications, can be associated with infant deaths and the factors associated with that death. Uncensored files containing addresses can often be geocoded to fairly precise latitude—longitude coordinates and linked with other geographically based files through the use of a geographic information system (GIS). At the time this assessment was in progress, zip codes were the only subcounty units available for the study. Most of the pregnancy outcome data described in this chapter came from the published vital statistics volumes, or from computer tabulations of 1990–1992 linked birth/infant-death files performed by the author. Linked birth/death files are available in many states. The following text and information have been extracted from the final report and are provided as an illustrative model (Zervigon-Hakes et al., 1994).

Infant Mortality

Infant mortality is a leading measure of the health and social conditions of a community. It is an indicator of the health of mothers, the effectiveness of the maternal care system, and the health and care of newborns and infants. The factors contributing to infant deaths are the result of both biological (e.g., low birth weight) and environmental (e.g., poverty, smoking, alcohol, and nutrition) events and conditions. The Office of Vital Statistics for each state would be the normal source of this information. National compendia of vital statistics are also available in a series entitled *Vital Statistics of the United States*. However, they are usually 4–5 years behind the current time. For this reason, unpublished data available from the National Commission to Prevent Infant Mortality was utilized for the national comparisons presented next.

Between 1985 and 1989, the county's infant mortality rate was 18.5 per 1,000, as compared with the state average of 10.8 per 1,000. The county's infant mortality rate was far higher than the national or state rate, but the average number of infant deaths each year in the county has declined by nearly one third—from 18.5 to 11.2 per 1,000 births, which is only slightly higher than the state rate. This change represents a drop in the average number of deaths from over 13 to about 9 per year.

A closer review of infant deaths within the closest 3-year period for which data were available (1990–1992) reveals that the overall rate of infant mortality among non-White births (10.9 per 1,000 births) is below the state goal of 14 per 1,000, and is above the overall state rate of 9.7 per 1,000 White births. Infant mortality among White births is higher than the state goal for this population. Infant mortality among Hispanics is lower than the state rate. Within two subpopulations, however, the rates exceed state goals among children born to White and non-White mothers ages 16–18.

Fetal Mortality

Fetal mortality refers to the death of an unborn occurring after the 20th week of pregnancy. These data are normally published by the state's Office of Vital Statistics. They are associated with medical and environmental risk conditions. Many are preventable through prenatal care and medical management. To study fetal death trends, it was necessary to look across a number of years. Even with this 4-year analysis, the numbers are still quite small for creating a per 1,000 comparative rate. Yet it is clear that non-White mothers are more likely to have a fetal death. The rate of White fetal death in the county has declined by nearly half since 1985–1988, but is still half again the state's year 2000 goal rate of 5 per 1,000 births. Non-White fetal deaths have declined only slightly over the same period, and remain far above the rate established as a state goal.

Neonatal Mortality

Neonatal deaths are those that occur within the first 28 days of life. The leading risk condition associated with neonatal mortality is low birth weight. Neonatal mortality, when combined with fetal mortality, is called *perinatal mortality*. The two are leading indicators of the quality of prenatal health care. Between 1985 and 1988 and 1988 and 1992, neonatal mortality increased slightly among Whites in the county. In contrast, the rate declined by nearly two thirds among non-Whites. The White rate remains above the state goal of 6.5 or less per 1,000 births; the non-white rate in the county for this period achieves the goal of 7 or less per 1,000.

Postneonatal Mortality

Postneonatal mortality refers to infant death after 28 days of life. Postneonatal deaths are more closely associated with environmental and socioeconomic conditions than those deaths that occur earlier. Good community heath surveillance, family support systems for at-risk families and children, nutrition, and well-baby visits are leading preventive measures used to lower postneonatal as well as child mortality. Leading causes include sudden infant death syndrome (SIDS), congenital anomalies, child abuse, accidents, and infection. Postneonatal mortality has declined sharply among White infants in Gadsden County, but has remained nearly unchanged among non-White infants. The rates in both racial categories for the 1988–1992 period were below the goals set for the state.

Causes of Infant Death

Vital statistics tabulations can also provide information on cause of death according to widely used International Classification of Deaths, Revision 9 (ICD–9). The general categories give only a sense of the types of causes of infant death. For example, the phrase "Conditions originating in the perinatal period" typically refers to babies born with a low birth weight. These data can provide a good indicator of the specific type(s) of interventions that may be necessary. Injury and poisoning were primary causes of infant death within the county in the not too distant past. If infectious and parasitic diseases had been a significant cause (they were not), water and other sanitary systems would likely be targeted for improvement. Currently, perinatal conditions (primarily low birth weight) are the principal causes of infant death within the county. This has intervention implications that will become clearer when the factors such as teenage pregnancy, which are strongly associated with low birth weight, are seen later.

Low Birth Weight Babies

Low birth weight—less than 2,500 grams, or 5 pounds 8 ounces—is a good measure of maternal and fetal health. It is an important potential contributing factor to poor child health, developmental delay, and disability. An infant born with a low birth weight is 40 times more likely to die in the first 28 days of his or her life, and 20 times more likely to die in the first year (Institute of Medicine, 1985). Very low birth weight—less than 1,500 grams, or 3 pounds, 5 ounces—is an even more powerful contributor to infant death and morbidity (poor health). A very low birth weight baby is 200 times more likely to die in the first 28 days of life, and those that survive often require intensive medical care and educational intervention to improve their outcomes.

Numerous studies have provided information on how to decrease the numbers of low birth weight babies through the provision of comprehensive prenatal care, which includes family planning, social service, and educational support for pregnant women at risk for a preterm birth. Nevertheless, these statistics have been the most resistant to change over time, both in Florida and the nation. Since 1984, Florida's low birth weight rates have ranges from a low of 7.4% to 7.7%. There is much work to be done to improve this unacceptable rate in communities and states.

Since 1989, the county's percentage of low birth weight babies has remained fairly stable—rising from 9.4% to 10.3%. This change represents 8–10 additional low birth weight babies per 1,000 born, or an increase of about 7 in the number of low birth weight babies each year. Because the county population is small, a change of 1% makes less difference in actual numbers than it would in a more populous county.

A closer look at low birth weight incidence by race and age in this county reveals higher incidence for adolescents and women over age 35, regardless of race. Data were not available on income level of families. It is likely that these findings are reflective of poverty rates among African-American and Hispanic families with young children, although a recent article found that large racial differences in low birth weight remain unexplained by income and other sociodemographic factors (Cramer, 1995).

Very Low Birth Weight Births

Among low birth weight children, there is an even more undesirable pregnancy outcome. Very low birthweight babies are 200 times more likely to die within the first 28 days of life and often need intensive medical care after birth (Institute of Medicine, 1985). Very low birth weight babies are more likely to suffer neurological abnormalities and disabilities and often need special education services to help their development. It is an important measure of the number of babies who will need specialized services.

The incidence of very low birth weight babies among non-Whites is typically higher than for White populations. Non-White babies are more likely to be very low birth weight. Those born very low birth weight start life more vulnerable to developmental delays and poor health outcomes. The overall rate of very low birth weight in the county has fluctuated considerably, largely because the rate among non-White births changed so much. The total rate, which matched the state rate in 1990, was twice the statewide rate in 1992. The non-White rate in the county, well below the state rate in 1990, has since risen higher than in any previous year since 1988. Both the non-White and White rates are more than twice those established as year 2000 goals.

BIRTH AND PREGNANCY SCREENING

As has been seen, mortality and birth weight outcomes are key indicators in the assessment of infants and their mothers' health. However, these outcomes do not exist in a vacuum. They are associated with other factors, such that some women are at greater risk of unfavorable outcomes than others. Knowing these associations and detecting them early are central to designing effective interventions. Within Florida, the desire to provide for the possibility of effective interventions statewide led to the development of two universal screens—one to be used at the first prenatal visit and the other to be performed at birth. These approaches to screening are readily adaptable to other locales. In addition, the individual variables that constitute the screens can be used alone or in combination as predictors of unfavorable outcomes, which is what was done in the Gadsden assessment. The following information on how the screens were developed serves to illustrate the development of a screen, and to provide empirical evidence of the association between commonly available indicators and pregnancy outcomes.

The mother's health, home environment, social and economic position, risk-taking behavior, and other demographic factors are all related to pregnancy outcomes. Birth certificates contain a wealth of information on factors known to be related to birth outcomes. The 1991 state legislature directed the Department of Health and Rehabilitative Services (HRS) to develop an infant screening instrument (F.S. 383.14) to identify infants with greater than average risk of having health problems. The department considered the relationship between postneonatal death and all the information available on the birth certificate. Postneonatal deaths, which occur between age 28 days and 1 year, are considered an indicator of morbidity or the child's general health, and survivors with the same risk factors as the fatalities are likely to require more intensive health care than other infants. Factors that occurred in at least 1,000 births, and that had an associated risk of at least twice the average risk of postneonatal death, were retained as screening criteria. There were 10 such factors:

- Birth weight less than 2,000 grams
- Abnormal conditions of the newborn
- Congenital anomalies of newborn
- No prenatal care
- Mother not married
- Mother smoked 10 or more cigarettes a day
- Mother less than 18 years old
- Mother non-White
- Alcohol used during pregnancy
- Mother's education less than 12 years and age greater than 18

Infants who weighed less than 2,000 grams at birth were 12.2 times more likely to die within the postneonatal period, compared with heavier infants. For this reason, these infants and those with anomalies or without prenatal care were assigned a 4-point weight on the screening scale. Other factors were assigned a weight of 1, except for low education, which was scored 2. The mother's education factor was treated differently in several important ways. First, the overall risk ratio was less than 2, which was an exception to the general rule, and this relatively low risk factor was assigned a scale value of 2. The scales developers defended this decision, saying,

> The basis for this is the assertion that the mother's education is more closely associated with infant morbidity than post-neonatal death so post-neonatal death is a biased proxy for morbidity in the case of mother's education. The emphasis given to mother's education is based on an assumed association with infant morbidity in addition to the association with post-neonatal death. Thus the predictors of death are not necessarily good predictors of other important nonmedical outcomes. (Thompson, Hopkins, & Watkins, 1993, p. 5)

The infant screen is accomplished by adding the scale points for each risk factor recorded on the birth certificate. If the sum is 4 or more, the infant is considered high risk. High-risk infants are 6.2 times more likely to die post-neonatally, compared with those who screen negatively, according to the HRS study. Throughout the state, this screening is performed in the hospital or birthing center when the infant is born, and enhanced services are offered to the families by the county public health departments. The screen can also be performed after the fact, using computer files containing vital statistics birth records.

Use of this screening during 1992 and 1993 for the county showed that 17.2% of the infants screened during the period were evaluated to be at risk and were therefore offered additional services. This rate is 25% greater than for the state as a whole.

For a service delivery program to be successful, not only must services be offered, but those services must be accepted by the population. As with most programs, participation is voluntary. Families are offered the choice of being screened and of receiving enhanced services. The "consent to screen" and "consent to be served" measures provide an important ongoing evaluation of the success of Healthy Start and its acceptance by those it attempts to aid. The county achieves better results than the state overall (91.9% vs. 71.8%) from families in terms of mothers' willingness to have their infants screened, as well as in the proportion of mothers of high-risk infants who consent to services (93.6% vs. 85.0%).

The state also uses a prenatal screening instrument. The Healthy Start Initiative law specified that a prenatal screen was to be developed to screen for "preterm birth or other high risk condition" (F.S. 383.14). The state did not wish to be limited to factors that appear on the birth certificate; otherwise, unlike the infant screen, no actual data would be available for analysis. Instead, an expert panel was convened to consider information from the literature, criteria from other states, limited analysis of certain internal data sets, and experience-based professional judgment of panel members. The final 16 scoring factors were arrived at by consensus. They were:

- Mother is African American
- Mother not married
- Unwanted pregnancy
- Alcohol used during pregnancy
- Unhealthy previous pregnancy
- Mother less than 18 or over 35 years of age
- Mother's weight less than 115 pounds
- Transportation problems
- Mother requires continuing care
- Sexually transmitted disease treated within last 6 months
- Mother smokes 10 or more cigarettes per day
- Education less than high school and age greater than 18
- Lacks safe place to live and food
- No previous pregnancy

- Moved more than three times during last 12 months
- Prenatal care began during third trimester.

After a year of use, actual data were available. The adverse pregnancy outcome was defined as delivery at less than 35 weeks gestational age and/or birth weight less than 2,000 grams (Thompson, Freeman, & Steele, 1993). The first nine items predicted outcomes as expected. The prenatal screening instrument has subsequently been revised in light of these findings and interested persons should contact the Health Program Office of the Department of Health and Rehabilitative Services and request the Prenatal Risk Screening Instrument, HRS-H Form 3134, June 1994. The assessment reported herein was based on the original prenatal screen, and therefore the fairly substantial revisions are not discussed.

Results of the latest available infant screening information for the county cover from April 1992 through May 1993. They show that, although 13.81% of the state's newborns scored 4 points or more, the proportion of newborns in the county identified as high risk by the infant screen was 17.2% (125 infants) during the period.

SELECTED RISK FACTORS IN THE COUNTY

The assessment conducted for the Healthy Start Coalition collected and reported results based on both birth and infant screens, as described earlier. There was also interest in examining separately the individual risk factors from which the screens were constructed. It is important to know which of the risk factors are common within the community being studied when designing an effective intervention strategy. The following risk factor information was drawn from a number of published sources or tabulated by the author from birth certificate records from 1990 to 1992 and included in the report to the coalition (Zervigon-Hakes et al., 1994).

Prenatal Care

Prenatal care is essential for minimizing the chances of preterm birth (Institute of Medicine, 1985); the earlier it begins, the better. The primary source of information for the onset of prenatal care is the birth certificate. In view of the elevated risks of prematurity, low birth weight, and other complications associated with pregnancy at very young ages, these indicators deserve careful attention. The younger the mother, the more likely she is to begin prenatal care late and receive fewer than 10 care visits. Further, the proportion of adolescent mothers 16–19 years of age who began prenatal care late, had no prenatal care, or had less than 10 care visits is higher than the proportion of adult mothers.

Further examination of these indicators by mother's race or ethnicity reveals important differences. Although every woman under the age of 16 received at least some prenatal care, for almost half of these women, care began in either the second or third trimester of pregnancy. Among adult mothers, particularly those 35 years old or older, the proportion of African-American and Hispanic mothers who obtained care late or not at all exceeded that among White mothers. Among all county women giving birth between 1990 and 1992, White women were most likely (86.5%) to have begun care in the first trimester, followed by African Americans (71.3%). Hispanics were the least likely to have begun care early, and over 10% of them received no care at all.

Adolescence

Adolescent pregnancy is associated with dropping out of school, a lifetime of depressed earnings, and an increased potential for welfare dependency. Infant mortality and low birth weight, nationally and within Florida, are higher among adolescents than other populations. Adolescents who receive quality prenatal care early and continually through their pregnancy are less likely to suffer higher adverse birth outcomes. Yet after the baby is born, the newborn and child mother are more likely than other mothers to have reduced earnings and reduced educational attainment. Higher rates of child abuse and neglect are found among very young mothers. Twenty-five percent of teens who bear a child are likely to be pregnant again within 1 year and 50% within 36 months. Mothers who have babies before graduating from high school are more likely to become long-term welfare recipients lacking education, work experience, and support.

Data for teenage mothers were examined in three age groups: those under age 15, those 15–19 years of age, and those under age 19. Nineteen-year-olds are less at risk because high school graduation often occurs at age 18. Because of their age, children 15 years or less who become pregnant should be considered especially at risk, and are likely to need special care and support.

Two types of analysis are included in this section: (a) adolescent births as a percent of all births, and (b) adolescent births as a percent of the adolescent population. The first statistic provides helpful information for policy analysis on the future parenting trends and parenting service needs. The second provides important information on adolescent pregnancy trends.

In the county, more than one birth in six involves a mother who is 18 years old or younger. The proportion of births to teens in the county (18.1%) is over twice the state average (8.1%) and would seem unacceptably high. This has been true for the past decade, and, unlike the state as a whole, there has been no improvement in these rates over time. Further, the proportion of county teenage females who gave birth during 1990 (11.9%) is two-thirds higher than the state average (6.96%) and is nearly three times the state goal for 1995. On a brighter note, the birth rate for girls younger than 15 years old was lower than for the state as a whole, and only slightly greater than the 1995 goal of 1.5 per 1,000.

Once adolescents have become mothers, they are three to four times more likely to become pregnant again while still a teen, compared with those with no previous pregnancy history (Zervigon-Hakes & Lockenbach, 1991). It seems likely that these young women have even greater needs for service during pregnancy and early infancy, due to the responsibilities and burdens of caring for another child and often having no spouse to assist. Repeat teen birth rates are very high in the county—at twice the rate for the state as a whole—and are about three times the year 2000 goal set by the state.

The incidence of teen pregnancy also varies by race. African-American teens in the county were more than twice as likely as White teens of the same age to have a baby. The average total number of teen births each year increased by over 10% among both Whites and non-Whites between 1985 and 1988 and between 1989 and 1992. Further, the data shown earlier indicate that babies born to African Americans are also at greater risk of low birth weight or death during the first year of life, suggesting a double disadvantage for these infants.

Age of Mother

There is ample evidence that risk of adverse outcomes varies with mother's age. Infants born to very young and very old mothers are more likely to experience health problems. For example, rates of infant mortality and low birth weight are often higher in adolescent populations (Alan Guttmacher Institute, 1981; Institute of Medicine, 1985). This has been evident in this county, where infant mortality and low birth weight rates were found to be highest among children born to mothers between 16 and 18 years of age. In contrast, *high-risk births*, defined according to the criteria described earlier for infant screening, have been more prevalent among older mothers, partic- ularly those between the ages of 19 and 35, among whom the proportion of high-risk births was nearly twice that among teenage mothers.

POPULATIONS OF GREATEST CONCERN

One of the required tasks in this needs assessment was the identification of priority groups for whom services could be specifically targeted. The infor- mation presented thus far suggests three such groups.

- Mothers less than 19 years of age
- Non-White mothers
- Mothers with less than a high school education

The data showed that each of these subpopulations had a higher rate of adverse outcomes, compared with all county women, with respect to three important indicators. The only exception was for teenage mothers, who had a lower percentage of infants screened as high risk at birth.

Although the raw information is important descriptively, the true magnitude of the increased risk of an undesired outcome for each of the subgroups is not easily discerned. The best way to form comparisons among subpopulations is to compute the odds of an event occurring within each group and calculating the ratio of these odds. The result is called an *odds ratio,* and tells how much more likely it is that one group will experience an event compared with another group. Odds and probabilities are not the same thing. A *probability* is the

Table 7.1 Odds Ratios for Specific Birth Outcomes for Selected Population Subgroups

	Infant Mortality	Low Birth Rate	High-Risk Births
Mothers < 19 years old	1.360	1.501*	0.463
African-American mothers	1.125	1.687*	3.515*
Mothers with < high school education	1.470	1.208	7.754*

Source: Florida Linked Birth and Death Certificate Records, author's tabulation.
*Less than 5% chance that the underlying odds ratio = 1.0.

number of cases experiencing an event divided by the total number of cases; it is commonly called a *proportion. Odds* are the number with the event divided by the number without the event. To illustrate, consider 10 children—2 born low birth weight and 8 not low birth weight. The probability of low birth weight is 2/10 or one fifth. The odds are 2/8 or one fourth. These ratios are similar to, but not the same as, risk ratios, which are the ratio of the probability of occurrence of the event in one group compared with another group. One of the primary reasons to use odds as opposed to proportions is that odds are symmetrical. For example, if a particular event has a .75 probability of occurring, then it has a .25 probability that it will not occur. The same information expressed as odds would be that there was a 3:1 chance of the event occurring and 1:3 that it would not. Similarly, odds ratios are symmetrical, whereas risk ratios (the ratios of two probabilities) are not. In other words, the ratio of the odds for persons with the trait to those without is the inverse of the odds of those without the trait to those with. This is not a property of risk ratios and provides a clear advantage for odds ratios.

Linked birth and death certificate records showed that there were 249 women who gave birth to a low birth weight baby during 1990–1992 and 2,234 whose babies were not low birth weight. The overall odds of having a low birth weight baby between 1990 and 1992 in this county were, therefore, .1115:1. Odds for African-American women were .1296:1 and .076:1 for non-African Americans. Dividing the odds for African Americans by the odds for non-African Americans yields an odds ratio of 1.69, which means that the odds for children born to African-American women were 1.69 times as likely to be low birth weight compared with other children. Table 7.1 shows these odds ratios for each higher risk subpopulation with respect to three key birth outcome indicators.

Between 1990 and 1992, adolescents had 36% greater odds than older mothers to have a baby die in the first year of life and had 50% greater odds to have a low birth weight birth. Alternatively, these teenage women were less than half as likely to have their birth screened as a high-risk infant. This was apparently the result of the screening instrument (described earlier), which scored 2 points for being over 18 and less than a high school education, but only 1 point for being less than 19 years of age. African Americans were 13% more likely than others to suffer an infant death, 69% more likely to have a low birth weight baby, and 3.5 times as likely to have a baby identified as potentially at risk on the universal screen. Mothers with less than a high school education were only slightly (21%) more likely than those with at least a high school education to have a low birth weight newborn, but were almost eight times more likely to have a newborn identified as high risk on the infant screen.

These numbers are important in revealing groups that should be targeted for the receipt of services. They also provide critical baseline data against which to measure the success of subsequent targeted services. If interventions are effective, these odds ratios should move closer to 1 over time. The before and after odds of events, such as low birth weight babies, can also be compared; if the intervention is working, the ratio of the after to before odds should be less than 1.

All of the numbers presented earlier are referred to as *point estimates*. That means that a particular value is the single best estimate of the relative odds of an event occurring. Often it is important to know whether a particular ratio is sufficiently different from 1.0 for the difference to be significant in a statistical sense. There are several different approaches to this question.

The asterisks in Table 7.1 indicate odds ratios for which, taking into consideration the number of cases in the study, there is less than a 5% chance that the underlying "true" odds ratio is actually 1.0—or, stated another way, that it is not simply the result of chance. Assuming completeness of coverage, there is no sampling variability in vital statistics data because they are complete counts, rather than samples. Therefore, calculations derived from the recorded events are parameters, not sample estimates. A *parameter* is a summary value belonging to a particular universe, as opposed to a *statistic,* which is a property of a sample. The most common use of a test of statistical significance, which is to determine how likely it is that a specific sample statistic is the result of unrepresentativeness of the sample, is not appropriate. However, if a particular population parameter is considered to be an unbiased estimate of a true underlying number, it may be appropriate to calculate how likely it is that a particular proportion or odds ratio is a good approximation of the actual value. One simple calculation is Chi-square for a 2×2 table. That is what has been done in this instance. The 47% greater odds of death for infants whose mothers have less than a high school education is the correct population value for this time period. There is no sampling variability. However, considering the marginal distributions in the associated 2×2 table, there may be a greater than 5% chance that the true odds ratio found over a long period of time is actually 1. Other evidence, such as odds ratios in other counties or the state or for different time periods, might be considered. All of these would help determine if there is an association between level of education and infant mortality, but would not be helpful if we were trying to compare Gadsden for this point in time with other locales. Confidence intervals can also be placed around odds ratios or proportions (see Kahn & Sempos, 1989, for details).

The data presented in Table 7.1 present strong evidence that services should be targeted at three groups of women in the county with higher risks of adverse birth outcomes: adolescents, African Americans, and non-high school graduates.

IDENTIFYING GEOGRAPHIC AREAS
WITH THE GREATEST NEEDS

The rules promulgated to implement the Healthy Start Coalition legislation also required determination of geographic locations of targeted population groups at risk of adverse pregnancy outcomes. Census tracts and zip codes were specifically mentioned in the regulations as suitable subdivisions of a county.

Basic Review of Census Geography

The sources for most of the information presented so far were vital records, other administrative records, and census data. The U. S. Bureau of the Census tabulates and reports information for a variety of geographic areas, ranging from the entire United States to a census block. Geographic entities used by the census belong to one of three classes: legal, statistical, or administrative. Legal areas include: the nation, states, counties, minor civil divisions, incorporated places, Native American reservations, congressional districts, and voting districts. Statistical areas include: regions, divisions, census county divisions, metropolitan statistical areas, urbanized areas, tracts, and blocks. Administrative entities include: school districts, traffic analysis zones, and zip codes. The list is not exhaustive. For complete details, refer to the *Geographic Areas Reference Manual* (U.S. Bureau of the Census, 1994).

Figure 7.1 shows graphically the hierarchy and richness of detail of the census geographic scheme. Although a complete discussion of census geography is beyond the scope of this chapter, certain concepts require elaboration. One of the most useful subcounty geographic areas for statistical purposes are census tracts/block numbering areas (BNAs). A *census tract* is defined as:

> *A small, relatively permanent statistical subdivision of a county in a metropolitan area (MA) or a selected nonmetropolitan county, delineated by a local committee of census data users (a CSAC) for the purpose of presenting decennial census data. Census tract boundaries normally follow visible features, but may follow governmental unit boundaries and other nonvisible features in some instances; they always nest within counties.*

> *Designed to be relatively homogeneous units with respect to population characteristics, economic status, and living conditions at the time the CSAC established them, census tracts usually contain between 2,500 and 8,000 inhabitants. They may be split by any subcounty geographic entity. (U.S. Bureau of the Census, 1994, p. G-11)*

Note that *census tract* is defined in metropolitan areas and selected nonmetropolitan counties and is designed to be relatively homogenous in a socioeconomic sense. In the remainder of the country, counties are subdivided into BNAs. The principal distinction between a tract and BNAs is that the latter

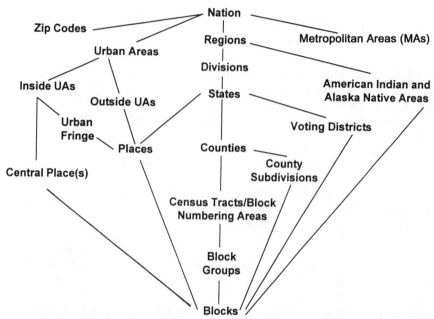

Figure 7.1. Geographic hierarchy for the 1990 U.S. dicennial census of population and housing. (From *Geographic Areas Reference Manual* [Fig. 2-1] by U.S. Bureau of the Census, 1994 Washington, DC: U.S. Government Printing Office. Copyright ©1994 by U.S. Government Printing Office. Reprinted by permission.)

are frequently county subdivisions of convenience, without any consideration of socioeconomic characteristics. Tracts/BNAs are further subdivided into *block groups* (BG), which are defined as "a combination of census blocks that is a subdivision of a census tract or BNA" (U.S. Bureau of the Census, 1994, p. G-11). A BG consists of all blocks whose numbers begin with the same digit in a given census tract or BNA. A census block is, "The smallest entity for which the Census Bureau collects and tabulates decennial census information; bounded on all sides by visible and nonvisible features shown on Census Bureau maps" (U.S. Bureau of the Census, 1994, p. G-11).

Census tracts/BNAs are one of the most useful subcounty areas for statistical purposes. This is because a great deal of information is tabulated and published at this level. For users with access to computing or microcomputing equipment, the block groups are also enormously valuable. Due to their enormous volume, information for these entities is not published; however, it is tabulated and presented in summary tape files (STF), the most useful of which is the STF3A series available on CD-ROM. STFs come in several forms and formats. The content of a particular set of STFs is specified by the number and letter (e.g., STF1C or STF3A). The most useful ones for most readers are STF1 and STF3. The STF1 series is basic demographic information collected from 100% of the population. The STF3 series contains information from the 1 in 6 sample of households that were asked detailed socioeconomic questions. A letter follows the number and specifies the level of the geographic detail provided. "A" is the most detailed. The "B" series contains zip code-based tabulations, which are often immensely valuable for needs assessment applications.

The compact discs contain tabulated data stored in a DBASE III format. Users with suitable software can extract cells of pretabulated information as required. The files are quite useful even without any additional software because each CD-ROM contains the bureau supplied "GO" software, which allows examination and printing of individual tables for any desired area. STF3As contain information for each level of geography from block groups, up through the entire nation. The CD-ROM also contains technical documentation.

Zip code boundaries provide an often useful alternative to census geography. There are two basic types of zip codes. The first is associated with a specific geographic delivery area; the other is associated with post boxes within a post office. There are three of the first type and three of the second type in the county.

For this needs assessment, locations with the highest risk of adverse birth outcomes were of primary interest. These data, tabulated from vital statistics records, were available for six zip code areas, including the three presented earlier plus three "post office box"-type zip codes. The number of births occurring to residents of the county between 1990 and 1992 was 2,483. Of these 73 (2.9%) had zip codes outside of the county due to either misreporting or miscoding. The three "post office box"-type zip codes were for post offices located in Greensboro (32330), Gretna (32332), and Midway (32343). Representing data associated with these three zip codes is problematic because they do not serve a specified geographic area. One approach illustrated here is to use the geographic boundaries of the three named places as the boundary for their associated zip code. This is actually a fine representation of the actual situation because many residents of these towns receive their mail at the post office, and persons living further away from town are more likely to have rural route delivery. Figure 7.2 shows the percentage of low birth weight babies by zip code.

As seen, the highest percentage of low birth weight infants occurred to mothers residing in (or at least receiving mail in) the Midway (32343) area, with 15.1%. The lowest, 8.7%, was for Greensboro (32330) post office boxes. This thematic map was shaded into three ranges that are shown in the legend box, although actual values are also shown for each zip code. Although this information could obviously be displayed in a table, a map provides spatial detail not available in tabular form.

Producing a Map

Desktop mapping of the type discussed here is becoming more readily available and will soon be fairly commonplace. Four basic resources are necessary to produce maps: a mapping program, boundary files, data to be mapped, and a suitable printer or plotter. All of the maps in this document have been black and white, although low-cost color in limited quantities is now

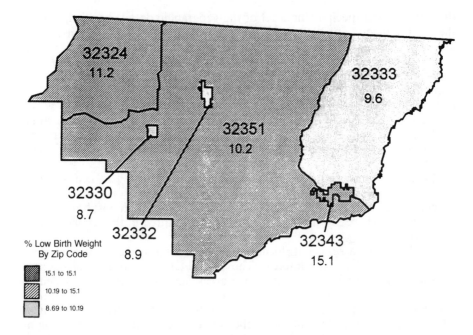

Figure 7.2.   Percent low birth weight babies, 1990–1992, Gadsden County Florida. Source: Vital
Statistics Records, authors' tabulations.

available. Boundary files for zip codes, counties, or census tracts are readily
available, but tend to be either expensive to purchase or time-consuming to
produce. The basic source of boundary files is the Census Bureau's TIGER/
Line files available on CD-ROM. These files require extensive and complicated
processing to be useful. Programs that convert these TIGER files into the
boundary files required for a particular mapping software are available. With
the software, suitable boundary files, and some data to map, the process is
relatively straightforward, although the learning curve for any particular program can be quite steep. Of course, the technical capability to produce maps
is only the first step in the effective display of geographical information. It is
difficult to draw a map and display data that are readily comprehensible to the
reader. Unfortunately, as with any visual or graphical display, it is easy to
mislead or misinform. For guidance on this subject, Edward Tufte's excellent
books, *Envisioning Information* (1990) and *The Visual Display of Quantitative
Information* (1983), are recommended.

PROJECTING FUTURE NEEDS

Up to this point, techniques to gather and present current and past information related to assessing the needs of infants and mothers have been dis-

cussed. The coalition's maternal and infant health care needs assessment was also required to estimate the number of women who will get pregnant each year in the coalition's service area and the number of these women who will have insufficient financial means to cover prenatal, labor and delivery, post-partum, and infant care. Strictly speaking, what is required is a projection, rather than an estimate. In conventional demographic usage, an *estimate* is a value derived on the basis of other information that is known for the time the estimate is being made. A *projection* is a value calculated for a future time period and for which there can be no actual concurrent data.

Projecting Number of Births

To develop a prenatal and infant health services plan in 1994, the coalition needed an estimate of how many women would become pregnant in 1994 and 1995. The best predictor of the near future is the immediate past. The projection is based on a 10-year average change in the general fertility rate, which is the number of births in a year divided by the number of women ages 15–44 in that year. County births have been generally stable or dropping. The average change in fertility between 1982 and 1992 was $-.41$. The 1994 projection was calculated by subtracting 2 years of average change ($2 \times -.41 = -.82$) from the 1992 fertility rate in the county. The resulting projection of a fertility rate of 84.38 in 1994 was multiplied by the number of women in childbearing ages (15–45 years) projected by the governor's office (9,907 women in 1994), and the result was projection of 836 births in 1994. The procedure was repeated for the 1995 projection. Of course, there are other ways to produce this kind of projection, such as fitting a curve or trend line to the prior data. Unfortunately, for a very near-term forecast, it makes relatively little difference which procedure is actually utilized. Any projection is merely a mathematical model and its accuracy depends on how well future reality matches the underlying assumptions. The rather extreme fluctuations in the county's recent fertility rates (72.8 in 1990, 90.7 in 1991, and 85.2 in 1992) suggest that the model is unlikely to work very well in this instance. Another complication is that the smaller the population to project, the larger the projection errors are likely to be. Avoid making projections if possible, and, if required, use them cautiously.

Projecting Need for Financial Assistance

Healthy Start Coalitions were also required by regulation to project the number of pregnant women who would lack sufficient financial resources for pregnancy-related expenses. Medicaid was considered a financial resource, and therefore Medicaid eligible women were not included in this projection. Pregnant women and infants to age 1 are eligible for Medicaid if their income is below 185% of poverty. Children ages 1–8 are eligible for Medicaid if their income is below 133% of poverty. Pregnant women in these categories refusing Medicaid and/or those unable to find a Medicaid participating physician will have difficulty getting quality prenatal, delivery, and postpartum and infant health care services. The working poor have difficulty purchasing insurance, and yet are those thought to be most in need of financial aid. This category includes pregnant women whose income is between 185% and 250% of poverty.

Projections of numbers of pregnant women needing financial assistance were calculated by assuming that the current proportion of pregnant women in each poverty level would remain constant in the next 2 years. Those women whose family income places them greater than 185% of the poverty level and less than 250% are considered to have the greatest risk of requiring additional financial assistance with their pregnancy-related expenses.

FROM ASSESSMENT TO ACTION

Unlike many research endeavors, needs assessments are not an end product, but primarily a tool for further planning and action. An assessment can serve many planning purposes including:

- identifying specific problem areas or unmet needs,
- aiding in the development of realistic goals, and
- establishing baseline data for later comparisons.

Upon completion of the assessment, the study team prepared and presented a report to the county Healthy Start Coalition, which was responsible for the design and implementation of a service delivery plan.

After reviewing the results, the coalition decided to focus on what it described as four major health problems. In each of these areas, the county's rate of occurrence was higher than for the state as a whole, as well as above state and national goals. The four problem areas identified were:

- excessive infant mortality rate,
- excessive incidence of low birth weight infants,
- excessive teenage birth rate, and
- excessive proportion of women not beginning prenatal care in the first trimester.

The coalition also examined the assessment results and identified three groups of women in the county with the poorest perinatal outcomes and for whom services were to be targeted. These specific population groups were:

- women less than 19 years of age,
- non-White women of childbearing age, and
- women with less than a high school education.

The coalition then established goals and strategies for meeting those goals. For example, the coalition desires to reduce the county's infant mortality rate to 9.5 per 1,000 live births by 1997, and to 8.5 per 1,000 by the year 2000.

The problem areas, goals, and strategies for achieving the goals were all detailed in a document entitled *Service Delivery Plan for Maternal and Infant*

Table 7.2 Health Problem: Infant Mortality. Strategy #2: Increase general community knowledge regarding the importance of prenatal care through public awareness campaign

Action Steps	Responsibility	Timelines	Evaluation or Measure
Produce regular newsletter to reach wide sector of public and private community, including: coalition members, health/ medical communities, Chamber of Commerce members, school officials, churches, civic groups, concerned citizens, etc.	Publicity committee and coalition staff	Quarterly, 7/95—6/97	Newsletters and mailing lists
Revise coalition pamphlet explaining what Gadsden Citizens for Healthy Babies, Inc., is and its role in the community	Publicity committee; coalition staff and executive director	Summer 1995	Revised coalition information pamphlet
Continue regular close contact with county newspapers to cover coalition news; write guest columns and editorials regarding maternal and child health	Executive Director, Publicity committee; coalition staff; community health providers	7/95–6/97	Local news articles, editorials, and guest columns
Participate in speaking engagement opportunities, such as invitations from community groups, civic clubs, churches, MOD kickoff breakfast, etc.	Executive director	7/95–6/97	Agendas and newsletters of civic organizations
Sponsor annual maternal and child health fair—"Healthy Children's Day"	HCD committee; Quincy Kiwanis club; sponsors	Spring annually	Minutes of planning meetings; posters; programs
Sponsors informational booth at community events, including Quincyfest, Havana Days, Operation Guard Care, church and school health fairs	Coalition committee; HSC staff; coalition members	7/95–7/96	Posters, handouts, etc.
Participate and maintain membership on community boards and civic organizations to integrate concerns of maternal and child health into other community activities	Coalition board members; coalition staff and executive director	7/95–7/96	Membership lists and rosters

Health 1995–1997 (Gasden Citizens for Healthy Babies, Inc., 1995). Each intervention strategy was clearly outlined in a tabular form, as in Table 7.2.

Table 7.2 shows the strategy and describes specific actions to implement the strategy, persons and groups responsible for taking the action, time when the action will be taken, and how the action will be measured or evaluated. Twenty-one strategies to address the health problem areas were developed and presented in a similar format. The service delivery plan also calls for monitoring many of the key vital statistics and indicators described in the chapter annually as they become available.

The coalition also decided not to target services initially to any geographic subarea of the county. One major factor in this decision is the effort and difficulty associated with obtaining subcounty vital statistics and other indicators. They did indicate that once they had more experience in assessment and health care planning, future initiatives might focus on interventions targeted to specific areas of the county.

SUMMARY

The needs assessment was the key ingredient in designing intervention strategies. As this chapter was being prepared, these interventions were only just beginning to be implemented. It will not be known for several years whether specific goals are achieved. A major concern is that the reduction of infant mortality in a small population area can be thwarted by just one or two additional deaths or by a reduction in the number of live births. Even if the goals are met, it will not be possible to "prove" that the improvements are the result of the interventions. This would require a controlled study. Nonetheless, this assessment and future ones will play a key role in monitoring, and hopefully improving, the health of pregnant women and their infants.

8

Assessing the Needs of the Elderly: Two Approaches

Susan Berkowitz
Carolyn C. Carter
Carolyn Graves Ferguson
Rebecca Reviere

One of the most outstanding aspects of aging in the late 20th century is the growing variation within the elderly population. The elderly are living longer and their population is becoming more ethnically diverse than ever before in U.S. history, and projections suggest that these trends will accelerate in the coming years. Agencies serving older individuals that aim to be proactive in their planning must monitor population trends to meet the changing needs of their changing populations.

Northern Virginia is no exception to these demographic shifts. Traditionally, this area has been fairly affluent, with a relatively young population due to the influx of government workers. However, like the rest of the United States, Northern Virginia is experiencing an increase in the size and diversity of the elderly population. In the late 1980s, in the face of these trends, two Northern Virginia Agencies on Aging—the Fairfax Area Agency on Aging (FAAA) and the Arlington Agency on Aging (AAA)—carried out needs assessments to obtain information on their changing elderly populations. In this chapter, these two projects are discussed: a longitudinal needs assessment with waves in 1984 and 1990 conducted by the FAAA, and a qualitative minority-focused needs assessment carried out for the AAA in 1989. Although the projects were carried out independently and were quite different in several respects, both were conducted under the auspices of the Gerontological Society of America's Postdoctoral Fellowship Program in Applied Gerontology (now renamed the Technical Assistance Program).

Under Title III of the Older Americans Act (OAA) of 1965, as amended, Area Agencies on Aging were created in the early 1970s to provide planning, coordination, advocacy, service delivery, and technical assistance to elderly citizens and their families at the local level. Agencies are either a part of local

The authors acknowledge the assistance of Ann Long Morris, Ed.D., OTR, Geriatric Director for the Elderly, American Occupational Therapy Association, Bethesda, MD.

For further details, see Reviere, R., Carter, C. & Neuschatz, S. (1994). Longitudinal needs assessment: Aging in a suburban community. *Physical and Occupational Therapy in Geriatrics, 12,* 1–15.

government, funded by joint jurisdictions (regional, multiregional, or state), or private organizations serving localities authorized to receive funding under the OAA. Although the OAA requires agencies to assess the needs of their elderly service population, no uniform procedures have been developed to guide the assessment process required for the "area plan for aging services"— an annual agreement required for agencies to receive funds. Needs are often measured in ad hoc fashion, often through public hearings or by selectively gathering the experience and educated observations of service providers. Both case studies described in this chapter utilized systematic methods of applied research in the assessment of elderly needs.

LONGITUDINAL NEEDS ASSESSMENT

The suburbs are graying, as individuals who moved out of urban areas in the 1950s grow older (Golant, 1990). Approximately 43% of the elderly live in the suburbs (U.S. Bureau of the Census, 1989). They "age in place" in settings designed primarily to house families rearing children, where rather spacious neighborhoods are tied together by the automobile (Oriol, 1989). Despite relative affluence, suburban elderly have unique sets of needs.

To be truly accurate, planning for those who are "aging in place" should be an ongoing, self-correcting process. Longitudinal research—a method of following the same individuals or like persons over a period of time, instead of studying different individuals at different points in time—provides an opportunity to study and explore the process of change (Shock et al., 1984). With information over time, agencies can efficiently allocate resources, plan programs, and develop policies that match the needs of their population. The FAAA began an ongoing research project in 1983.

Baseline

In 1983, the County Board and the Commission on Aging requested that the agency conduct a county-wide survey of the status and needs of its growing elderly population. The goal of the study assessing the area elderly's well-being was to profile the human service needs. To meet this overall goal, there were four specific objectives: (a) identify problem areas and unmet service needs experienced by elderly residents to determine what were perceived as their most important problems, (b) assess the extent to which the elderly population of the area utilized existing human service programs and agencies, (c) ascertain the degree to which chronic illnesses interfered in daily activities and measure personal well-being, and (d) develop a priority listing of unmet human service needs and estimate the number and type of residents experiencing each type of problem (Fairfax Area Agency on Aging, 1984).

Instrument. The researcher for the initial survey round reviewed several possible survey instruments. The Older American Status and Needs Assessment Survey (OARS) was chosen as the core instrument because it had been used before in the area, thus at least potentially facilitating comparison with earlier results.

According to county policies and procedures governing research, the instrument had to be reviewed and approved by several county agencies whose expertise included statistical analysis, evaluation, and automation. Some of these agencies made suggestions for modifications, particularly in the sections on social resources, emotional well-being, and service utilization. The refined instrument was piloted on 20 elderly individuals to test for appropriateness of length, question reliability, and ease of administration.

Sample. The Department of Social Services divides the county into four service areas. A separate representative sample of all persons 55 years and older, generated by random-digit dialing, was drawn from each service delivery area. An earlier study done in the area resulted in a 25% refusal rate. To correct for this anticipated level of response failure, respondents were oversampled by 25% to yield the desired number. Persons living in nursing homes were excluded, but those living in senior housing or foster care homes were included.

Interviews. Initial telephone contacts were made over a 1-month period. There were 29,596 calls made to 23,242 telephone numbers. At least four calls were made to numbers for which there was either no response or a busy signal. Calls were made from 9:00 a.m. through 9:00 p.m., Monday through Friday, to reach persons who might be employed. Seven hundred forty-four households were reached, of which 612 agreed to personal interviews and 132 refused.

A second phone contact was made to those who had agreed to participate to establish a specific date and time for the interview. Three hundred ninety-two households finally agreed to be interviewed. Some households had more than one person of the appropriate age, producing 510 individual respondents. In-person interviews, using the adapted OARS instrument, were conducted by trained interviewers.

Results. Findings demonstrated that most older residents in the area were under 70, female, White, married, unemployed, and had high incomes when compared with their national cohorts. Most respondents enjoyed relatively good health and had access to a personal automobile for most activities. Older individuals were even more likely to be female and unmarried, and also tended to be less well educated and poorer, and were more likely to have physical problems than younger elderly respondents.

Using and communicating findings. The results of this first round of the longitudinal study were widely disseminated and were a basis of program, policy, and funding decision making for the Board of Supervisors. Findings were utilized to obtain funding for contractual health prevention programs designed to promote and maintain good health among this relatively healthy population. Based on an interest in pursuing lifelong learning by the highly educated elderly respondents, the Commission on Aging's Education Committee cosponsored the development of a Learning in Retirement Institute, the first of its kind in the area.

On the basis of the profile of county elderly as well educated with high incomes and relatively good health, program activities were initiated to recruit, train, and retain older persons as resources for the community. The volume of volunteer referrals, placement, and job development for elderly citizens culminated in skilled staff for a Volunteer Development Unit—now a division of the agency.

Many of the baseline findings on the profile of the population were utilized in a report developed by a Board of Supervisors' appointed citizen committee that made recommendations for addressing the elderly population's most pressing needs. In 1987, the board adopted the report as county policy. Recommendations were used to justify funding requests and to guide program development. The document was incorporated in subsequent policy recommendations that addressed the human service issues of target populations of all ages and need.

Follow-Up

Six years later, faced with an increasing number of elderly in the population, limited funds, and a federal mandate to conduct a needs assessment, the agency applied for and received a grant for a postdoctoral applied research fellow. As part of a larger project, the researcher was charged with investigating the possibility of conducting a follow-up to the baseline study. Because two of the authors of this chapter were directly involved in the follow-up, more detail is provided in this section.

Although the earlier study was designed to make it easier to reinterview the elderly sample, no one specifically provided for a follow-up. Thus, the first task of the later study was to ascertain the feasibility of conducting a follow-up to the baseline survey. There were two determining factors for this decision:

1. The availability of the baseline questionnaires and data. During the interval between interviews, the agency moved to another location and the questionnaires were archived. The data tapes stored on the county mainframe had been erased because county agency procedures for permanent storage were not followed. However, the original questionnaires were found, and it was possible to match the informed consent forms with names, addresses, and ID numbers with corresponding questionnaires that had only ID numbers for reasons of confidentiality. Most were matched fairly easily, but others had been miscoded or misfiled, and further contact with those respondents was impossible. For those that could be matched, questionnaire data from the baseline research were once again coded and entered.
2. A sufficient percentage of respondents from the baseline round was available and willing to participate in a second interview. An examination of those responding to a question about their willingness to be contacted again revealed that 425 of the original respondents (approximately 85%) had answered positively.

After the agency director was satisfied that the follow-up could be completed, the agency planner and researcher took the idea for the project to the advisory body of the agency. Commissioners discussed the advantages and disadvantages of the project, reviewed the preliminary questionnaire, and made suggestions for revisions. Throughout the project, commissioners were given status reports and continued to provide feedback and input to the project.

The project was directed by the researcher and the chief planner of the agency. Close contact was maintained with the agency director and staff through both oral and written communication. The researcher attended staff meetings with the planner to discuss the project and solicit assistance and feedback from staff. Most staff were supportive of the project from the beginning, and more than half were involved in some way—from recruiting volunteers to interviewing to inputting data.

Instruments. The instrument was modified slightly to give more detailed information on social resources, financial problems, and service utilization. Otherwise, it was as similar to the baseline as possible. The following areas were in both questionnaires: demographic data, household composition, perceived social support, housing, transportation, physical health, functional limitations, well-being, income and income sources, financial problems, utilization of services, and perceived needs. In addition, the follow-up questionnaire included information on marital status change, residency patterns, and work history.

A telephone contact form was developed to assist interviewers in processing their calls and to give information on the status of all the original respondents. The form served as a flow sheet to allow for easy evaluation of what to do and which questions to ask in different situations. Categories were differentiated to note who had moved, died, become ill, and other. In addition, there was a category for those who only wanted to participate with a telephone interview. For example, if interviewers reached a household where the original respondent had died, they turned to a blue sheet to record information from a second person if available; if the respondent was too sick to come to the phone, the interviewer turned to a green sheet to record information from a proxy about the condition of the initial respondent. In this way, the researcher was able to develop a profile on those who were not followed up and gather reasons for attrition.

As in the earlier study, instruments were circulated for comment through specific county agencies. County procedures dictated that the County Office of Research and Statistics approve all surveys asking county residents for information. This step is similar to a university Human Subjects Review Board; it is essential, although often tedious. This stage of the process took more time and negotiation than expected because the county's requirement for sensitivity to the community and research requirements for reliability and validity had to be worked out. In the end, acceptable changes were made, and the survey was approved for implementation.

Volunteers. If carefully screened and trained, volunteers can save countless hours and dollars for the research team. Volunteers were utilized in every stage of the longitudinal needs assessment. The agency had an efficient and effective volunteer coordinator who was often able to match job needs with volunteers who had appropriate skills and expertise. For example, one volunteer created a database listing names and addresses of all those available for re-interview. Volunteers were also recruited to serve as interviewers for the project.

The written job description of volunteer interviewers identified: the goal of the job, tasks to be undertaken, approximate number of hours and duration of the job, qualifications, volunteer benefits, and supervision and other types of support. The interviewer job was attractive because it was short term: It required a minimum of 20 hours and a maximum of 60 hours over a 4- to 6-week period. Interviewers averaged 20 hours on the job.

Each volunteer's name was entered into the agency's volunteer database. Volunteers received accident, personal, and excess automobile liability insurance coverage while engaged in agency interviews. The agency's volunteer coordinator provided project staff with a service log to enable volunteers to account for their activities and the number of hours they worked.

Interviewers. Sixteen volunteers served as project interviewers. Because the target population was elderly, elderly volunteers were used whenever possible. The purpose of doing so was to create greater trust and understanding in the interviewer–respondent relationship. It was felt that this would elicit more valid information. Interviewers for this follow-up round were obtained from a pool of existing agency volunteers. The volunteer services coordinator circulated the job description, and the volunteer newsletter ran an ad soliciting workers. In addition, the volunteer coordinator called interviewers who had worked on the earlier survey, and several agreed to participate in the follow-up. The planner of the project wrote a letter to representatives serving on the commission requesting they consider taking a short-term volunteer job as interviewers. The volunteer opportunity was also opened to agency staff who wanted to participate in the research.

At the time they agreed to volunteer for this project, most volunteers were involved in many other activities, including full-time jobs outside of the home. Eleven of the 16 were over the age of 50; most were over 65. Seven older volunteers were volunteer long-term-care ombudsmen and were already screened, trained, and selected to be the "community presence" and to advocate for elderly citizens residing in local long-term-care facilities and their families. The remaining four older volunteers were three commission representatives and a volunteer who administered the Medical Forms Assistance Program. Two of the younger volunteers were also volunteer long-term-care ombudsmen, and the remaining three interviewers were paid agency staff.

At the project's completion, interviewers were thanked with a formal letter of appreciation, individually acknowledged at the annual agency volunteer recognition awards ceremony, and individually listed in the acknowledgments of the final written report.

Training. Volunteers were required to attend one of the two 2½-hour sessions conducted by the researcher, the chief planner of the agency, and an older worker enrolled in the Seniors in Training for Employment (SITE)—a subsidized older worker program. The SITE worker served as assistant project manager of the interviews. He piloted the interviewing process by conducting a few phone and in-person interviews prior to the training and discussed his experiences during the training. This was built into the training program to put the volunteers at ease about their upcoming jobs. It also provided the research team with an opportunity to pretest questions and correct problems prior to carrying out the interviews.

Sessions were arranged at two different times to accommodate schedules; one was held in the morning, another in the evening. After introductions, volunteers were given a packet containing an interviewer manual designed for the project by the research fellow, copies of the form for calling respondents, and the questionnaire.

The first part of the training session introduced the agency and the project. The team explained the nature of survey and longitudinal research and the importance of confidentiality. Interviewers were given a written "Interviewer Instruction Guide," designed as both a training tool and a resource for use in the field. The guide was divided into six sections: (a) a general overview of the survey as a research tool; (b) instructions for beginning, implementing, and concluding the interview; (c) a summary of hints, suggestions, and guidelines; (d) a description of how to make and record the phone contact; (e) question-by-question specifications of procedures for coding the instrument; and (f) a copy of the questionnaire, on which interviewers practiced and took notes during the training.

Because volunteers were expected both to contact respondents by phone and to conduct the in-home interview, they had to become familiar with two different instruments: the telephone contact form and the questionnaire. Each section of both forms was read, explaining skip-and-answer patterns. After a brief discussion, each volunteer chose a partner, and they interviewed each other with the project directors available for answering questions and helping with difficulties. When all groups had completed role playing, problems and uncertainties were discussed.

A brief overview of available agency services was provided, and packets of related information were distributed for interviewers to leave with each respondent whom they visited. "What-if" scenarios were discussed. Although it was made very clear that interviewers were not to offer advice or assistance, the team wanted them to recognize immediate service needs and bring them to the agency for follow-up. They were encouraged to become effective listeners and to be sensitive, but noncommittal, about problems perceived or expressed during their visits in the respondents' homes.

The agency volunteer coordinator spoke to the interviewers about volunteer liability and the volunteer service log. She also gave each interviewer a set of agency volunteer business cards to sign and leave at each participant's home. This provided additional credibility for the interviewers.

The final part of the training involved assigning volunteers a group of respondents. Volunteers were presented with a list of approximately 24 names, addresses, and telephone numbers with corresponding record number—the only identifier used on the survey instrument. To make the work of the interviewers easier, every attempt was made to ensure that they did not have to travel far to conduct the interviews. To this end, both respondents and interviewers were sorted by zip code and the closest possible match was made. This was a large task made difficult by the fact that interviewers and interviewees were not evenly geographically distributed. If interviewers strongly preferred another area, they were encouraged to switch with another interviewer. In most instances, this was done successfully.

Hours and phone numbers of agency contact persons were provided, and interviewers were encouraged to use this support system whenever they felt it was necessary. Finally, instructions were given for turning in their materials and final debriefing when they submitted their interview/volunteer annotated log.

The interview process. Volunteers began by calling the names on the list, following the telephone flow sheet. Interviews with consenting respondents were conducted in their homes; they lasted an average of 1 hour, with a range from 45 minutes to 2 hours. Each interviewer was responsible for up to 24 contacts in 5 weeks. Interviewers had names and phone numbers of the planner and SITE worker and were encouraged to call if any problems or questions arose about logistics. A few interviewers called if they ran into problems, but most handled reluctant or angry citizens on their own. The SITE worker called interviewers if there had been no contact within the 2 weeks since interviewing began.

The team arranged that the face-to-face interviewing would occur in early fall—during the month of October or the first week of November at the latest. This established an "end time" before the holiday season. Interviewers who found they were unable to meet the deadline turned their lists over to the planner or SITE worker, who identified other volunteers to do their interviewing. Some volunteers who had completed their interviews took on a few more names. The SITE worker also served as a backup interviewer, and a second SITE worker began assisting with interviews as the deadline drew closer. Of the 425 original respondents who agreed to be recontacted, SITE workers attempted contact with or interviewed 85 individuals; 16 volunteers attempted contact with or interviewed 340 individuals.

Relatively few problems arose during the interview process, and most were resolved in the field by the volunteers. The team believes that so few problems occurred because volunteers were carefully screened and trained. The telephone contact may also have eliminated problems because it served to screen individuals reluctant to participate in the project.

The interviewers produced an excellent product. Questionnaire data were thorough enough to eliminate all need for recontact for clarification, even on written responses to open-ended questions.

Attrition. Attrition over time is one of the major problems in longitudinal studies. According to Norris (1987), the prevalence rates of responses can be skewed, the ability to generalize responses to the target population can be reduced, and/or relationships between different variables of interest can be influenced by attrition. Further, there had been no contact at all with the baseline respondents since they were interviewed 6 years earlier. Some phone respondents who refused the re-interview indicated that they were unclear as to the purpose of the study, and others said they could not recall having been interviewed for the previous study 6 years earlier. To summarize attrition patterns for this study, those who agreed to be re-interviewed matched the full baseline study sample fairly closely. However, the follow-up sample was more likely to be White and married, less likely to be widowed and more likely to have more education and higher income. In contrast, those who refused re-interview were more likely to have lower incomes, and be female, unmarried, widowed, living alone, and to have fewer years of education. These differences may have influenced the results, although probably not to a very great degree.

Results. One hundred thirty-two individuals responded to both rounds of surveys. The following is a brief summary of the replies of the respondents for whom complete data was obtained and on which most later policy decisions were made.

Demographics. The median age of the sample was 71.5 years; 60.6% was female, and 97.7% of the sample was White. As expected, there was a decrease in the number of married individuals and an increase in the number widowed. Living arrangements also changed. Although most respondents lived with their spouses at both panels, more lived alone by follow-up. There was a slight decrease in income over time.

Health status. The three most common chronic conditions at both times were arthritis, high blood pressure, and glaucoma. In the second interview, circulatory trouble, stroke, and "other" were reported as increasingly interfering with activities. There were reported increases in the number of doctor visits, use of prescription medications, and hospital days. In addition, respondents reported more need for help in all activities of daily living. Previously, the largest category of need was for house repairs; later, reading, climbing stairs, cleaning house, grocery shopping, walking, and house repairs reached that same level. The largest increases in need were for house repair.

Housing and transportation. Although most respondents lived in their own home and had for some time, 22% fewer preferred a single family home. Approximately 40% expressed interest in housing designed for the elderly. At follow-up, there was a slight shift from driving self to other forms of transportation, but most transportation needs were met by individuals driving themselves.

Needs and problems. Most respondents reported "no problem" when asked about their financial situation; after that, housing was most often reported. There were increased service needs for yard work, information, and housework. Overall service use was low at both times, with the exception of recreation and information and referral.

Using and communicating findings. The Commission on Aging endorsed the final report; the support by this appointed citizens advisory board was crucial to future utilization, lending credibility and support for the findings and, in particular, establishing ownership for the findings. Thanks to the commission's advice since the study's inception, their hands-on assistance with the study, and their endorsement, the reliability of the findings was not questioned.

Citing findings that yard work and housework were frequent service needs, the agency planning staff with AT&T and local government submitted a grant to support a program to have volunteers provide home repair and other home-based services. The grant was awarded and implemented as a public–private service providing volunteer home maintenance, yard work, and minor home repair services (volunteer in-home services) housed at the agency and supervised by a private Caregiving Coalition.

Similarly, to fill a gap in service created when a telephone reassurance program was eliminated by the National Red Cross (during a critical time of reductions in that organization), local government agreed to support and oversee an all-volunteer program. This program—telephone reassurance to homebound elderly—provided continued preventive, low-cost, supportive in-home service to isolated and/or frail elderly.

Findings also suggested increasing needs for assistance with house work and minor home repair. In response, the volunteer friendly visitor program that serves isolated elderly clients received unquestioned funding support.

The finding of increased need for information among the elderly was important to management in local government as they made budget recommendations. As the local administration went through a budget reduction and categorical funding exercise, community education expenses (staff and operating costs) associated with the Community Education Division received an "essential" status while most other services were modified, reduced, or eliminated.

A county-wide approach to the delivery of human services using a central intake system was also supported by the study findings. The central intake system, part of the human services redesign for the county, is implemented formally in at least one section of the county. Such a system addresses the needs of many target populations, including the elderly population, for greater access to information and referral to a greater degree. The central intake system fosters informed decision making and consumer empowerment consistent with the philosophy of citizens taking on more responsibility for themselves.

In 1992, the federal government implemented a requirement that any application for funding for support services in HUD Section 202 housing (a program to subsidize elderly housing) must be supported by the local Area Agency on Aging. Based on findings from the longitudinal needs assessment, staff and commission members were keenly aware of many citizens' increasing preference for moving to retirement-specific elderly housing over staying in their own home. As a result, the agency carefully reviewed applicants' requests for funding, ultimately certifying one housing proposal's plan for support services and denying certification of another based on a poorly constructed plan for support services.

Study findings regarding housing were also communicated to the Virginia Housing and Development Authority and used to support the first for-profit housing developer in obtaining tax credits to construct 240 units of elderly housing in a portion of the county where this housing was much needed. Tax credits, available to developers on an annual basis but limited in number throughout the state, enable builders to credit tax expenses from rental units— a cost savings that is passed on to the (elderly) renter. Competitive tax credits were granted to this housing developer.

This study's findings have been crucial during these times of fiscal constraint and fewer governmental resources, with particular relevance for (a) devising strategies for private sector involvement, (b) devising strategies for volunteer program development, and (c) forming public–private partnerships. For example, the longitudinal study suggests that the levels of functioning and independence of many residents was still quite high—at a median age of 71.5 years. Therefore, it concluded that persons over the age of 70 are viable community resources with needs, but also with energy to pursue solutions.

Elderly citizens—the target population—continue to be the best advocates for volunteer programs, lifelong learning programs, and opportunities for paid employment. Public comment and public hearings continue to support the need to call on elderly as resources both in the traditional roles of sharing employment skills and in nontraditional volunteer and paid positions such as second or third careers utilizing newly developed or underutilized skills and talents. Further, employers are learning the value of older workers who have a lifetime of experience, strong work ethic, loyalty to employer, low absenteeism, and, sometimes, a willingness or desire to work flexible or part-time hours while accommodating the needs, budget, or workload of the company.

Advantages and disadvantages of the present approach.

Cost savings. The low cost of this needs assessment was due to extensive use of volunteers, subsidized work training staff (SITE older worker program), staff borrowed from other agencies, and operating expenses (telephone, office supplies, etc.) made available by the host agency for the research. Areas of expertise that were provided "in kind"—at no cost to the research project— were: face-to-face interviewing, survey instrument review, use of a mainframe computer, graphics for final report, data entry, and editing of report at various stages for various purposes.

Grant funding for lead researcher. The Fellowship Program provided the agency with an opportunity to apply for a grant to underwrite an innovative approach to supplying full-time research expertise for a 3-month period. The agency had to agree to supply matched funds and in-kind services. This made it possible to combine the best resources to conduct the research.

Location of lead researcher. Having the lead researcher on-site for the vast majority of the research project led to good communication between and cooperation by the researcher and team on the best approaches for moving from one stage of research to another. Located with the staff who were providing services to the target population and being involved with the target population through participation in training elderly volunteers, and briefing the commission, the researcher was quickly integrated into the subject. A cooperative spirit was engendered.

"Same people" approach to a longitudinal study. This research used the same people over time, rather than substitute "like people," as in some longitudinal studies. All subjects were community-based, reducing the impact of other factors such as institutional regulations, controls, and biases. However, to the limited extent that some of the regional respondents were now institutionalized, this probably also influenced the findings.

Ancillary benefits to community. This research study was done in the community—in the homes of the target population. This process enabled citizens and taxpayers to learn more about the resources available to them; it also enabled interviewers—who were also citizens—to become an extension of the county's provision of service: providing resource materials and making referrals to professional staff where appropriate. Interviewers were also encouraged to express their concerns or observations in writing, providing the direct services staff of the agency the opportunity to become aware of citizens' needs with the permission of the community resident.

Tendency toward greater attrition. In addition to using the same people over time, which offers a natural limitation to the number of persons who may be followed over time, there was no interim contact with individuals studied at baseline over the 6 years. This lack of contact did not generate familiarity, trust, or a willingness to participate among those who may have been physically or mentally able to be re-interviewed, but who perceived the re-interviews to be an imposition, invasion of privacy, or of questionable purposes. As a result, several potential respondents questioned the legitimacy of the survey, and whether they had in fact been interviewed earlier, and were surprised or skeptical when requested to be re-interviewed.

Lack of specific plans for follow-up survey. The disadvantages to lacking plans for follow-up include a greater possibility of lost data, such as when the original mainframe tapes were erased, difficulty in reconstructing a few aspects of the original research design(methodology, implementation, etc.) for comparison over the 6 years, and a lack of provision to maintain contact with baseline respondents.

Respondent characteristics less like those of general target population. The follow-up sample was less like the overall elderly population in the area than was the sample at baseline. A drawback to using a longitudinal study is that the same people followed over time may be less likely to reflect the profile, trends, and problems of those in the general target population who are catalysts for or participants in change. For example, original respondents who moved away may have done so due to economic hardships in their own lives or in the community. Those who remained in the community since baseline 6 years earlier may have been better able to afford to continue living in the community.

MINORITY-FOCUSED NEEDS ASSESSMENT

In the year 2050, an estimated 30% of those 65 years and older in the United States will be African American, Hispanic, Asian American, or Native American. Because minority elderly tend, on average, to be poorer, in worse health, and in need of more assistance with activities of daily living than White elderly of the same age, they can be expected to have more intense and somewhat different service needs than the traditional clientele of many agencies serving the elderly. Although the proportion of different minority elderly populations and their level and specific configuration of needs will vary from region to region, in the coming decades, the elderly service delivery system in most parts of the United States will be called on to adapt to a more ethnically and racially diverse clientele.

The Older Americans Act (OAA) of 1965, as amended, encourages targeting OAA-funded services to those in greatest socioeconomic need, especially minorities, in recognition of the greater vulnerability of these elderly populations. Despite this, service use among minority elderly is, on the whole, lower than would be expected (Gallagher, 1988). This suggests that race and ethnicity are important, yet often unacknowledged, factors affecting the dynamics of service utilization. Although outright discrimination may still figure as one cause of minority underutilization of these services, in most cases the causes are more subtle and complex. Because most service providers consider their services open to all, they may not be aware of the web of barriers faced by minority elders, such as: lack of knowledge of available services, paperwork requirements and other bureaucratic impediments, fear, language and cultural barriers, and a history or reputation of discrimination (Harel, Mc Kinney, & Williams, 1987; Markides & Mindel, 1987; Stanford, 1980).

Recent years have also witnessed increasing interest in enabling elderly persons to remain in their homes or reside in other community-based homelike residential settings rather than having to turn to institutions. This has been inspired, in part, by cost considerations, as institutional long-term care for the elderly and disabled continues to absorb an ever-growing share of Medicaid dollars. However, another part of the impetus for this trend comes from the expressed desire of most elderly to remain in their own homes for as long as feasible—a sentiment supported by broad cultural values favoring maintenance of independence and individual choice.

The minority-focused needs assessment grew out of a convergence of concerns about barriers to minority service utilization and factors supporting continued community residence for the homebound elderly. In 1989, personnel at the Area Agency on Aging recognized that the elderly population in their service area was becoming increasingly racially and ethnically diverse. The county's long-standing African-American population was gradually aging in place. Although many in the younger generation had moved to other communities in the area and beyond, the older generation remained heavily concentrated in two relatively stable neighborhood clusters. Thus, although still not quite equaling the percentage of elderly in the county's population-at-large (over 17%), by the late 1980s, more than 9% of African Americans in the county were 60 or older, and the percentage was expected to rise steadily in the coming years.

Over the course of the previous several decades, the county experienced several waves of in-migration from Central and South America, Southeast Asia (Vietnam, Cambodia, Korea), Afghanistan, and Ethiopia. Because the needs of youth and families with young children were more visible than those of the elderly, various county and private social service and health agencies tended to focus their energies on the younger segments of these populations. Nevertheless, agency personnel knew there were elderly persons in these minority communities with extensive unaddressed needs that often remained "invisible" to service providers. To be proactive in shaping a service strategy that incorporated these groups, the agency wanted to gather the information necessary to properly inform policymaking and program development in this area. With this aim in mind, the agency applied for and was awarded a grant to have a Postdoctoral Fellow in Applied Gerontology assigned to their agency for the summer of 1989. The goal was to determine the unmet service needs of homebound minority elderly in the county and to devise ways of better meeting these needs. One of this chapter's authors was the researcher; another is the assistant director of the agency and served as the point of contact with the funding agency.

The fellow met with the director and assistant director of the agency to develop a more concrete plan for conducting the needs assessment. Agency staff restated their overall goals for the needs assessment and offered the researcher their full support and assistance, including all-important access to their considerable detailed knowledge of county agencies and community organizations. Agency personnel largely left the choice of appropriate needs assessment methods to the research fellow. The guiding parameters were that the field portion of the study had to be conducted in a 5- to 6-week period, and had to rely on the researcher as the primary interviewer. Given these restrictions on time, resources, and personnel, as well as her training and experience as an ethnographer, the researcher suggested that the needs assessment rely primarily on qualitative, in-depth methods of community observation and intensive interviewing. A preliminary intensive interview guide was designed, and the instrument was made available for agency comment and review well before the project actually began.

Considerable additional clarification and refinement of the scope of the research questions occurred during this initial meeting. Interested in understanding impediments to utilization of all types of services, not just in-home services, agency staff indicated that they did not wish to restrict the definition of *homebound* only to those meeting strictly medical criteria for homeboundedness. They also wanted to obtain information about elderly persons who were physically capable of leaving their homes, but, for whatever reasons, never or almost never did. Thus, the working definition of *homebound elderly* was purposely kept very broad, permitting a distinction between the "medically homebound," who might need additional in-home services, and the "socially homebound," whose situation could, at least potentially, be overcome.

Because limitations on time and personnel made it impossible to study the full array of elderly minorities in the county, a second key issue addressed at this meeting was deciding the specific minority groups to be included in the needs assessment. After considerable discussion, three groups were chosen: African Americans, Hispanics, and Vietnamese. The rationale for selecting these groups is provided next as part of the sampling discussion.

Agency staff wanted the researcher to begin the needs assessment project by updating a somewhat out-of-date guide to in-home services available to senior citizens in the county. Developing the guide as a prelude to the larger needs assessment would serve a double purpose: providing a valuable resource for the community while familiarizing the researcher with the type and range of in-home resources available in the county and across the larger metropolitan area. This list could be a basis for assessing the minority respondents' knowledge of existing services, as well as a means to disseminate this information to the target population.

As is so often the case, the minority-focused needs assessment project, as it finally emerged, was designed to serve multiple purposes. Its two main purposes were to: (a) assess unmet service needs and determine the barriers to utilization of available services by homebound elderly African Americans, Hispanics, and Vietnamese; and (b) make concrete recommendations to the Area Agency on Aging and the Department of Human Services on how to better serve these elderly minorities. A third, subsidiary, purpose was to disseminate information regarding available services to the target population.

The researcher and agency assistant director participated in a 2½-day conference sponsored by the granting agency, which gave researchers and agency partners the opportunity to iron out plans and clarify mutual expectations concerning the intended products of the project, time lines, and types of support the agency would provide. A "mini-contract" or memorandum of understanding was drafted; it outlined project goals, methods, products, and resources, and established time lines and target dates for completion of specific tasks and products. Both parties signed it. Developing this document helped to specify the components of the project and their interrelations while nurturing a spirit of teamwork that proved invaluable in the coming months.

Sample

The idea of creating a probability sample of all minority elderly in the county was never seriously entertained. The decision to select a purposive sample of three homebound elderly minorities hinged primarily on three factors: (a) limitations on time, resources, and personnel, which limited the number of interviews that could be conducted; (b) the agency's willingness to support a needs assessment that would collect more in-depth data on a few, selected groups; and (c) the researcher's strong preference for using qualitative, quasi-ethnographic methods.

The first major decision concerned which three minorities were to be included in the study. Agency personnel felt strongly that African-American elderly, representing the single largest minority population in the county, should be one of the respondent groups. The agency offices are situated on the edge of one of the two well-established African-American neighborhoods in the county. Two senior centers are located in these neighborhoods, and serve a predominantly African-American clientele. Although it appeared that African-American elderly in the county were relatively well served in certain regards, there was evidence of areas of unmet need. Also, agency personnel suspected that a history of racism in certain private agencies might have continued to affect utilization of services by African-American elderly. In addition, from a purely practical standpoint, the strength of ties to community organizations, especially churches, within the African-American community would make it easier to generate a list of homebound elders in a relatively short time span. Finally, although not African American, the researcher had worked in

African-American communities before and was comfortable with the idea of conducting interviews in these neighborhoods.

Although composed of persons of different national origins, taken as a group, Hispanics represented the second largest minority population in the county. According to 1980 census figures, which by 1989 were badly out of date, about 6% of the county's population was Hispanic, of whom 14% were 60 or older. A Cuban-American program manager employed at the agency had an extensive network of contacts with other Hispanic service workers in the county, and with representatives of a variety of ethnic associations, churches, and voluntary groups. Thus, she could facilitate entry into the community and provide some names of elderly homebound Hispanics. In addition, the researcher speaks Spanish, is often taken for Hispanic, and is reasonably knowledgeable about Latin cultures.

The choice of which Asian minority group to include in the study was the most difficult. Several different national groups were represented in the county population, including Vietnamese, Koreans, Cambodians, Indians, and others. Unlike Hispanics, these groups do not speak a common language, and only in the broadest sense possess a common culture. Consequently, it made no sense to treat all Asian-American elderly as a single group. Vietnamese elderly were selected primarily because they represented the single largest Asian nationality in the county's population, although still only a minuscule percentage of the total population. Agency personnel were acquainted with a few Vietnamese community leaders and service workers in the county who could facilitate community entry. Two part-time multilingual Vietnamese aides employed at two of the county's senior centers were already on the county payroll and available to act as translators. One of the senior centers served a mixed population, which included a number of elderly Vietnamese who might also be able to provide names of homebound elders who could be contacted for interviews.

Once the target populations were chosen, a two-step network approach was used to generate the sample. First, agency personnel provided the researcher with names of clergy, community leaders, members of civic and ethnic associations, neighborhood activists, and county workers in each of the minority subcommunities. The researcher contacted these community key informants, explained the purpose and sponsorship of the study, and asked to meet as soon as possible at a time most convenient to them.

These in-person meetings with key informants in each of the minority subcommunities served multiple purposes. First, they were a way to build trust; the researcher knew the critical importance of establishing direct face-to-face contacts in minority communities. Before releasing potentially delicate information, such as the names of homebound elderly, these key informants needed a sense of the human being to whom this information was being entrusted. Second, these meetings provided an opportunity for the researcher to develop an understanding of the social organization of the three ethnic subcommunities, as well as the strength and nature of each group's linkages to the larger service delivery system and political structure. This contextual information, important in interpreting the interview materials, also provided the basis for devising a respondent recruitment strategy tailored to the characteristics of the specific minority subcommunity.

Once the ice was broken, these key informants were asked to provide names, addresses, and telephone numbers of homebound elderly persons or to suggest others who might be able to supply these names. Because few people had a list of homebound elderly already on hand, few of these meetings actually yielded specific information. More often, these key informants needed additional time to think or put together the needed information, or else suggested another person or organization they thought better able to help. The researcher followed a "snowballing" approach in which one referral led to another. Thirty-five key informants, including clergy, county refugee workers, heads of ethnic mutual aid associations, and leaders of community-based coalitions, were contacted in this way, most during the first 2 weeks of the project.

These initial discussions with some key informants also revealed that the study's definition of *homebound* might be difficult to communicate across cultural boundaries, and would probably require reconceptualization before it could be properly applied to these minority populations. For example, although considered socially homebound by the study definition, some older Vietnamese and Hispanic women who left their homes infrequently were simply conforming to cultural expectations appropriate to women of their age and social class in their countries of origin. The researcher explained that, although there was nothing intrinsically "wrong" with remaining at home, it was important to know, not just assume, these women's reasons for not leaving their homes.

Finding Respondents

The same basic snowballing approach used to contact key informants was employed in locating elderly homebound respondents. Because of time constraints, the sample was limited to 48 homebound minority elders, 16 from each group. However, because the three subcommunities were so disparate, the process of generating the respondent sample worked very differently in each of the three.

The African-American community proved to be the easiest to access. County employees volunteered the names of five or six neighborhood and community activists—informal leaders who were able to provide the names of a number of elderly homebound persons. Churches maintained lists of homebound elderly parishioners for friendly visiting by church volunteers. The directors of two senior centers also supplied names of homebound persons, including some who had stopped coming to the senior centers. Once interviewing began, the researcher asked respondents for names of other homebound friends, relatives, and neighbors. The lists of contacts quickly began to snowball, reflecting the interwoven quality of social networks in the county's African-American neighborhoods. It took only a few weeks to complete the in-home intensive interviews with the 16 African-American respondents. Potential sources of referrals were barely tapped; many more interviews could easily have been arranged were time not so limited.

Although language was not a barrier for the researcher in the Hispanic community, this was the hardest of the three groups to penetrate. Various points of approach were tried. The researcher and Cuban-American program manager at the agency discussed the study with a Hispanic human services aide (also Cuban-American) at one of the senior centers who said she knew several homebound older persons. Rather than provide their names and addresses, she preferred to contact them herself and arrange for the interviews. This ultimately yielded just two referrals, and only after some prodding. The director of a private Hispanic advocacy and social service agency offered to put all her agency's resources at the researcher's disposal. However, she left her job shortly thereafter, and her successor was less able to help. Other groups were temporarily disbanded or their officers were out of town. Several church-related groups said they did not know of any older homebound persons. A Hispanic county extension service worker who primarily worked with young families agreed to accompany the researcher on several interviews with elderly homebound family members of her clients. She arrived late and was unable to keep the appointments, promising to provide the names and addresses for the researcher to contact on her own, but never did. A volunteer for a Central-American refugee relief organization agreed to draw up a list of potential respondents, but proved virtually unreachable in the ensuing weeks.

The names of the 16 elderly Hispanic respondents were drawn from eight separate referral sources. Nine respondents were referred either by the Cuban-American program manager at the agency (three she knew personally, three from the Meals on Wheels rosters) or her bilingual colleague in the Adult Services Division of the county. Because the referral networks were thinner, it took several weeks longer and considerably more effort to locate and interview the sixteen Hispanic respondents than it had for the African-American respondents. The process was marked by many more false starts and frustrating dead ends.

Several important characteristics of the county's Hispanic population help explain the difficulties of finding elderly respondents.

- The Hispanic population is comparatively young, and the problems of the elderly were not very visible or salient.
- At the time the needs assessment was conducted, a significant share of the Hispanic population was composed of officially unrecognized refugees from Central America who were ineligible for most forms of assistance and wary of any contact with the authorities. Those who had applied for amnesty under the terms of the Immigration Reform and Control Act of 1986 had often been ill-advised by attorneys to avoid use of any services so as not to jeopardize their claims to residency. In some cases, children legally in the United States had brought in their elderly parents illegally. The tenuous and ambiguous legal status of many of the community's residents created a defensive posture toward anyone, however well intentioned, who asked personal questions. The situation also put Hispanic social service delivery organizations in a difficult double bind of wanting both to serve and protect their constituents.

- Rapid turnover of personnel and lack of coordination among different agencies and organizations serving the Hispanic community made for a rather porous organizational structure, which appeared to lack much reach or spread in the community. Those organizations that did reach certain subgroups of the community (e.g., churches, relief organizations) may have withheld names in an effort to protect their clients.
- The county's Hispanic population was recently arrived and marked by considerable "within-group" differences of social class, nationality, and educational level. Most of the social service delivery personnel and agency directors were well educated and from middle- or upper-class Latin-American backgrounds, whereas much of the service population was Central American, poor, and had little, if any, formal education. A true community had not yet coalesced, which impeded the ability to act in concert.

Unexpectedly, despite language barriers making it necessary to rely heavily on the use of interpreters, the Vietnamese community was less difficult to access than the Hispanic community. In a conscious effort to reach all segments of the elderly Vietnamese population, and not just the better educated and more highly placed refugees who had migrated after the fall of Saigon in 1975, the researcher contacted a variety of bilingual persons as points of approach into the community. The researcher spoke with two senior center directors and their bilingual Vietnamese aides. Both aides were briefed on the purpose of the study and then asked to contact elderly homebound Vietnamese in the county and arrange for interviews. They also agreed to serve as interpreters when necessary. An activities director at a senior citizen's apartment building provided names of homebound residents and introduced the researcher to an elderly Vietnamese resident fluent in English who was pleased to serve as an interpreter. Several Vietnamese social workers and a Vietnamese extension service worker provided contacts and translation. The researcher was invited to attend a meeting of a Vietnamese Senior Citizens Association, at which she made a presentation explaining the study and enlisting the association's help in locating respondents. After her presentation, the researcher was flooded with requests for various types of assistance (including help with complicated legal immigration issues), but obtained no leads on elderly homebound persons in Arlington, although she was given names of persons in other parts of the area. Contacts with the head of a Vietnamese ethnic association and a Vietnamese employee of the local Red Cross provided useful information on the organization of the ethnic subcommunity, but yielded no specific names.

Although marked by class, religious, and political differences, the Vietnamese community in the county was clearly more cohesive than the Hispanic community, and this was reflected in a greater ease of recruitment of respondents into the study. Despite a few false starts, respondent recruitment went comparatively quickly and reasonably smoothly. However, 14 of the 16 Vietnamese respondents were referred by county workers of one kind or another. Moreover, because so much of the negotiation was handled by the interpreters, the dynamics underlying recruitment remained somewhat obscure. For example, several respondents obviously agreed to be interviewed mainly as a way to see their previous extension worker and refugee intake worker again. In other cases, ties went back to family or political loyalties established in Vietnam.

Refusals

None of the African-American respondents refused to be interviewed. The high response rate was largely a function of having used the names of trusted community residents in making the initial telephone contacts. Only one interview was difficult. The respondent, in a relatively advanced stage of Alzheimer's disease, was clearly incapable of giving the interview. Although she lived with her husband and his sister, the latter claimed to be unable to answer questions for her sister-in-law. Finally, the husband reluctantly agreed to be interviewed on another day.

Three of the potential Hispanic respondents contacted by the senior center aide apparently refused interviews. The aide was not specific about their reasons for refusing. Not having been a party to these conversations, it is hard to know exactly how she presented the study or how strongly she appealed for participation. Interestingly, none of the Hispanic respondents contacted directly by the researcher refused to participate. Two elderly Vietnamese declined interviews, on the grounds that they had already endured enough interrogations. The senior center aide who tried to persuade them differently believed they were afraid, associating any sort of interview with unpleasant past experiences in Vietnam. All things considered, once respondents were located, the refusal rate was quite low.

Key Characteristics of Respondents

Of the 48 respondents, 85% were female and 15% were male. Ages ranged from 60 to 89 years; the average age was 74. In view of how they were recruited, they cannot be considered in any way statistically representative of homebound African-American, Hispanic, and Vietnamese elders in the county.

In the African-American subsample, all but 1 of the 16 respondents were female. Their average age was 78. Six of the African-American respondents were married, six were widowed, three were never married, and one was twice divorced. Five had no children. In keeping with the diversity of the African-American community in the county, which historically has had a fairly stable middle and lower middle class (Stanford, 1978), the respondents represented a range of educational levels and occupational histories. Although some had little formal education, two had attended college. Four of the women had been domestic workers, but an equal number had held white-collar jobs. Living situations varied, with a predominance of female-centered arrangements. Twelve of the respondents lived in their own or family homes, and only three resided in rental housing. One woman had lived in the same house since 1910, and several other respondents had been in their homes for 40, 50, or more years. Long-standing residence in the same home created strong ties with certain neighbors, who had become "just like family" and had been integrated into caregiving networks.

The Hispanic respondents included 12 women and 4 men, ranging in age from 61 to 88 years, with an average age of 75. Nine were from Cuba and three from Peru. The others were from Bolivia, Colombia, Nicaragua, and Guatemala. They had been in the United States between 3 and 39 years, averaging just over 18 years in the country. Four of the respondents were married, eight widowed, two separated or divorced, and two never married. All but one had children. Most of the Cubans had been of relatively high social status and educational level in their own country, as had the sole Colombian respondent. Peruvian and Bolivian respondents came from more modest social origins as shopkeepers, market vendors, and artisans. Only one of the respondents, a Nicaraguan woman, had been brought to the United States to work as a domestic. The diversity of backgrounds should caution against overgeneralization about Hispanics. However, for the reasons detailed earlier, the sample was clearly skewed toward more established groups and away from more recent, lower status immigrants from Central America.

Only 2 of the 16 Hispanic respondents spoke English well. Interestingly, they represented opposite ends of the social continuum. A few others, mostly men, could manage a few English phrases, but most of the women, including some who had been in the United States for well over 20 years, did not even know this much. One widow proudly proclaimed that her late husband had promised her she would never have to learn English. Others said they had come to the United States too old to be expected to master a new language. For a few, not learning English seemed to symbolize resistance to the sociocultural dislocations of their situation. Eight of the Hispanic respondents lived alone, although two were grandmothers occupying apartments next door to their daughters and grandchildren. The others lived in a variety of mostly familial, female-centered arrangements.

Fourteen of the Vietnamese respondents were women and two were men. Their average age was 70, and they had been in the United States from fourteen months to fourteen years, with a mean of seven years in this country. Eight (including both of the men) were married, seven were widowed, and one was divorced. Although the respondents came from a variety of backgrounds, all best efforts notwithstanding, the subsample was still somewhat skewed toward those who were relatively highly placed in Vietnamese society before the revolution: One man had worked for the American embassy, a second had been an accountant for a French firm, and another (more recent immigrant) was a union leader. Husbands of female respondents, most now widows, had been a teacher, school principal, accountant, employee of the American army, and head of a farm cooperative. Only one was a farmer in Vietnam. Among the female respondents, one had been a pharmacist and another was the niece of the former King of Vietnam; however, at least two of the women interviewed were not literate in Vietnamese. In any event, whoever they may have been in their homeland, most refugees who fled Vietnam after 1975 had to leave everything behind. Unlike those who were younger when arriving in this country, with rare exceptions, those already well along in years had neither the time nor the energy to start over again from nothing. Many had suffered an enormous declassement as part of an already painful process of adjustment to a foreign environment. Their families were scattered all over the United States and the world. A few had children still in Vietnam about whom they were terribly worried.

Only 1 of the 16 Vietnamese respondents could speak English reasonably well. A few others could haltingly speak a few phrases, but not really enough to communicate. Most respondents had been exposed to some efforts to teach them English when they first arrived in the United States, but had since forgotten even the rudiments of what they had learned. They said, "I am too old to learn a new language" and "I get ashamed." Most had given up on the idea of pursuing their English studies any further. Seven of the Vietnamese respondents lived with their spouses, and one lived with her husband and teenage son. Two resided with their sons, another with an acquaintance to whom she paid rent, and five lived alone. All but 2 of the 16 respondents lived in rental units, most in subsidized housing.

Interviews

Interview questions were open ended, following the same basic outline for each respondent. Data were gathered on: (a) sociodemographic characteristics (age, residence, work history, immigration history), (b) health status, (c) functional capacity, (d) informal helping networks, (e) knowledge of existing public and private services, (f) utilization of services, and (g) perceived unmet needs for service.

The researcher conducted interviews with all the African-American and Hispanic respondents; most of the latter chose to be questioned in Spanish. Monolingual Vietnamese respondents were interviewed using interpreters. Unless the respondent objected, interviews were tape-recorded. Three Vietnamese respondents requested that the microrecorder not be used. The researcher took notes during the session and added comments later as necessary. As is often the case in intensive, open-ended interviewing, interviews varied in length and tone according to the respondents and the concerns they wished to express. The shortest lasted about 45 minutes, the longest about 2½ hours. Among the Vietnamese, especially, interviews had the feel of formal visits, with accompanying rituals of greeting and offering of tea and sweets. In some cases, when homebound persons were unable to answer questions, their caregivers were interviewed instead.

The method of intensive interviewing has both advantages and drawbacks. It lacks the standardization of close-ended questionnaires and it is more dependent on the individual skills and training of the interviewer. Alternatively, intensive interviews can provide a richer and more holistic picture of people's lives. They also give respondents greater ability to define issues in their own terms rather than in terms imposed by the researcher. This freedom of expression is particularly important for groups that diverge from the cultural mainstream (Berkowitz, 1989).

Results

Seventy percent of African-American respondents were homebound primarily for medical reasons, as compared with 50% of the Hispanics and only 13% of the Vietnamese. Put another way, about one third of the African Americans, half of the Hispanics, and three quarters of the Vietnamese might be considered "socially homebound," in that they were physically capable of leaving their homes, but did not. Both knowledge and utilization of services were highest among the African-American respondents, intermediate among Hispanics, and lowest among the Vietnamese. However, even in the most knowledgeable group, 30% knew only about basic financial assistance programs such as Social Security, Supplemental Security Income (SSI), Medicaid, and Medicare. They were largely unaware of other available supportive services, including senior centers, adult day care, companion and homemaker services, Meals on Wheels, in-home nursing and bathing, transportation, and other services such as home-delivered groceries.

All three groups expressed needs for better or more appropriate transportation, reasonably priced homemaker and in-home nursing care services, broader medical insurance coverage, and mental health services. Despite several cases of Alzheimer's in both the African-American and Hispanic samples, almost no one in any of the three groups knew about Alzheimer's disease or about services available for Alzheimer's patients or their caregivers.

Extrapolating needs from respondents' comments was not always a simple, straightforward process. The researcher often had to interpret the respondents' statements and then translate these into definable needs for specific services. Well-educated, White, middle-class respondents are practiced in articulating their needs in terms readily comprehensible to service providers. In contrast, minorities, the poor, the frail elderly, and other disadvantaged groups are not used to being asked what they want or need, and often cannot translate their felt needs into the available service nomenclature.

For example, several elderly homebound Vietnamese women said they did not go out of the house because it made them feel dizzy. A few noted they had tried to take the bus, but had become confused, frightened, and dizzy, and had hurriedly returned home. Some complained of getting severe headaches when they ventured into the wider environment. Putting these together with other statements pointing to the traumatic effects of cultural dislocation, separation from family, and prolonged refugee status, the researcher interpreted these somatic complaints as indicating a generalized sense of cultural and physical disorientation—a feeling of being completely overwhelmed upon leaving the sanctuary of their own homes. The researcher discussed this interpretation with several Vietnamese social service workers and one other anthropologist, all of whom basically agreed. This still left the question of which services could reasonably address these symptoms and feelings of cultural dislocation. Although provision of the right kind of transportation assistance would certainly help, sensitive, culturally appropriate mental health services were probably also needed to address the larger problem. The researcher did not know enough about Vietnamese culture to suggest what form these services might take, or how they could be most effectively presented to the potential clientele. Designing a service like this would clearly require the expertise of a highly trained bilingual Vietnamese mental health professional.

The point is that these respondents did not simply say, "I need this or I need that." If presented with a list of needed services, it is unlikely any of them would have indicated a need for mental health services or even really known what that meant. At most, they might have stated a need for transportation. But given the "apparent" availability of various transportation services, their answers might have been read as indicating a lack of knowledge of existing options. Inferring service needs would have been impossible without benefit of the knowledge of the respondents' lives and circumstances gathered in the intensive interviews.

The ability to evaluate responses in a wider community context also proved important in "deconstructing" an initially puzzling finding from the African-American subsample. Many respondents expressed a strong need for transportation services, saying they had to impose on relatives and neighbors who often took off time from work to provide rides for them. Although most knew about a door-to-door van service operated by the Red Cross, they complained that it was inconvenient or too much bother to make appointments in advance. Their answers seemed to ring a bit hollow. Finally, one woman alluded to the Red Cross' unfavorable reputation in the African-American community. "Honey, some people think they may not like our people very much over there." During World War II, the Red Cross had maintained separate blood supplies for African Americans and Whites, and had refused to mix the two. Older African Americans, still stinging from the slight, were essentially boycotting the van service and all other services provided by the organization. Again, it would have been difficult to make meaningful sense of this response set without knowing and understanding the ramifications of this critical piece of history.

Among elderly Hispanic respondents, not knowing English was the central, but not the only, impediment to obtaining information about and using services. For the Vietnamese, in addition to the language barrier, cultural disorientation was also an important factor. Both elderly Hispanics and Vietnamese had to depend on bilingual mediators in their dealings with the service delivery system. When children could not act in this capacity, in the absence of a bilingual social service worker or someone else to serve this bridging function, these elders were effectively cut off from access to all but the most basic services. This was the situation of some elderly Hispanics, and a majority of elderly Vietnamese in this sample.

By contrast, most elderly African-American respondents had long-standing ties to church and neighborhood. Many were also embedded in strong informal helping networks that incorporated friends, neighbors, and fellow parishioners, as well as relatives. These networks served as a source of information about services and a bridge to the service delivery system. African-American respondents were the least socially homebound of the three minorities, primarily due to the strength of these networks in providing informal support and facilitating linkage to the wider system.

Recommendations

One of the two main goals of the minority-focused needs assessment was to develop recommendations on how to better serve these elderly minorities. Just as the "raw data" needed interpretation before inferences could be made about service needs, crafting realistic and useful recommendations based on the findings required more than an understanding of the barriers to service utilization in the three minority groups. It also required insight into the organization and culture of the County Department of Human Services (DHS). The researcher had been developing an understanding of the structure and dynamics of the DHS while interviewing key informants in the three minority subcommunities and compiling the in-home service directory. Moreover, throughout the study, the researcher maintained an office at the agency and often met both formally and informally with staff to discuss the meaning and implications of the emerging findings. Staff supplied important information on different aspects of the DHS and other county agencies. Toward the end of the field phase, these meetings also provided a forum for brainstorming recommendations. The active involvement of agency personnel—with their knowledge of the internal politics of the county—was essential to developing a set of recommendations that stood a chance of being seriously considered for implementation.

Selected recommendations for changes in policy and practice developed for the minority-focused needs assessment are presented next, paired with the specific findings and rationale supporting them.

- Hire qualified minority bilingual/bicultural personnel at all levels of the service- delivery system, especially where gatekeeping and case-management functions are crucial.
- If and when elderly services are collocated, create a central information and referral station, and hire part-time bilingual personnel to staff the station and answer the phone during specified hours.

Findings and Explanation: Both Hispanic and Vietnamese elders, especially but not exclusively those who lacked the assistance of bilingual relatives, were falling through the cracks of the service system at critical junctures where there were no bilingual or bicultural social service workers to mediate for them in the larger system. This was happening most at pivotal points of entry into or exit from one or another part of the system. Therefore, it was recommended that the county make a concerted effort to hire qualified bilingual, bicultural personnel and to place these individuals in strategic positions where these linkage functions were especially critical. At the time, a plan was being considered to collocate all elderly services in one building and to create a single point of entry into the system. The second recommendation suggested that if and when that collocation occurred, special efforts should be made to staff the information and referral station with bilingual personnel during certain times of the day. Although it was recognized that this would not overcome all barriers to information-seeking, staff felt it would help, especially if knowledge that this service was available in their native language were to diffuse into the community.

- Hire a Vietnamese-speaking social worker in the adult services division.

Findings and Explanation: This recommendation is a more specific outgrowth of the findings presented previously. The absence of a Vietnamese-speaking worker in this division meant that most elderly Vietnamese, when transferred out of the refugee services division that did employ a Vietnamese worker, failed to make the linkage to continuing services. Conversely, the presence of bilingual Hispanic workers in both the refugee and adult services divisions meant that these linkages were made to a far greater degree for Hispanic elderly once they entered the system. In the context of the county service delivery system, one strategically placed individual could make a big difference.

- Hire bilingual/bicultural workers to deliver culturally appropriate geriatric mental health services to Hispanic and Vietnamese elderly.

Findings and Explanation: When asked what services they lacked, several of the Hispanic respondents expressed a need to talk in Spanish with someone who would understand their emotional and psychological problems and be able to help. Many Hispanic respondents complained of loneliness or isolation and had few, if any, local kin ties or other social supports. As discussed earlier, several socially homebound Vietnamese women said they did not leave their homes because they felt dizzy when they went outside; others said they were afraid of "offending" or "bothering" Americans. Many of these respondents had endured stays in refugee camps. Their family networks had been ripped apart and sometimes spread all over the world by the ravages of war and migration. The researcher and agency personnel decided these people were suffering so much emotional distress they should have help; in both cases, to be of any real value, that help needed to be of a very particular and sensitive kind.

- Hire an outreach worker for the agency with bilingual capability. If hired, the worker could be responsible for disseminating comprehensive information about services for the elderly and could provide names of specific contact persons to extension service workers and workers at the Central Entry for Refugees and Limited English Proficient Programs so the latter can help their elderly clients link up with services other than those they directly provide. Ideally, this should be done in person and in conjunction with a training session.

Findings and Explanation: At the time, the agency was seriously considering hiring an additional part-time outreach worker. Given the findings from this study, it seemed important to hire someone who was bilingual and able to address the linguistic and cultural barriers to service utilization by Hispanic elderly. Although it would have been wonderful to find someone with capabilities in a number of languages, it seemed unrealistic to ask that the person be multilingual. The suggestions for the specific activities this outreach worker might perform came from the realization that many county extension workers, as well as workers in other units serving refugee and limited English-speaking populations, did not consider the elderly members of the families they served their clients, or were unaware of what culturally and linguistically appropriate services were available for the older persons in their service population. Just providing these workers with information would be helpful, but (especially for the Hispanic workers) not nearly as effective as establishing a direct, personal line of communication between these workers and workers at the senior centers or agency. It made all the difference to the Hispanic workers that they have the name of a specific individual (preferably Spanish-speaking) to contact. Hence, the emphasis was on providing specific names, doing things in person, and holding a training session as ways to create personal connections while conveying important information.

- Distribute information about services for the elderly to targeted ethnic associations, community organizations, and church groups (which specific groups or organizations should depend on the particular minority group). Establish direct, personal contact with members of these organizations, and explain the importance of serving the needs of the elderly, as well as children and youth.

Findings and Explanation: All three minority subcommunities had organizations and informal leaders who mediated (with varying degrees of success) community members' linkages to the wider service structure, although the specific persons or organizations that fulfilled these functions varied from group to group. For example, in the African-American community, churches were crucial; in the Vietnamese community, ethnic associations were pivotal. It made sense to utilize these "indigenous" organizations in disseminating information. Moreover, the prevalent cultural style in all three groups was responsive to working through personal contacts, rather than utilizing impersonal or formal channels. In addition, especially for the Hispanic and Vietnamese respondents, the idea of providing social services to the elderly was unfamiliar, sometimes even completely novel. For example, a thoughtful Vietnamese social worker in the refugee division acknowledged that she had routinely looked on grandparents as an exploitable resource for families with young children. "Until I spoke with you, I never considered these elderly people might have needs of their own." Older Hispanics reluctant to express their own needs would often say, "The government here already does so much more than in my country. How could I ask for more?" Consequently, as a means of both providing information and calling attention to their situation, it was important to emphasize to these organizations that elderly persons have legitimate needs that the service system is designed to address.

- Disseminate information on Alzheimer's disease or send speakers explaining Alzheimer's to community and church groups in minority communities, and include information about caregiver options and available programs so that informal community leaders and family members can be alert to the symptoms of the disease, its patterns of progression, and ways of caring for patients.

Findings and Explanation: Few people in any of the three minority subcommunities knew about Alzheimer's disease (its manifestations, symptoms, progression), how to care for an Alzheimer's patient, how to access services, or which services were available. In some cases, Alzheimer's patients were treated as if their behavior was willful; as a result, dangerous as well as abusive circumstances had developed. Although "technically" available, information about the disease and available resources had clearly failed to penetrate the minority communities in a meaningful fashion. This recommendation again suggests that "indigenous" organizations and individuals serve as the point of contact for disseminating critical information into the community.

- Find a way to more effectively utilize the unique skills and talents of existing bilingual, bicultural staff now serving a mixed English-speaking and limited English-speaking clientele.
- If bilingual, bicultural personnel are expected to perform interpretation and mediation functions beyond those strictly defined as part of their job requirements, include this as one of the key elements in their job descriptions and evaluate them accordingly.

Findings and Explanation: These may well be the most controversial recommendations of all. Knowing the head of the DHS was free to accept or reject any or all recommendations, the researcher decided to risk being seen as overstepping her bounds in order to point up the difficult situation of many bicultural, bilingual personnel. Several workers with invaluable linguistic and cultural skills were serving mixed or predominantly English-speaking clienteles as a function of the internal division of labor in their agencies or departments. At the same time, these workers were under pressure from former minority clients to continue to mediate for them in the service system. Had they not done so, the clients would have fallen through the cracks in the system. In addition, these former clients had become attached to these workers as individual patrons and did not understand the rules of the bureaucracy. Consequently, they tended to interpret the workers' protestations that they could not help them any longer as personal rejection. This put obvious pressure on these workers not to sever the relationship. Moreover, although performing these mediation and translation functions was not part of their official job description, nor explicitly acknowledged in their performance appraisals, these workers believed they were still "unofficially" expected to be doing these things. Hence, the workers quite understandably felt locked into a structural double bind. Because existing county personnel policy precluded allowing these workers to serve an exclusively monolingual or monoethnic clientele, the recommendation had to be phrased in a more open-ended fashion. It was agency personnel who suggested that these functions could be included as key elements in the job description, thus ensuring that workers would be given credit for what they were currently doing on their own.

Utilization and Dissemination

To effectively disseminate the results of a needs assessment and utilize the information to bring about change, the agency staff must be vested in pushing for changes and must "keep the ball rolling." For the momentum of the process to be maintained, staff must seize every opportunity to disseminate the information to those in decision-making and policymaking positions, regardless of the amount of time that may have passed since the study was completed. Those who are strongly committed to utilizing the results to effect change will keep the recommendations in the forefront while maintaining a modicum of patience and ongoing flexibility. The process cannot end after the final report is completed.

Although most of the recommendations were purposely focused on or targeted to specific units or services within the DHS, staff realized that such additions or changes had a price tag, and that action would come slowly in a bureaucracy. As noted, many of the recommendations focused on increasing the number of staff and building their capacity to serve minorities. However, these recommendations came at a time when budget cutting and belt tightening were just beginning.

Clearly, those recommendations that would directly impact programs and services controlled by the agency were most easily and readily implemented. Prior to the needs assessment, the adult day care center supervised by the agency had been unable to serve any non–English-speaking participants. As a result of the needs assessment findings, a "Survival Spanish" class for staff, the adult day care center, and the Geriatric Clinic was arranged to enable them to better communicate with and be culturally sensitive to the needs of participants. Shortly thereafter, when a vacancy occurred at the adult day care center, a Spanish-speaking mental health worker was hired. This person was able to do outreach to Hispanic communities, and to work with social workers who have Spanish-speaking clients to encourage and facilitate their participation at the center. This staff person also now provides mental health counseling to Hispanic participants at one of the senior centers.

Another recommendation was to hire an outreach worker with bilingual capacity. Although the agency has been unable to gather support for increased staff so far, it decided to respond to this need in several ways. Program staff and volunteers have been used to translate materials into Spanish and Vietnamese. To distribute information about services to targeted ethnic associations, community organizations, and church groups, the agency has worked with the Hispanic and Vietnamese task forces to assist with outreach and staff participation. These two groups consist of county employees who work with these two populations in a variety of capacities. As a result, several organizations and church groups have invited staff to present information to their members. By informing the employees about available programs and services, the agency has created linkages to persons who would not otherwise be reached.

The recommendation that focused on disseminating information and educating community leaders and family members in minority communities about Alzheimer's disease was a result of the researcher's finding that there was little known about the disease, its symptoms, progression, or community resources, particularly among the African-American community. One of the staff who served on the board of the local Alzheimer's Association chapter disseminated this information to the board; the two worked together to submit an application to a foundation to fund a half-day respite care program for persons with Alzheimer's or other forms of dementia. This program was funded and is located in one of the existing senior centers in one African-American community. Residents in this community are familiar with the senior center, so it did not pose a threat as an "unknown." Funding also provided staff to do outreach in the community and to educate African-American community leaders and residents about the disease and available resources.

The agency was also able to use the recommendations that focused on staff training and cultural sensitivity as a vehicle to provide technical assistance to its subcontractors to enhance service to minority communities. For example, when it was discovered that transportation was a barrier to service in one African-American community due to a misperception that dated back to World War II, staff were able to work with some members of the community to remove the barrier. The senior center in that community normally received transportation services from the local Community Action Program (CAP). When the driver was on vacation, however, makeshift plans often fell apart. Staff convened a meeting between the CAP, the Red Cross, and the senior center to arrange for the Red Cross to provide backup service. This small change completely altered the community's view of the Red Cross, and put it in a more positive light. In addition, community members now access Red Cross service for transportation to medical appointments and for grocery shopping. The agency also worked with the contractor who provides personal care services to do outreach among Hispanic communities and to hire bilingual home health aides to provide service in these communities. In addition, the agency's contract with the legal services provider now includes a provision that a bilingual attorney provide service to Spanish-speaking participants at senior centers.

The only way any changes were going to happen outside the agency would be if there was a significant buy-in at the highest levels of the department. When the researcher submitted her recommendations to the agency, staff also asked that she submit them to the Chief of the Division of Social Services, and to the Director of the Department of Human Services. She subsequently scheduled appointments with each to discuss her recommendations.

For the most part, the director was open and receptive to many of the recommendations. In contrast, the division chief viewed some of them as stepping beyond the bounds of practicality and as implicit criticism of her leadership. Despite this, a Vietnamese-speaking worker was hired into that unit some time later. This occurred, in part, due to pressure from the agency based on the study recommendations and, in larger part, due to an unanticipated vacancy in that unit and the immediate need to fill the position from within the department.

The recommendation to provide cultural sensitivity training was adopted for all county personnel who interact with minority and limited–English-speaking clients. All persons in supervisory positions received a training session on managing a diverse workforce. Another training session, open to all staff, was offered on Understanding Arlington's Multicultural Elderly Population. Subsequent training sessions were targeted to serving particular minority populations. Although these outcomes did not result only from the minority-focused recommendations, the latter certainly played a part in raising the level of awareness of minority issues and concerns in the county.

In addition to these specific programmatic additions and modifications, some general changes have been made in policies and practices at both the agency and departmental levels. These are, to some degree, attributable to the findings and recommendations of this needs assessment. For example, it is now standard practice to have minority representation on all interview panels for hiring. It has also become departmental policy to advertise vacancies and information about available programs and services in newspapers and publications targeted to specific minority populations. In addition, both the agency and department routinely involve community leaders from targeted populations to serve on any advisory group, task force, or planning team to ensure access to and participation from those groups.

A somewhat unique recommendation dealt with those elderly who were socially homebound as a result of the need to meet familial obligations. Many older minority women stayed at home to take care of their grandchildren, and therefore could not attend senior centers and other programs. The researcher recommended that a senior–tot center be established, where seniors could come and bring their grandchildren. Discussions are still underway between one senior center and the department that operates several child recreation programs to see whether this can occur. Those discussions are exploring the possibility of the agency providing transportation for both the seniors and their grandchildren. In addition, a county board–appointed Citizen Advisory Commission has just completed a reexamination of all services provided by the County. Information regarding the senior–tot recommendation was shared with the commission, and subsequently was incorporated into a recommendation to the county board that a multipurpose center be created in the county to serve both seniors and children. This is yet another example of the serendipitous impact of disseminating results to a wider audience, beyond the scope of the original intent of the needs assessment.

Strengths and Weaknesses

On balance, especially considering the impact made by the minority-focused needs assessment in relation to its modest scope and cost, its strengths greatly outweigh its weaknesses. However, as in almost any needs assessment, compromises had to be made and certain choices precluded others. If it were to be done over again, certain things would probably be done differently.

Using a qualitative approach. The needs assessment's greatest strength might also be considered its strongest weakness. Taking an in-depth qualitative approach to understanding the barriers to service utilization and the reasons why the respondents were homebound allowed the researcher to sensitively probe into many important areas of their lives. The picture that emerged for each group was deeper and more holistic, as well as more nuanced and culturally specific, than would have been possible employing more standard, quantitative methods. Furthermore, it would have been difficult to make meaningful sense of many of the responses without an understanding of the larger cultural and community contexts in which the respondents were embedded. This basic approach was justified because all three of the elderly minorities diverged from the cultural mainstream, and thus needed to be able to tell their stories in their own terms.

By the same token, employing in-depth methods of interviewing placed a clear upper limit on the number of interviews that could be conducted in a relatively limited time period. Researchers holding to stringent quantitative standards might well turn up their noses at the results of 48 interviews. Also, to be maximally useful, good in-depth intensive interviews require a highly skilled and experienced interviewer. Although it would have been possible to train additional interviewers in this technique, it would have been extremely difficult and demanding.

Sample. Selection of a purposive, nonrepresentative sample was closely tied to the choice of an in-depth qualitative approach. Designing a stratified random sample of elderly minorities would have been an exceedingly challenging task that would have more than absorbed the resources available for the whole project. Moreover, it is not clear that it would have been worth the effort in yielding the needed results. Nevertheless, the sampling strategy that was used also had its weaknesses. First, only three groups could be chosen for the target population. Although the criteria for selecting the three were reasonable, they were also at some level arbitrary. When the researcher was asked, "Why Vietnamese? Why not Cambodians?", all she could answer was that the Vietnamese community in Arlington was somewhat larger. The repercussions of focusing on some groups as opposed to others were not trivial because the study results and recommendations were, for the most part, aimed at the specific groups selected. A generalized heightened sensitivity to cultural difference in the service delivery system would presumably aid all minority groups, but hiring a Vietnamese-speaking worker would not help Koreans or Cambodians to access the system. The situation was clearly complicated by the diversity of groups in this polyglot population.

Second, the strategies utilized to locate homebound persons in the three communities probably resulted in a bias toward persons who, despite being homebound, were better connected to the community or the service delivery structure than others. Trying to reach homebound persons in these communities "cold," especially in the Hispanic and Vietnamese communities, would

have been close to impossible. Asking respondents for "second-order" referrals to other homebound persons helped mitigate this bias, but did not overcome it altogether. Consequently, the results are probably skewed in the direction of underestimating the extent of social homeboundedness and
overestimating the level of knowledge and utilization of services in all three
groups. For both the Hispanic and Vietnamese respondents, this tendency was
reflected in a sample clearly skewed toward more established groups and away
from poorer and less well-educated Central Americans or Vietnamese boat
people, whose service needs were probably greater than those of the respondents. Unfortunately, these limitations could only have been overcome, if at
all, with considerable diplomacy and a great deal more time and effort.

Use of interpreters. The fact that the researcher does not speak Vietnamese
and most of the Vietnamese respondents were unable to converse in English
clearly made it necessary to use interpreters with the Vietnamese respondents.
Although this was not planned in advance, it turned out that whoever made
the initial contacts with the homebound respondents accompanied the researcher on the interview and served as interpreter. Under the best of circumstances, relying on interpreters adds another layer to the interview process. In
this case, the situation was further complicated by the interactive format of
the intensive interview as well as having to depend on five different individuals,
with varying levels of education and degrees of mastery of English, to act as
interpreters. Although they could be prepared for the types of questions they
would be asking, the interpreters could not be given a specific list of questions
to ask. They had to be ready to follow the flow of the dialogue and construct
the next question based on the response to the last. This is a difficult skill to
master under any circumstances, all the more so with delicate issues of translating across cultural and linguistic boundaries. Although it would have been
difficult to arrange and probably somewhat uncomfortable given the status
differences among them, holding a single joint training session for all the
interpreters would have been a good idea. From a purely methodological standpoint, using just one individual to serve as interpreter would have been even
better; however, doing so would also have at least partially undercut the process
used to recruit respondents and, as a consequence, would most likely have
lowered the response rate. As it was, the researcher worked with the interpreters on an individual basis, debriefing with them after each interview and
commenting on any apparent issues or difficulties that arose during the interviews. This seemed to work reasonably well, but it would probably make a
purist somewhat uncomfortable.

Close working relationship with agency personnel. The structure provided
by the Fellowship Program greatly enhanced the working relationship between
the researcher and agency staff. The program required that the agency interview prospective researchers to facilitate the best possible "match" for the
project. This process accomplished two goals: to crystallize the goals and
objectives of the needs assessment, and to determine whether the approach
and desired outcomes of both the researcher and the Agency were compatible.
The program also required that the researcher and the agency's primary con-

tact participate in a 2-day work session to further define the project goals, boundaries, and respective roles. These requirements helped avoid misunderstandings and barriers that often plague such endeavors.

Open communication and flexibility were necessary and ongoing components of the study. Meetings were held weekly, or as needed, to discuss progress and resolve any issues or problems as they arose. Additionally, the researcher was required to submit progress reports to both the agency and the program, which facilitated communication and provided a system of checks.

The working relationship was further enhanced by the fact that the researcher lived in close geographic proximity to the agency. The agency maintained ongoing contact and input from the researcher after the formal completion of the project, which aided tremendously in efforts to implement some of the recommendations and, in some cases, refine or redefine the strategies. To have a researcher come from a distant location would have necessarily restricted or prohibited some of the outcomes.

Independent status of the researcher. Although the agency contributed part of the researcher's stipend, external funding allowed the researcher a degree of independence she would not have enjoyed as either a county employee or a direct contractor. Not having to follow a prescribed set of procedures or conform to established hierarchies enabled the researcher to move easily across departmental and divisional boundaries and sometimes to take short cuts in making contacts and collecting information. Key informants felt they could speak to the researcher more freely because she was not beholden to anyone, and several expressed their hope that their views would reach receptive ears they could not easily (or at least directly) reach themselves. This "insider–outsider" status helped the researcher by facilitating the development of a comprehensive picture of the county-wide social and health service delivery system for the elderly, which in reality was divided among a number of separate departments, divisions, and agencies. Even in a relatively small county, personnel from one agency or division did not always know specific staff in another and were sometimes poorly informed about services that others could offer their former or current clients. Consequently, one of the more valuable unintended consequences of the needs assessment was that the researcher helped create linkages among county employees and agencies serving the elderly. It may also be true that the county was more receptive to the researcher's recommendations because she was an "outsider," and therefore had no vested interest in the outcome or implementation of the recommendations.

SIMILARITIES AND DIFFERENCES OF THE TWO APPROACHES

The two needs assessments described in this chapter were intentionally presented together as a means of highlighting and demonstrating the numerous similarities and differences that can be discovered when comparing the goals, approaches, methods, and results of other assessments. The intent here was not simply to present two approaches to studying the needs of the elderly, but rather to exemplify the many issues and considerations that must be addressed, and to form the basis for determining the focus and desired results of a given needs assessment.

As previously mentioned, both needs assessments were carried out under the auspices of a Postdoctoral Fellowship Program. Based on this sponsorship, both were conducted in a prescribed time period (essentially 8 weeks), with limited planning time and a relatively restricted level of funding (approximately $6,000). Both efforts focused on a county level, and were supported by and housed within county government agencies. They are different, yet very efficient, ways to succeed on relatively limited resources.

Each of the studies relied on the use of an "outside" expert rather than using existing staff. In both instances, the researcher developed a close working relationship with the sponsor agency, and was also able to achieve a high degree of cooperation from other departments and agencies. The researchers for both studies were locally based, which allowed the working relationships to continue beyond the program's time frame. In fact, both have "lived on" in many different ways, and continue to do so. For example, both researchers continue to work with their respective agencies to strategize and rethink approaches to implementing their findings and recommendations. This chapter and, indeed, this entire book are also products of this ongoing collaboration.

SUMMARY

Both counties are in the metropolitan Washington, DC, area. The geographical similarity means that both counties have a similar service base, although they focused on different segments of the population. It should be noted, however, that those who may conduct similar needs assessments in other suburban areas may find different target populations and results. Many people have an image of "the suburbs" that is not true in the Washington, DC, area. Often the population in the suburbs is as heterogeneous as the city population. Because of the similarities in the two service bases, unquestionably either county might have done the other's study under their same set of circumstances.

The methodological approaches of the two studies were very different. One agency conducted a longitudinal needs assessment, which meant there was an earlier base from which to work, whereas the other conducted a qualitative assessment, with no prior research base. Consequently, the two studies used different sampling and data collection approaches, which necessarily produced different types of results. Based on these different approaches, the two agencies used the resources and skills of the researchers differently (e.g., interviewing, data analysis, etc.). Despite that both areas have similar services bases, and despite that both are studies of the elderly, these were very different yet equally valid approaches.

The target group for one study was the mainstream population (White, middle class), as a result of the original sample. The other focused on a specific subsection of the population (homebound minorities)—those not so easily reached and not likely to be in the service loop. The ease of accessibility to the two target populations significantly impacted the use of resources. For example, Fairfax made strong use of volunteers, in many cases cohorts of the target population, whereas Arlington had to rely on paid assistance from interpreters to reach some segments of the target population.

Although the initial purpose of each assessment differed greatly, both projects used their findings for many purposes. The results of each of the studies were, purposely, presented in different ways based on the overall goals of each project. The longitudinal project developed no specific recommendations; the results were reported as results of a survey, yet policy and program changes did occur. Conversely, the minority-focused project was intentionally designed to produce program and service specific recommendations, and the same thing happened—policy and program changes were effected.

Despite the similarities and differences presented here, the key to the success of each of these needs assessments was that both pushed for action. In both, agency staff, with the ongoing communication with and assistance from the researcher, continued to advocate for changes and modifications based on the results and recommendations from their respective assessments. The process did not end when the final reports were submitted, nor will it end in the foreseeable future.

III

DISSEMINATION AND FUTURE STRATEGIES

9

Using and Communicating Findings

Carolyn C. Carter

Historically, needs assessments have been heavily focused on the research phase, frequently providing no indication of if or how the findings are disseminated and used, or what impact they have made on the target population, policy, or services. A review of numerous needs assessments conducted from the late 1970s through 1989 showed that most authors provided varied levels of detail on the type of needs assessments conducted, but little information on the application or outcome of the study. Pages of numbers and percentages were supplied with little or no discussion of the implication for application, policy, or action. The reader was often left asking, "So what?" Similarly, Newcomer (1994) observed that evaluators typically spend 95% of their time conducting a study and writing the findings section while spending 5% writing recommendations. In contrast, their audience typically devotes 95% of their reading time to the recommendations.

Needs assessments do not end with analysis of the data. This chapter addresses practical approaches to achieving such an end. To be most useful and to have an impact on policy, program development, and service delivery, findings must be communicated and disseminated to various audiences. Otherwise, the needs assessment will not have fulfilled its mission no matter how well the research was done. This chapter outlines ways to communicate and effectively apply findings. Details on how to use and communicate findings are presented on five basic elements: the audience, draft findings prior to study completion, presentation, dissemination, and implementation. The first section of the chapter discusses the concept of identifying who the audience is and what it wants to know, including considerations of how to communicate with the audience. Knowing the audience is key to understanding and actualizing the subsequent sections of this chapter. The second section presents an unconventional method for communicating and using findings—that is, drafting preliminary conclusions prior to the study's analysis and completion. Third, suggestions are offered on how to most effectively present findings to allow different audiences to learn the most from the research, with a focus on writing the final report. The fourth section provides techniques for effective dissemination of the needs assessment study findings. Last, recommendations for implementing the results are provided to maximize the likelihood that findings will be utilized.

DETERMINING THE AUDIENCE

Audiences have different needs for information and they process information differently (Karsten & Kasab, 1990). Although various levels of difficulty and inclusion are appropriate, presentations that have general appeal to audiences are

- solid, with a research foundation;
- practical;
- innovative or interesting;
- applicable to the audience and elsewhere;
- clear editorially and graphically; and
- attractive.

For professional audiences such as academicians, service providers, and administrators, emphasis on the details of methodology and analysis should be included in explaining the research components of the study. For other members of the audience such as the general public, the target population, and elected officials interested in the bottom line, a brief overview of the research design may be sufficient.

Gauge the level of detail of research to share with the audience. Newcomer (1994) has encouraged a review of audience characteristics. Is the audience fully conversant with technical vocabulary and the nuances of policy and program operations? Audience characteristics, such as education level and type of professional training, may affect the research strategy and reporting format preferred. Audiences differ in their interests. Remain flexible and use interchangeable materials and varied presentation styles, especially while on the speaking circuit. Answers to the following questions provided by Newcomer about audience characteristics should shape strategies for communicating with specific audiences:

- Who is the audience? Is it the general public, stakeholders, or both? The level of detail and types of media will vary depending on what the audience wants to know and what it thinks is important.
- Are they visual or auditory learners? Identify the audience's capacity and willingness to understand and retain different amounts and types of information.

Karsten and Kasab (1990) suggested the following analysis of the audience:

- Know the audience before disseminating information.
- Identify audience's information needs and desires.

- Determine how the audience acquires information, increasing the likelihood of reaching the target audience by using existing, familiar channels. For professional audiences, look at journals they read, conferences they attend, and organizations they join or support.
- Identify people respected by the audience, and learn their names and professional affiliations. The audience considers these people credible. Brief these individuals ahead of time to obtain additional support from these leaders.
- Find out the audience's reactions to those competing for funds, support, and resources, and plan an approach to the audience that appeals to their preferences or priorities.
- Be sensitive to cultural differences, and identify the appropriate languages for audio or visual communication.
- Determine if the audience includes persons with disabilities and select dissemination techniques that accommodate their physical challenges. For example, plan ahead for an interpreter, develop large print brochures and handouts, or equip the sitting area with space for a wheelchair.

DRAFTING FINDINGS PRIOR TO STUDY COMPLETION

Well before the final results are analyzed, the research team and stakeholders will likely have a good idea of what the major findings will be. The final report is not constructed only as the last stage of the study. It may be a good, if somewhat unconventional, idea to begin drafting findings as they emerge, allowing additional time and opportunity for testing reactions before the report is released, especially if some of the emerging findings are controversial or unanticipated (Newcomer, 1994).

Drafting preliminary findings before the final report is constructed is recommended for two main reasons: (a) it keeps the group focused on the why, how, and what of the study's purpose, and (b) it mitigates the last-minute rush to categorize, prioritize, or find appropriate ways to describe findings in the final report.

There are other practical reasons for developing preliminary findings to a needs assessment, such as preparing stakeholders for strategies they may want to implement in promoting or responding to findings. For example, suppose the goal of a needs assessment is to identify the most pressing needs of developmentally disabled adults to promote independent living in the community. A preliminary finding might be drafted to read, "Based on what we have found thus far, it appears that for developmentally disabled adults in this area finding a job is the single greatest barrier to living independently in the community." Vocational rehabilitators, adult educators, and employment agencies may contemplate and develop plans for changes in the infrastructure necessary to provide more jobs for developmentally disabled adults.

Preliminary conclusions should be marked clearly as *draft* and *preliminary*. Preliminary audiences should be chosen judiciously. In addition, only those findings that are particularly well-founded and not likely to be overturned by additional analyses should be released in this way.

PRESENTING THE FINAL REPORT AND OTHER VENUES

Once the analysis is complete, the research team and stakeholders are anxious to share findings. This requires devising a plan for addressing what the findings tell various audiences and deciding how results can have the greatest meaning or substance. The plan should specify which information might be highlighted and presented in greater detail.

One of the most effective vehicles for communicating information to a heterogeneous audience is the final report. A written report is the traditional means of communicating research and analysis, translating the results of applied research to audiences for consumption. Although not the sole means of sharing findings, the final report is the most widely circulated document associated with the needs assessment. This makes it vital that the report be reasonably brief, readable, and timely in its release.

A needs assessment study will never leave the shelf if it is a wordy, obtuse document laden with jargon or unnecessary detail. Nor is a document viable when the information is outdated because the findings may no longer be applicable or, at a minimum, may be perceived to be unreliable in the current environment.

The final report should be adaptable to different types of presentations of findings, both written and verbal. Following are the basic elements for a written final report. They may also be applied to verbal presentations to audiences of different sizes and interests, as well as other written means of communicating the study's findings.

Constructing the Final Report: An Outline

The final report—the written document that conveys information to audiences about the study from its inception to conclusion—should include basic sections that appeal to most readers. Stakeholders and audiences have expectations that there will be a final report following the analysis of findings. Final reports for general consumption should not exceed 30 pages of text, including graphics and excluding acknowledgments, table of contents, bibliographies, and appendices. Brevity is best for a greater likelihood of reading. To reach a wide and varied audience, the report should be written at approximately a high school reading level. Interest in detail on statistical analysis and technical approaches is primarily limited to audiences such as academicians, research practitioners, and funding sources. These details are best dealt with in the appendices or by a section on how to obtain information on request. Presentation of detail is discussed later in this chapter.

Using the following outline, the various sections should be adapted to reflect the particular nature of the needs assessment. Depending on the project, the final report may have a proportionately larger section devoted to describing one or another aspect of the findings or process. For example, in reading a needs assessment of a lower income, ethnically diverse community, the audience may be particularly interested in learning how the research team approached a community with cultural differences, language barriers, and different value systems. In this instance, the final report should contain a more substantial narrative in the Methods section describing how the target population was approached. Conversely, a more traditional study using questionnaires with predominately White, English-speaking, educated, middle- to upper-income respondents requires a more limited description of how the target population was approached.

The following section outlines the various parts of the final report.

Executive summary. An overview of the study, the executive summary should have the capacity to be used as a stand-alone or tear-off document containing all the essential information on the study, even if the audience never reads the whole report. This section should be brief, about three to five pages in length, based on 30 pages of text for the final report. Brief one-paragraph answers to the following questions should be included:

- Who was the target population?
- What was the study about?
- What were the major findings? It is important to select key or predominant findings, reserving discussion of data analysis for the Findings section.
- What geographical area was studied, and why was it selected?
- Why was it important to conduct the study?
- How and by whom was the study conducted? This should be a brief description of methodology, which should be discussed further in the Methods section of the final report.
- Recommendations (if applicable). If recommendations in the final report have been developed for policy, program development, or service modifications, the last part of the executive summary should list at least the most important of these recommendations.

Graphs and tables or charts are generally not included in the executive summary. Often detailed and space-consuming, these are more appropriate for the Findings section of the final report.

Background. Describe the evolution of the needs assessment. To do this, set the backdrop to the study: Describe the target population, the demographic characteristics of the general population in the area, and the characteristics of the geographical area (e.g., rural, urban, suburban). Describe the overall political or social climate of the area. For example, is it a prosperous suburb with a large revenue base or a conservative area with a diminishing number of residents? Discuss the impetus for the needs assessment. Answers to these questions should be included:

- Who conducted the needs assessment and how was it funded? Describe why the agency conducting the study is equipped, capable, or appropriate to assess needs of the population at this time.
- What were the driving forces or motivations behind the study? Possible answers include directives from elected officials or management or funding available from grants. Did law or regulations require an assessment of need?

- How is the target population similar to or different from its counterpart in other geographical areas? How do these characteristics make this target population appropriate for a needs assessment study? Include a brief review of studies of similar target populations and their implications for the present study.

Methods. This section of the final report focuses on how the study was conducted. The choice of and rationale for research method(s), who participated, and how the data were analyzed should be briefly described in this section. Use of technical or research jargon should be limited. The following questions should be answered in the Methods section of the final report:

- Which method or methods were used to assess the target population's unmet needs, and why?
- Who conducted the research? Was the research staff recruited and trained and how was that accomplished? What materials were provided to the research team to conduct its work (if applicable)? In what ways was the researcher supported by the agency?
- Who developed and/or selected instruments and why? How were the instruments selected? Were the instruments piloted? Were issues of reliability and validity addressed?
- What sample criteria were used?
- What analytical techniques were chosen, and why?

Include references to additional information on methodology or offer examples in the event that the reader is interested in more detail. Consider including in the appendix copies of the instrument(s) or statistical charts. Also, let the reader know that additional information on the methodology is available upon request. Provide the reader with a specific address, phone number, and with the cost of the materials, if applicable.

Findings. This section should describe the results of the analyses and discuss their implications. What needs were found? What does it mean? Focus on answering the research questions as fully as possible. The presentation should be understandable to the general audience.

As with the Methods section, minimize the use of jargon and technical terminology. Percentages and degrees of variance from the overall population or from previous studies on the target population should be included in this section. This shows the needs of the target population in relation to others, putting findings into perspective. Graphs and charts will help the reader. Most important, tables and graphs should be well labeled.

Recommendations. This section is included in the final report only if recommendations have been developed as part of the process. If the timing is right, the final report is an appropriate vehicle for answering the question, "So what?", by including recommendations immediately after the findings. The general audience may expect recommendations in the final report, and stakeholders may want to use these recommendations to create or modify policies, or affect program development or service delivery. However, there may be reasons why recommendations are not made at the same time as the report is completed or are not included in the report. Responses may be referred to a citizens' group, for example, or there may be political reasons for withholding the release of recommendations. For example, an elected official might want to time recommendations to coincide with a political campaign. No matter when recommendations are released, they should be stated clearly.

Newcomer (1994) suggested addressing these questions in constructing recommendations:

- Are recommendations understandable and unambiguous?
- Are officials who should take action clearly identified?
- Is a reasonable time frame for action provided?
- Are recommendations numbered?
- Are recommendations brief? One or two sentences are usually sufficient. Lengthy recommendations are difficult to absorb and are more likely to leave the reader with the impression that the recommendation is not feasible.
- Are recommendations followed by succinct summaries of findings that support each of them?

Carefully select the language of recommendations to reflect appropriate content and avoid cultural, age, ethnic, or gender bias. Prioritizing results is an essential part of developing recommendations. The order of recommendations should reflect the most pressing or important needs based on findings, and ranking these conclusions should utilize the input and support of the stakeholders. Stakeholders may consider political or administrative factors, including external and internal factors discussed in chapter 5, in determining the order of recommendations.

The summary of findings supporting each recommendation is included in the Recommendations section. The discussion of recommendations in the executive summary is shorter, but the specific language of the recommendations should be identical in both sections. Consider including a few recommendations that do not require immediate funding. This gives officials and other stakeholders the opportunity to support the needs of their public or target population in concept or through actions that do not obligate expenditures. Including these recommendations can be important when officials and other stakeholders have limited or no resources or when the adoption of recommendations will encourage sharing the financial burden. Recommendations can be carefully phrased by using language such as "encouraging efforts to," "participating in public/private partnerships to," or "identifying low-cost measures to implement."

Other considerations. In addition to the main body of the report outlined earlier, other sections of the report that are important and practical for the reader include: acknowledgments, a table of contents, and a bibliography. In addition, appendices may contain tables, graphs, charts, a sample survey instrument, a flow chart showing such things as response rates, a reading list, and instructions on how to obtain additional information on the study.

Finally, several people should be lined up to proofread the final report. Select individuals with an eye for detail to catch the little mistakes, and include someone with excellent knowledge of grammar—possibly an information officer or someone who routinely proofs information before it leaves the agency. Volunteers with editing experience may help with this task. Persons unfamiliar with the study are helpful in reading the final report for comprehension and flow. Be ready to revise and rewrite. Few draft final reports require no further revision or change. Assimilating comments and perspectives of different reviewers, including stakeholders, is important to producing a document in which all have an investment. Build in the time required for making revisions to the final report.

Other Ways of Presenting Findings

The order and content of the final report, as described above, can be used in other presentations. The circulation of the final report may generate requests for additional types of presentations of the findings.

Karsten and Kasab (1990) offered suggestions for effective oral dissemination in four areas: personal communication, formal presentations, exhibits, and using visual aids. It may be helpful to refer to their approaches for personal (informal) and formal communication in planning for the presentation.

The importance of considering the types of presentations is driven by the characteristics, needs, and abilities of the audience described in the beginning of this chapter. The reporting vehicles should be tailored to the preferences of different audiences. Findings may need to be packaged in several different formats (Newcomer, 1994). There are a number of techniques to accomplish these basic goals and each one should be examined for appropriateness, affordability, and effectiveness in sending forth the study's messages.

DISSEMINATING FINDINGS: TECHNIQUES

Presentation of findings focuses on the means of reaching the audience about the results of the needs assessment. This section on dissemination centers on how that information reaches the audience and motivates them to take appropriate action.

Karsten and Kasab (1990) defined the overall goal of disseminating results as encouraging others to use the results of the work. Newcomer (1994) suggested that effective dissemination means that the right people get the right information in the right format to convince them that action is necessary. Dissemination also serves a useful purpose in educating the audience to the meaning of the research findings as well as how they can be applied. Others may use the needs assessment as a model for assessing their target population.

This section outlines specific goals and objectives for developing effective dissemination strategies for the needs assessment. Consider why, how, when, what, and by whom dissemination will occur to encourage the use of the study's findings. Practical approaches to dissemination are suggested in this section, such as media for dissemination, specific techniques for different stakeholders, and tips on what to include in various types of dissemination materials. Early in this chapter, the tools for analyzing the audience were provided. Knowing the audience is a critical first step to the effective dissemination of findings.

As with the presentation of findings, dissemination should be included in the planning strategy for the needs assessment. Waiting until the study is complete may mean that options for dissemination are too limited to be effective. Although a preliminary dissemination strategy should be in place, be prepared to modify the approach for dissemination as the needs assessment develops.

Planning Dissemination Strategy

Karsten and Kasab (1990) suggested that an appropriate dissemination strategy can be developed by addressing these questions during the initial planning process and revisiting them periodically throughout the project:

- What information does this study offer for dissemination?
- Who are the potential users of this information?
- What products or services from the recommendations will audiences use?
- How will the research team and stakeholders disseminate results?
- When should dissemination take place?
- What resources will be required to disseminate?

Begin to tell people about the project at the very beginning, and continue to keep stakeholders posted and the general public alert to the study's progress. Chapter 5 discusses whom to include and when in planning a needs assessment. Plans for effective dissemination also begin at this time, including the same people or organizations.

Timing and targeting findings are critical for effective dissemination. Plan to disseminate findings when the audience is ready to receive, interpret, and use the findings. To raise visibility and enhance attention, Newcomer (1994) posed these questions in timing dissemination:

- When does the audience meet?
- When must they take action to have change occur within the desired period of time?
- If legislation is required, when does the legislature meet, and how long does it take to draft appropriate language and get support for new legislation?

Karsten and Kasab (1990) posed this question: Is the dissemination plan responsive to external schedules such as publication deadlines and conference dates?

Identifying or Creating Media

There are a range of options to enhance the display and dissemination of the results and recommendations. What media are available to most effectively communicate the information to be conveyed about a study? Before choosing the best methods for dissemination, carefully consider the type of materials the audience would use before committing to developing products for dissemination.

To determine the most effective ways to relay information, ask the following questions of key informants or audience members:

- What is the audience's level of interest in the study? If minimal, basic, or unknown, a brief presentation without audiovisuals may suffice. Consider using the three- to five- page executive summary for dissemination to this audience.
- How does the audience like to receive information, and what products might be useful or appealing?
  - The audience may not process information on the spot, but may use the information later.
  - Pay particular attention to the appeal of the dissemination product. Is it something that will attract the audience?
  - Label all tables and graphs so they can be easily read, and highlight the most significant, dramatic, or surprising findings through simple shading or exploding pie charts. Sophisticated graphics, if available, may detract from the most important messages and those the audience wants to recall.
  - Personalize results whenever possible. Anecdotes are good tools for sharing the experience. The audience is likely to respond to and recall findings to which they can personally relate.
  - Maintain some levity and introduce humor in the presentation. Findings can be dry, so a light mood may make the information more palatable. Analyze the audience and needs assessment to determine what degree of humor, if any, is appropriate.

What to Include

Several factors determine what to include in the dissemination of the needs assessment: the type and size of the audience, the time spent with the audience, their time frame for digesting and using information, and the products available to use.

Who will deliver the message, and what is that person's influence in getting the message and information across to the audience? If the audience is the target population whose needs were assessed, does the presenter have credibility with those members of the target community? If the audience is composed of policymakers, does the presenter understand the political, economic, and social context of the area? Does he or she have the skills to present findings diplomatically and appropriately for policy consideration?

Once presenters are identified, are they equipped with resources? Use the following criteria for choosing resources:

- Evaluate resource suitability for the audience.
- Examine costs of different media, and determine whether less expensive means of effective communication can be used.
- Include options such as computer graphics, brochures, media articles, press releases, exhibits, visual aids, audiotapes, videotapes, radio, television, or online access.
- What "talk document" will be used? This is the handout or report delivered to the audience and from which the presenter speaks or to which he or she refers to frequently. Consider the final report or executive summary as possible talk documents. The executive summary is more appropriate for providing basic information. The final report is appropriate if the audience is interested in more information and an in-depth understanding of the study, or wants to devote time to reading and discussing the needs assessment.
- What is the time frame for disseminating information? Can action relating to policy or programs be implemented immediately, or is there a funding cycle determining the timing for stakeholders? Are recommendations going to require support from a large number of persons to receive political or social backing, and how long will it take to garner that support?
- How quickly can resources be produced? Develop a production timetable, and allow extra time for mistakes. Be informed about others' production schedules such as those of graphics departments, printing offices, and public affairs departments. Are other vendors for graphics or printing an option?

Follow up with an audience that has shown an interest in a particular aspect of the study. Get back to the audience as soon as possible with information. Offer to mail information or meet with the audience another time. For instance, if the audience is interested in knowing how to recruit volunteers to conduct professional interviews, consider developing a detailed description, video role play, and discussion of recruitment, screening, training, and support provided. Offer to present this information to the audience at a future meeting date.

Stakeholders as Disseminators

Stakeholders have been involved with or informed about the process and findings throughout the study. Therefore, stakeholders may be particularly appropriate for communicating the results. Vested in the study, they often enable or promote action on recommendations. This section examines the ways different stakeholders can be effective disseminators.

Decision makers and elected officials. By virtue of their ability to influence policy, funding decisions, and program development, those in positions of power can be extremely effective disseminators. Performing this function may also benefit them by crediting them with the call to action for community betterment or with the initiation of new legislation or policy.

Because elected officials and persons making high-level decisions have competing demands on their time and attention, they may have to be motivated to be actively involved in the dissemination effort. Offer these stakeholders encouragement as well as the tools to participate in the dissemination of the study.

Officials are interested in the outcome, not a discourse on the process. They prefer to be perceived as rescuing the target population from further suffering and need the simple facts of the study: Who has the need, what is their need, and how will the need be addressed?

Timing can impact the willingness of decision makers and elected officials to become disseminators of information and to take on visible ownership of the project. If initiating recommendations or instituting change is politically popular, they may want to schedule the dissemination for a time close to a campaign for election or reelection. Decision makers and elected officials may be in the right position at the right time. Specifically, they may sponsor legislation, support new policy, or introduce regulations to bridge the gap in a critical need of the target population. If funding is required, the official needs to show the benefits of lower costs now, rather than projected higher costs of unmet need later.

Sponsoring groups. If the needs assessment was supported by foundations, grants, or initiated by government mandate, the stakeholders in these organizations are highly motivated to illustrate the study's value. They are invested personally and professionally in disseminating the results of the study and in showing what differences can be made by identifying and demonstrating their need. Their motivations may include a desire to enhance their own credibility or to build community support, or concern about obtaining future funding.

The agency or individual funded to conduct the needs assessment may be concerned about documenting their credibility and track record with the funding entity, which can determine chances of receiving future awards. Employers relying on the funding to support their organization through foundations and grants may reward or promote employees for a job well done on a needs assessment study.

Concern over reduced or lost funding is a reality for the survival of some agencies. For example, the Older Americans Act mandates that needs of the elderly be assessed to determine funding for discretionary services. Area Agencies on Aging are required annually to submit formal proposals for funding to the State Units on Aging, including a description of how, when, and what needs were identified in determining that year's request for service priorities. If this requirement is not met, the Area Agency on Aging runs the risk of reduced funding or disciplinary action.

The desire for community support may be critical to a community business' viability. For example, the hypothetical Community Chest Corporation (CCC), funded by donations, has historically used donations to fund discretionary local community programs. The CCC conducts and disseminates an annual needs assessment to determine the distribution of donations to local organizations. A poorly conducted or misunderstood study of need could reduce the next year's pledges to the CCC. The community may perceive that this organization is not capable of communicating or disseminating appropriate information on the type or degree of community need.

The target population. Consumers both expect and desire input on issues that concern them. The target population's investment in making use of the needs assessment is natural (Reviere, 1990). In a review of studies of family needs, Sung (1992) noted a growing awareness of systematic needs assessment demanded by human service consumers to achieve action and accountability. These observations may suggest that the target population, having a personal interest in the benefits of needs assessments, can be the greatest advocates for their own need.

The target population may be effective disseminators for a variety of reasons:

- Knowledge of need and ability to share many real examples.
- Ability to communicate information to certain audiences. They may be better able to convey messages in the target population's own terms, in their language, and be better trusted by members.
- Enthusiasm for the results of the needs assessment. The target population can display genuine enthusiasm about discovery or confirmation of need, especially if there is any chance that their needs may be addressed. Anecdotes are useful for those willing to tell their story.
- Likelihood of affecting change. The target population may be involved in designing and implementing solutions to fill the gaps in need.
- Ability to create solutions to documented need. Low- or no-cost efforts may take root within the target community once the need is acknowledged.
- Overcoming reluctance to accept assistance. Attitudes about the responsibility for success or failure, or about the causes of need may influence the degree of willingness or resistance to accepting subsequent services (Martinez-Brawley & Blundall, 1991).
- Surprising responses to the needs assessment. Unexpected reactions from the target population to the needs assessment can be effective in peaking interest in the study.

Community leaders. Religious and civic leaders are often ethically and professionally committed to helping fill gaps in documented need. They often have good rapport with different segments of the community. As communicators, they may be effective in disseminating information to a willing target audience that already knows them—sharing customs, language, and culture. They are likely to elicit feedback and interest from their constituents. Karsten and Kasab (1994) recommended that target audience analysis include determining the names and professional affiliations of respected people whom the target audience considers credible authorities on the subjects addressed in the study.

Elected officials, the media, and the general public perceive community leaders as spokespersons for the target population. These individuals may also be more articulate and accustomed to dealing with officials or the press than the target population that they are serving or representing. The type of dissemination used by community leaders will be based on their "inside" knowledge of the most effective ways of conveying the information the target population wishes to know concerning its impact on their lives and their community.

Groups residing, serving, or conducting business in the community may want to sponsor or fund volunteer projects. Community leaders of the target population can be effective in suggesting appropriate project involvement and may offer useful suggestions on how to help the target population, for example volunteering with Big Brothers if there is a documented need for male role models for young boys in that community.

As community leaders, service providers are often willing and compelled, ethically and professionally, to utilize the findings of a needs assessment study. In most instances, they perceive it as their duty to do something about the recently documented need. They are also effective communicators and may be further motivated to engage in the dissemination of findings if there is the prospect of obtaining additional funding to increase services. A greater need for service could be realized and their business could expand.

Other beneficiaries and unanticipated results. Persons other than stakeholders may benefit from the needs assessment and may be discovered and identified as a population with specific characteristics of their own. For example, an assessment of service needs of crime victims in Jacksonville, Florida, determined that for each rape victim, 1.25 persons have a need for support. Changes in program development and service delivery may address not only the needs of rape victims, but also those of this serendipitously identified constituency (Blomberg, Waldo, & Bullock, 1989).

The findings from needs assessments may differ from what at least some stakeholders anticipate. Flexibility is required to carry out the message when this occurs. For example, in the 1980s, the bedroom community of Fairfax, Virginia, was burgeoning with new single-family homes. A needs assessment of the elderly conducted in 1984 (see chapter 8) showed that 67% of the elderly population preferred to stay in their own home, a finding consistent with other national studies. However, a later follow-up assessment of the same population revealed that only 46% of the elderly subjects preferred to live in their own home, and nearly a fourth indicated a preference for living in a retirement home. As a result, developers and builders have approached county planners and community leaders about building elderly housing.

IMPLEMENTING RECOMMENDATIONS

Communicating a study's results through preliminary findings, a final report, presentations, and effective dissemination ensures that the knowledge is reaching the audience in the format, content, and manner most likely to be well received. This section of the chapter focuses on the implementation of recommendations and ways to maximize the use of findings.

Because the needs assessment is "a systematic and ongoing process of providing usable and useful information about the needs of the target population to those who can and will utilize it to make judgements about policy and programs," implementation is the culmination of the process. Implementation demonstrates that the goals of the needs assessment have been accomplished.

Implementation of findings is framed with broad reference to policy and programs. More specifically, implementation is directed at one or more of three avenues: (a) introduction of new policy or change in existing policy, (b) development of programs, and (c) new or modified service delivery. Action in any or all of these areas suggests that the needs assessment has realized its intended goals.

The development of recommendations was discussed earlier in this chapter. Effectively constructed recommendations are likely to suggest implementation strategies. They prioritize desired policy, program development, or service-delivery changes; are politically, economically, and procedurally appropriate and timely; and specify who should act on implementation.

Stakeholders should be involved in developing recommendations because, with the interests and institutional positions they represent, they may have a better perspective than the researcher on how best to translate results into focused and politically feasible recommendations for changes in policy and practice. Participating in interpreting results and shaping recommendations also sensitizes stakeholders to difficulties involved in drawing conclusions from the data and will reinforce their ownership of the findings. Positive consequences will be fostered for follow-through in the implementation of the study's results (Berkowitz, 1993).

Recommendations do not have to be formally adopted to be implemented. Findings from the needs assessment can be implemented in the community with the assistance of the stakeholders, regardless of whether recommendations have received formal endorsement or official support from persons in positions of power. The following sections address informal and formal strategies for implementation.

Informal Implementation

Earlier in this chapter, the target population's role as disseminators of findings through implementing low- or no-cost solutions was described. Similarly, community leaders should be prepared to respond with suggestions and alternatives once the need is documented or acknowledged. For instance, a volunteer Neighborhood Watch program may be established as a new service in the community following findings that the greatest concern to local citizens is the fear of crime. In this example, the community acts in response to documented needs without a formal recommendation and plan for implementation.

In a review of various models of community involvement in the practical application of needs assessments, Rothman and Tropman (1987) found that community ownership was an important key to the implementation of results. Stakeholders likely to be instrumental in the implementation of findings on an informal level include:

• the target population—potentially direct beneficiaries of the action taken and where the need has been identified.

- community leaders—who, through presence in the community and expertise (service providers) and trust (clergy, block captain), are likely to implement solutions to meet needs.

In some cases, the same members of the target population and the same leaders can participate in both formal and informal implementations. In other cases, the individuals may be different. For example, community leaders who have credibility with the media may not be those who are most influential with neighborhood residents.

An example of the community leader's role in the implementation of recommendations is seen in a study of health problems of an Arab-American community. Clergy, community leaders, and health professionals who translated and provided cultural interpretation for Arab patients and health care providers were in the best and most expedient position to respond to the most important health services including family stress, adjusting to the United States, managing acute illness, coping with adolescents, and marital stress (Laffrey, Meleis, Lipson, Solomon, & Omidian, 1989).

Kaufman (1990) noted that, in using findings based on assessed need, case managers responsible for developing long-term-care service plans for functionally impaired elderly must integrate the supportive efforts of the clients' social network (i.e., community, family, church) into the overall service approach. This level of response was seen again when Dean (1992) described the responsibility that community college personnel felt for utilizing the findings of needs assessed in their organization. With nominal group technique, they identified a range of strategies to improve performance by administrators, faculty, and support personnel, not all of which necessitated changes to official policy and procedures.

Formal Implementation

In some cases, implementation is the expected follow-up to the adoption of written, formal recommendations. Implementation of findings assumes a more formal avenue when the recommendation is approved or endorsed, leading to "official" policy change, program development, and/or changes in service delivery. Official endorsement of recommendations may support appropriation of funding. Implementation through formal channels is likely to be more visible to the community than informal implementation because a powerful body—such as elected officials or policymakers—is involved. When implementation is enhanced by visibility, individuals or agencies may be held accountable. Persons in positions of power may announce plans to implement recommendations at a public meeting, including recommended funding or policy changes to delivering service. Following the news, persons in power, the general public, the target population, the media, and others may hold individuals or agencies accountable for implementation. It becomes evident why clearly identifying offices or officials who should take action in the development of clearly constructed recommendations is so important. The following hypothetical scenario demonstrates this point. The Local Housing Authority (LHA) needs to recommend spending priorities for federal Community Development Block Grant (CDBG) funds. The LHA requests that staff assess the neediest low-income neighborhoods experiencing blight. The LHA accepts the findings from the study and recommends that two communities receive funds from this year's CDBG allocation. The LHA—political appointees and stakeholders in the needs assessment—justified their recommendations through objective means, and received credit for helping these two communities where voters reside.

SUMMARY

Three factors stand out in using and communicating the findings of the needs assessment: (a) the audience has a role in shaping the how, what, when, and where of presentation and dissemination; (b) stakeholders have a role in the presentation, dissemination, and implementation of the study results; and (c) planning is essential for communicating findings before the study begins, during the study, and after the study is completed. Utilizing these three tenets in communicating the study's findings greatly enhances the opportunity for turning research into action.

10

Building for Future Needs Assessments

Rebecca Reviere
Susan Berkowitz

Needs assessments can be powerful tools for improvement if plans are carefully and thoughtfully made, appropriate methods are designed and implemented, and findings are prioritized and translated into policies, programs, and plans to improve the lives of the target population. This book has outlined practical approaches to planning, choosing methods, and disseminating findings of needs assessments. In addition, three chapters of case studies have been presented that illustrate actual needs assessments and their different target populations, methods, uses, strengths, and weaknesses. The rest of this chapter takes a step back from the details of the practice and presents a synthesis of larger lessons learned about needs assessment. The discussion is informed by a comparative reading of the case studies, combined with the main points from each of the other chapters. More specifically, the benefits, foundations, processes, and alternative approaches of needs assessment are evaluated. The chapter closes by anticipating future efforts.

BENEFITS OF UTILIZATION AND FOSTERING COOPERATION

Needs assessment is the systematic and ongoing process of providing usable and useful information about the needs of the target population to those who can and will utilize it to make judgments about policy and programs. As demonstrated throughout this book, data from needs assessments can be utilized in various ways. A needs assessment can identify gaps in service and it can shape the future of service delivery. The findings may provide the support to create a task force that will further develop and refine recommendations, devise potential solutions to a documented problem, or modify an existing budget. The results of a needs assessment might convince decision makers that a new program should be created. After this program has been in operation for a while, decision makers in another locality may decide to create a modified version of the program to serve a similar target population.

The authors acknowledge the helpful information on the National Incidence Study of Child Abuse and Neglect (NIS-3) provided by Dr. Andrea Sedlak, Associate Director of the Human Services Group at Westat, Inc., who is Westat's Project Director for this study. The study is being carried out under contract with the National Center on Child Abuse and Neglect (NCAAN).

By serving as an "open door" to various constituencies, a successful needs assessment can also strengthen ties among groups. If done collaboratively, as recommended, the process of conducting a needs assessment and disseminating the findings may enhance relationships among sponsoring organizations and other agencies, stakeholders, the target population, and the community as a whole. Continued cooperation among agencies, organizations, and stakeholders that first came together to work on a needs assessment may produce multiple long-term benefits. Sharing information and resources in one project can lead to other mutually profitable joint ventures. If a project has gone well, lines of communication have been opened that can benefit all involved. For example, if elected officials found that the results of a needs assessment were useful, they may become more interested in promoting a particular area of service provision.

The needs assessment can also reinforce the agency or sponsoring organization's rapport with the target population. If members of the target population have been positively involved as stakeholders in the conduct of the project and the resulting development of policy and programs, they should be receptive to further cooperation. Alternatively, if the expectations of the target population were unrealistically high, communications were strained, or members of the target population felt they were portrayed negatively, later attempts at serving that group would almost certainly be made more difficult.

The visibility acquired by the agency or organization sponsoring the needs assessment can also be valuable for improving public relations in the general community. If community members come to see the target population as deserving (Martinez-Brawley & Blundall, 1991), the topic as timely, and the approach as appropriate and cost-effective, they will be more likely to perceive the effort positively and thus support further efforts for this population.

THE FOUNDATIONS OF NEEDS ASSESSMENTS

Stepping back from the concrete requirements of carrying out and implementing a needs assessment allows focusing on the foundations that support these basic efforts. The three foundations of successful needs assessment are: (a) a positive climate, (b) adequate resources, and (c) relevant expertise. If these basic underpinnings are missing, it makes little difference whether or not one attends to the details of planning meetings or writing final reports.

Positive Climate

A *positive climate* refers to the need to have favorable environmental conditions surrounding the needs assessment. Because the project is dependent on the larger context in which it occurs, the relationship between the needs assessment and the wider system should, ideally, be supportive and facilitative. A positive climate includes favorable conditions in both the internal organizational and external political environments.

Internal Organizational Environment. Two primary considerations affect the internal organizational environment: (a) the support of the management of the agency or organization sponsoring the needs assessment, and (b) the culture of the agency or sponsoring organization. The support of the management of the sponsor of the needs assessment is important both because of the power and resources it commands, and because the degree of managerial acceptance of the project can influence the tone for the rest of the organization. For these reasons, the role the administration plays in conducting the needs assessment and implementing the findings, and the quality of the relationship between the administration and the research team, are important components in a smoothly conducted project.

If the assessment was initiated from within the administration, the administrative role should be fairly clear and straightforward. However, in situations where the needs assessment was initiated from elsewhere in the organization or mandated from outside, the administration will have less vested interest in the project; resulting support may be tepid at best, and nonexistent at worst. In chapter 6, Miller and Solomon discuss the difficulties inherent in attempting to carry out a needs assessment with an outside mandate. The funding agency, the Centers for Disease Control (CDC), required a needs assessment for continued support, but administrators and many staff of the AIDS service organization were not convinced of the reasons or the need to carry out the project. In these cases, to maintain interest and backing, the administrators will have to be persuaded of the relevance of the needs assessment. Listening carefully to administrators' concerns (over money and community perception), incorporating their suggestions, anticipating their objections, and clarifying the projects' aims will help ease their objections and enlist administrative support. The more closely the administration identifies with and promotes the project, the easier it will be to secure resources and cooperation. Lack of collaboration and support from administration can kill a project completely. The quality of the administrative–research relationship is helped by a clear definition of role and ongoing communication among all involved.

The culture of the organization can also be salient in conducting a needs assessment. Organizational culture is the way of life of the organization. It includes: (a) the organizational structure, (b) purpose or function, and (c) style. The structure of the organization or agency refers to its parts and their interrelationships. Chapter 5 discusses the importance of becoming familiar with the organizational chart of the agency or organization sponsoring the needs assessment. Knowing the organization's lines of authority, patterns of communication, and budgeting procedures and prerogatives alleviates confusion and helps prevent wrong turns, especially when operating in a large bureaucracy. If the organization is coherent and unified, the project will run more smoothly. If the organization does not function smoothly, coordinating the necessary assistance, funding, and backing for a needs assessment may be difficult.

Second, the climate is much more supportive when there is a good fit between the goals of the agency and those of the needs assessment. If the agency's purpose is well-defined, a needs assessment can help fulfill it. If the agency or sponsoring organization is struggling for self-definition, the needs assessment can either help focus that purpose or else cloud the question even more. In other cases, staff may see their primary mission as service delivery and thus resent the efforts required for a successful needs assessment.

Third, the style of the organization is another key aspect of organizational culture that can affect a needs assessment. Needs assessment is conceived of and initiated in an existing organizational context with its own distinctive cultural personality, so to speak. It is important to recognize and work with that style in achieving the goals of the needs assessment. Three aspects of organizational style are particularly important: trust, stability, and efficiency.

Trust. Trust might seem an odd issue to consider in conducting a research project, but it influences whether individuals follow through on commitments and adhere to agreed-on plans and policies or attempt to undermine the project, consciously or unconsciously. Earlier possible sources of resistance were noted from those in the sponsoring organization who resent time spent on research rather than service delivery. Staff may show up late for meetings, misrepresent the amount and quality of their work, and repeatedly miss deadlines. Much of this resistance can be overcome through open negotiation, clear communication or training, and shared vision. A real problem arises if, even after negotiation, colleagues are still unreliable and either overtly or covertly antagonistic. Although such situations will hopefully be rare, they may occur. It is best to openly discuss issues and attempt to counteract effects of a lack of trust when necessary.

Stability. Needs assessments are usually long-term projects requiring oversight. Even under the best of circumstances, it can be difficult to keep up with and ahead of the requirements of running a project. When the organization is in a state of flux, it can be almost impossible to maintain the continuity to produce a polished product. If the organization is moving to a different location, the workforce is being restructured, the administration is being reorganized, or major budget changes are pending, postponing the project for a more opportune and stable time might be wise. Even small changes to the normal routine, such as holidays, academic calendars, or a new computer system, can disrupt a project.

Efficiency. Efficiency is how well the organization usually runs. If deadlines are rarely met or the organization sputters from crisis to crisis, all the friendly communication and trust in the world will not make the climate an easy one in which to work. Insiders recognize the strengths and weaknesses of their organization. If there is a history of projects that are started only to be forgotten a few months later, would yet another project be any different? Are there available resources to ensure follow-through for the needs assessment?

The issues of efficiency, trust, and stability are important organizational characteristics to consider. Some organizations are very stable and have a trustworthy and efficient staff. Working in an agency where these characteristics are in short supply makes completion of a needs assessment more difficult, but not impossible. Carefully choosing a responsible research team, scheduling in ways that best match the organizational calendar, and building in extra time for frustrating setbacks can help overcome many problems.

External political climate. The importance of sensitivity to the external political climate has been repeatedly stressed. *Need* is defined as the gap between real and ideal conditions that is *both* acknowledged by community values and potentially amenable to change. The existence of need may not mean that the community accepts the responsibility for ameliorating the need. The fact that homeless people are sleeping on the streets while others sleep comfortably in their beds does not mean that the latter feel obligated to act on the situation. This is a matter of community values, and the prevailing political atmosphere may not support an ethic of benevolence toward those who do not, or cannot, maintain community standards of living.

The move to reinvent government aims at lessening or decreasing the role of the federal government while shifting responsibility for the disadvantaged to state and local governments and nongovernmental organizations. At the same time, the prevailing philosophy stresses individual and family initiatives for self-help. In this social and political climate, needs assessments may appear almost archaic. However, as governmental safety nets fail, the responsibility necessarily falls on other organizations to catch those falling through the cracks. In this atmosphere, needs assessments may have an important role to fulfill by directing scarce funds to those most in need. However, this role is made more difficult when research funding is under attack at the federal, state, and local levels. Increasingly, social scientists will have to turn to the private sector or to nongovernmental agencies for research dollars.

Adequate Resources

Considerations of resource adequacy must come before the commitment to conduct a needs assessment. This issue is discussed in chapter 5, but it is more than a planning consideration. To be successful, social scientists doing needs assessments require resources to conduct research, disseminate the findings, and eventually implement any new programs or policies the findings may suggest. Two basic resource considerations are especially important:

- *Funding.* Substantial funding may not be necessary, but stable funding is needed to sustain a needs assessment. Social researchers preparing to launch a project may investigate currently existing or new sources of funds. Garner (1989) suggested that obtaining new funding or transferring existing funds for a project requires internal, and possibly external, support for that project, evidence of previous fiscal responsibility, and clear vision and purpose. Support and consensus from stakeholders both inside and outside the organization ensures that the needs assessment is perceived as relevant and important and that cooperation is forthcoming. A history of prior success with budgeting and financial management convinces those doing the funding that their monies will be wisely and safely spent. A clear purpose for monetary requests, coupled with well-articulated goals for the needs assessment, suggests that funds will not be wasted on superfluous issues.
- *Personnel.* A needs assessment is rarely completed by one individual. In most cases, a team of researchers and stakeholders works together over the

course of the project. The research team may be composed of agency staff, outside consultants, volunteers, or some combination of these, and the composition of the team will change depending on the immediate tasks and skills required. Most groups have a small core of dedicated workers and a larger fringe of those who are involved from time to time.

Personnel selections usually require careful screening for the necessary skills and commitment to the spirit of the needs assessment. Various types and levels of abilities are needed during the course of a needs assessment, and tasks are completed more efficiently if there is a good match between abilities and task requirements. It is generally easier to utilize existing skills than to try to teach staff new skills, especially in the middle of a project. Using untrained or poorly trained staff can compromise the quality of data collected and subsequent policy and program decisions. Researchers often find they must balance their need for assistance with the time required for training and overseeing personnel who do not have the necessary skills for the requirements of the needs assessment.

Relevant Expertise

Applied research such as needs assessment demands a special combination of skills in methodological design, data collection, and analysis, coupled with the ability to translate findings for practical and policy application. Relevant expertise requires that the researcher: (a) be physically available and psychologically committed; (b) have the necessary methodological, organizational, and interpersonal skills; and (c) be able to work in cooperation with stakeholders. Planning, conducting, and implementing a needs assessment is easier if the researcher is physically available during much, if not all, of the process. This is not an issue for an in-house researcher, but may be if the researcher is hired as a consultant or through a short-term grant. The case study chapter on assessing AIDS-related needs (chapter 6) discusses the difficulties experienced when the project's consultant is only available on a part-time basis.

Second, the researcher must either possess or be able to draw together the necessary combination of methodological, organizational, and interpersonal skills for conducting a needs assessment. These include the ability to design and conduct applied research, choose and use suitable analytic techniques, and draw practice and policy conclusions and craft recommendations from the data. When one person cannot fulfill all these functions, it is important to seek additional expertise.

The researcher must also be able to work in the existing organizational structure as well as with various stakeholder groups. Academic researchers have the luxury of carrying out research projects entirely within university walls. This ivory tower approach to research is perfectly acceptable and respectable, but rarely does it work for conducting a needs assessment. Researchers who pursue a stakeholder-based approach to needs assessment may need to be willing to compromise the strictest standards of scientific rigor, relinquish complete control of the effort, and cope with potential conflict among stakeholders, and between stakeholder and researcher goals (Berkowitz, 1993). Even so, the benefits of stakeholder participation outweigh the drawbacks. When members of the target population, elected officials, informal community leaders, and researchers work together, it generates greater interest in and support for the research and heightens motivation to utilize findings. Researchers may trade some degree of scientific control, but gain more customized products with better fit among measurement, interpretation, implementation and ultimately, utilization.

THE ONGOING PROCESS OF NEEDS ASSESSMENT

The foundations discussed earlier are the building blocks that support a solid needs assessment. In addition, projects require a good deal of time and effort that, at times, can appear overwhelming. Even under ideal circumstances, difficulties arise and motivation wanes. This section discusses three ongoing processes that contribute to the maintenance of the momentum and the ultimate success of the needs assessment:(a) thoughtful planning, (b) adaptable scheduling, and (c) creative problem solving.

Thoughtful Planning

Thorough and careful planning lays out a clear direction for the conduct and implementation of a needs assessment. Strategic planning provides an overview of influences outside the immediate sphere of the needs assessment and inside the project system. This vantage point allows for a proactive approach as researchers simultaneously take an "inside–out" and "outside–in" view of their project (Kaufman & Bowers, 1990). Strategic planning is carried out in conjunction with project planning that elaborates the specific stages of the project. Solid planning gets a project off on the proper path, keeps it on track, and leads to the desired conclusion.

Although the best planning can be complicated by unanticipated events, viable plans can be adapted to unexpected contingencies because they: (a) provide for continuous monitoring of forces with potentially disruptive impact, and (b) establish ongoing evaluation of the progress of the project. These two features of planning build in a mechanism for anticipating barriers and problems before they become overwhelming and derail the project completely.

The projects described in chapter 8 illustrate the benefits of thorough planning. Both of the needs assessments of the elderly were supported, in part, by an outside funder that provided for and required a written plan, signed by both agency directors and researchers, before the project could begin. Although written with different degrees of specificity, these plans gave a clear direction for the projects even before the researchers officially entered the agency setting.

Adaptable Scheduling

The inclusion of stakeholders in a needs assessment often demands nontraditional scheduling. Meetings and interviews cannot always be accomplished between 9:00 a.m. and 5:00 p.m. In addition, because it can take a great deal of time to hear and incorporate the suggestions of all concerned stakeholders, researchers should have realistic expectations about the time frame of the project. If ongoing stakeholder participation is built in from the early stages, the rhythm of the process will require less adjustment later, as new voices join the process.

Planning, despite its directional nature, is not necessarily a linear process (Pancer & Westhues, 1989). Researchers are often simultaneously attending meetings with stakeholders, drafting research instruments, and making notes for the final report. Chapter 9 discusses the importance of considering final products during the planning phase. This allows for efficiency and streamlining, and for iterative feedback. Being aware of the requirements for final products early ensures that plans and methodological designs can be fine tuned as they develop. For maximum success and minimum confusion while juggling various tasks, researchers need to keep a firm hold on the ultimate purpose of the needs assessment.

Creative Problem Solving

The third ongoing process of needs assessment is creative problem solving. Researchers should be willing to suspend their normal activities and reorder or rethink their priorities and roles as the need arises. Miller and Solomon (chapter 6) were able to redirect their energies as the project required. When staff needed training, they developed training procedures, although that was not part of their original plan. Sometimes creativity involves making the existing situation work for, not against, the project. Berkowitz (chapter 8), in dealing with a seemingly unrelated and time-consuming agency request that she produce a listing of available services, incorporated that knowledge into the needs assessment instrument.

Overall flexibility is a basic and critical requirement of planning, scheduling, creative problem solving, and, indeed, the entire needs assessment process. Researchers, agency professionals, or students may feel a strong need to be in strict control of every aspect of a project to ensure that it goes as expected. After it is set in motion, a needs assessment develops a life of its own as different personalities, time constraints, and obstacles emerge. The social scientists responsible for the needs assessment are often operating simultaneously in both a reactive and proactive mode: they must keep working toward the planned goal, yet flexibly respond to changes and problems as they arise. This ability to adapt to new and changing circumstances throughout a needs assessment should result in a needs assessment that closely fits the situation as it evolves, rather than merely matching demands as they appear.

ALTERNATIVE APPROACHES

Most needs assessments have been one-shot, relatively small-scale, local endeavors designed to provide local decision makers with information on specific populations or groups in their jurisdictions. The results are typically not disseminated beyond the local area, presumably on the assumption that they have little value or applicability to anyone or anywhere else. This "localism" has contributed to an unduly narrow vision of the field while fostering an ad hoc, "seat of the pants" approach to needs assessment methods. In drawing out common themes and issues from the case study chapters and methods discussion in chapter 2, 3, and 4, the next section outlines various ways in which these "localistic" tendencies can be usefully addressed.

Assessing National Level Needs

Although the four needs assessment projects described in the three case study chapters address needs at county, subcounty, and neighborhood levels, there is no reason that needs assessments cannot be conducted at the state, regional, national, and international levels. Table 2.1 shows how a needs assessment might be carried out for a statewide target population. The scope of the needs assessment largely depends on the level of the policymakers to whom the study is addressed. Congress as a body will want information on the unmet needs for services of at-risk families throughout the nation, although individual congresspeople will still take a special interest in knowing about families in their home districts and how they compare with those in the rest of the nation. Similarly, state legislators will want information on the status of relevant constituencies in their states. The primary reason that needs assessments have tended to be local efforts is that they have been commissioned largely by local entities, such as city or county governments. By contrast, studies contracted or undertaken directly by federal and state agencies, which are designed to directly or indirectly determine the nature and extent of need for certain types of services, are not generally regarded as needs assessments. But what else are they?

The congressionally mandated National Incidence Study (NIS) of Child Abuse and Neglect, sponsored by the U.S. Department of Health and Human Services, is designed to estimate the total number of children who are abused or neglected in the United States over the course of 1 year. The NIS methodology assumes that cases officially reported to and investigated by Child Protective Services (CPS) agencies represent only the "tip of the iceberg," and that considerable numbers of children are recognized as abused or neglected by community professionals, but are not investigated by CPS. For this reason, the NIS obtains data about abused and neglected children investigated by CPS as well as those recognized by sentinels and professionals who work in schools, hospitals, day care centers, law enforcement agencies, and other agencies. The cases submitted from all sources are unduplicated, and estimates are given in terms of the number of abused or neglected children during a specified time frame.

The sentinel methodology used in the NIS permits assessment of the unmet need for child protection services in the population. The NIS data indicate the numbers of abused and neglected children recognized by community professionals, and reveal the extent to which CPS agencies reach these children. In addition, two substudies are being conducted to identify whether professionals are failing to report cases to CPS, or whether CPS is screening out these cases.

Although Congress probably did not have a "needs assessment" in mind when it mandated NIS–3, a needs assessment is essentially what it has gotten.

Defining as needs assessments major national studies that investigate the scope of a problem and the extent to which and manner in which it is being addressed by the service delivery system substantially widens the vision of what can be encompassed by the term.

Reconsidering Methodological Approaches

Apart from redefining the scope of the concept of needs assessment to include national level efforts, another way to promote greater methodological awareness in needs assessment is by considering what might have been done differently in any given study.

Chapters 2 and 4 argue that, resources permitting, it is often preferable to combine methods rather than use a single method in assessing needs. In chapter 6, Miller and Solomon see their use of multiple data collection methods as mostly a strength, but also, in part, a weakness of their needs assessment. Their study of AIDS-related needs of women in an urban housing project employed a range of primary and secondary data collection methods, roughly in the following order:

- community observations designed to determine the extent and specific location of drug use and prostitution activities;
- interviews with local police community affairs officers and leaders of neighborhood and tenant associations about risk activities in the neighborhood;
- key informant interviews, by telephone and in person, with representatives of service provider and other community organizations about their experiences with the community, and the needs as well as perceived barriers to service utilization among different groups of women residents;
- review of available epidemiologic data and other census tract data on community characteristics as well as existing literature on similar types of needs assessments conducted in New York City; and
- anonymous in-person intercept interviews with a convenience sample of 212 women 18 years of age and older in a single housing development. The women were paid $15 if they completed the interviews, which covered knowledge of and personal exposure to AIDS-related issues, sexual history, risk behaviors, risk-reduction efforts, and barriers to risk reduction.

Miller and Solomon consider the greatest strength of their multimethod approach to be that the different methods produced convergent, although not entirely identical, answers to the questions being asked about needs. Hearing different respondent groups give similar answers in several different ways increased confidence in the accuracy and validity of the findings.

However, use of several different methods was also partly (although not entirely) an unplanned, ad hoc adaptation to immediate "on-the-ground" pressures. Chapter 2 emphasizes the importance of developing a coherent, comprehensive research design to serve as a blueprint for executing a needs assessment. A good design, in which the specific mix of methods fits together logically and synergistically, does not happen by chance. Once the research process is underway, the plan might require adaptation. Miller and Solomon acknowledge that better planning and a clearer conception of the methodological direction of the project from the outset would have eliminated some of the "trial and error," and would have saved the time and expense of using at least one method (observation) that ultimately proved unworkable. Following a coherent plan would also have allowed the activities to have been carried out in a more logical and useful sequence. For example, the review of epidemiologic data and other secondary sources could have preceded the other steps, and so provided a basis for later activities.

As seen in chapters 2, 3, and 4, to fulfill their functions properly, methods should be applied correctly and appropriately fit their stated objectives. Qualitative methods such as observation have a role to play, but should be used correctly. The researcher as well as those who actually carry out the methods must have the proper training and level of skill to apply any given method. Because qualitative techniques such as observation are less formal and superficially more "intuitive" than more structured methods, their use may seem to require less training. If anything, the opposite is true. By relying on a single researcher with extensive experience in qualitative methods, the minority-focused elderly needs assessment described in chapter 8 avoided this pitfall, but also limited the number of respondents who could be interviewed.

If multiple methods are employed, it is important to recognize that different methods reinforce one another only insofar as each is used appropriately. Mixing methods produces benefits through "triangulation" of sources, which enables multiple, independent ways of getting at the same question or set of issues. However, mixing methods cannot neutralize the poor use of one or more of those methods. Even if this means accepting certain limitations, it is better to employ one method well than to use two or more methods poorly.

It is interesting to speculate on how, for a given needs assessment, use of different methods might have yielded different findings, or at least somewhat different perspectives on the results. The Florida maternal and child health needs assessment discussed in chapter 7 used analyses of vital statistics and demographic census data to determine the priority groups of women in a particular rural county who should be targeted to receive services. Calculating the odds ratios for three negative birth outcomes (infant mortality, low birth weight, and high-risk births) isolated three priority groups of mothers: those less than 19 years old, African-American mothers, and mothers with less than a high school education.

Would interviews with community service providers and county public health officials have corroborated these responses? Use of different methods with different groups of respondents, in combination with analysis of secondary census data, often produces answers that are different, although perhaps variations on a common theme (Laffrey, Meleis, Lipson, Solomon, & Omidian, 1989). One could argue for the greater objectivity of secondary demographic data over the potentially biased subjective perceptions of service providers. Alternatively, it would be equally compelling to hold that service providers' perceptions are more valid, because the latter are in a position to identify the salient psychological, familial, and social characteristics making some groups of women better candidates than others for successful intervention. Using both methods in combination would probably have produced some degree of overlap in responses across the two methods. However, the service providers probably would have defined target categories in somewhat different terms.

Chapter 8 presents an example of how, because of different foci and methods, two studies in contiguous counties revealed rather different pictures of the needs of the elderly. One was a longitudinal sample survey of the general elderly population; the other was a qualitative study of three groups of homebound minority elderly that relied mainly on intensive interviews and community ethnography. The longitudinal survey yielded a portrait of a reasonably affluent, well-educated, mainstream elderly population with relatively few serious unmet needs. The minority-focused assessment discovered varying degrees of knowledge and utilization of services among African-American, Hispanic, and Vietnamese homebound elderly. It also revealed serious unmet needs in these populations, as well as significant linguistic and cultural barriers to service use, especially among the Hispanic and Vietnamese elderly.

The two counties are similar enough in demographic characteristics and service base that, had either study taken the other's approach, the results would probably have been quite similar. In other words, if the minority-focused study had surveyed a random sample of the overall elderly population of the county, there would have been few minority elderly (let alone homebound minority elderly) in the sample, and the overall picture would not have been too dissimilar to that in the other county. By the same token, if the longitudinal researcher had been given the task of determining the unmet service needs of homebound minorities in the county, she might have adopted an approach closer to (although probably not identical to) that taken by the other researcher.

Three general points follow from the prior discussion: (a) different methods can legitimately yield different perspectives on need; (b) there is no intrinsic relationship between the substantive focus of the study and the methods that can be applied to assess need (i.e., the same methods can be used to study maternal and child health needs and needs of the elderly); and (c) needs often have to be inferred, rather than read directly from the data.

This last point—on inferring needs—requires elaboration. Data rarely "speak for themselves." Inference, interpretation, and extrapolation are often required in moving from the raw data to an assessment of the target population's needs—and, from there, to a judgment of how these needs should be addressed. The Florida maternal and child health study provides a rather obvious example of inferring need, assuming that the demographic groups with the highest risks of poor birth outcomes should be targeted to receive services. The *neediest,* by definition, are those who fall into the highest risk categories.

It is less obvious that inference may also be needed in interpreting interview responses. The idea that respondents simply need to be asked what they need, or what the target population needs, is rather naive (cf. Harlow, 1992). Notions of need are filtered through different groups' perceptual frameworks. When members of the target population are unaware of the full range of services available to them, even if asked directly, they may not recognize a need because they cannot identify a specific service that would satisfy it. When questions ask about issues that are viewed as indicating weakness or dependence, respondents may be unwilling to admit their needs. The result may be a false picture of a target population with no unsatisfied needs. Alternatively, as in the elderly longitudinal example, evidence that basic needs are largely met can lead to addressing respondents' higher level needs, such as continuing education.

Moreover, respondents may not recognize conditions or events they experience as reflecting need. The researcher in the Arlington minority-focused needs assessment heard from many of her homebound elderly female Vietnamese respondents that they rarely left their homes because they got headaches and felt dizzy and weak whenever they went outside. Consulting with Vietnamese professionals and others, the researcher used her knowledge of these respondents' traumatic life experiences as refugees to infer that the dizziness, weakness, and headaches were symptomatic of feelings of cultural disorientation and fear. Based on this inference, she further recommended that culturally appropriate mental health services be developed by the county.

The process of moving from symptoms to diagnosis to the suggested "prescription" or remedy unavoidably involved several levels of inference. To address possible objections, the researcher in the prior example took pains in the final report to document both the empirical bases for these inferences and the assumptions that underlay the inferential process. That way, readers could judge for themselves if the interpretations were reasonable.

The larger lesson that may be drawn from this is that analysis of needs assessment data should avoid making naive assumptions that the data necessarily "speak for themselves." To do so is to abrogate researchers' responsibility to make meaningful sense of what they have found. By the same token, it is important to clearly indicate the assumptions that were made in analyzing and interpreting the data, and to thoughtfully present any recognized limitations in the methods that affect the findings.

ANTICIPATING THE FUTURE

Because the needs of target populations will almost always change over time—some slowly, others quite rapidly—needs assessment should ideally be an ongoing process rather than a one-time endeavor. Needs are not fixed, but are relative to context. Just as policies and programs may be initiated as a way to meet needs, changes in policies and programs can, sometimes unintentionally, create new unmet needs. For example, tightening eligibility criteria for receipt of food stamps may produce problems of malnutrition and hunger among segments of the population whose nutritional needs were being adequately met only a short time before.

Needs assessments gain power as knowledge accumulates. In comparison to data collected at a single point in time, information gathered over time is richer and more attuned to changing problems and needs. Even if the sponsoring organization is not in a position to conduct a formal longitudinal study or a study with several repeating phases, there are other ways to obtain data useful for tracking the changing circumstances and needs of a target population. Secondary sources, including newspapers, agency reports, and statistics from school systems, health departments, and birth and death registries can provide information on relevant ongoing developments in the target population. Maintaining and periodically updating a file of relevant clippings, statistics, and reports can serve this purpose.

Although this kind of monitoring cannot, and is not meant to, substitute for a full-scale needs assessment, it provides an inexpensive yet reasonably direct way to keep a finger on the pulse of what is happening to the target population. For example, those interested in the recreational needs of the residents of a given community should track changes in the age ranges, family structure(s), and racial and ethnic composition of the population. If there is a large influx of young Mexican families, a new study should not be needed to justify adding soccer games and Cinco de Mayo celebrations to the standard fare of Little League and Fourth of July fireworks.

Data do not stay current forever—the elderly get older, new immigrant groups move in, and disease patterns change. A variety of factors, including resources, community support, and the target population, can and will influence the decision of when to initiate another needs assessment. Regularly revisiting the data from a prior needs assessment in light of changing conditions helps signal when the earlier information becomes seriously outdated or is no longer adequate or appropriate for characterizing the target population(s). At a certain point, especially in situations of rapid social change, or when a 10-year difference in age in the target population makes for very different needs, the findings from the last needs assessment are no longer useful for accurately estimating or projecting needs. This is one cue that the time may be right to begin the needs assessment cycle again.

References

Alan Guttmacher Institute. (1981). *Teenage pregnancy: The problem that hasn't gone away.* New York: Author.

Altman, D. (1994). *Power and community: Organizational and cultural responses to AIDS.* London: Taylor and Francis.

Bailey, K. (1994). *Methods of social research* (3rd ed.). New York: The Free Press.

Basu, J., & Keimig, P. (1990). The use of computerized need projection methodologies to implement health planning policies. *Journal of Health and Social Policy, 22,* 19–38.

Berkowitz, S. (1989). *Assessing the unmet service needs of elderly homebound Blacks, Hispanics and Vietnamese in Arlington: Recommendations for improving delivery and overcoming barriers to utilization.* Final report to fellowship program of Gerontological Society of America, Washington, DC.

Berkowitz, S. (1993). *A guide to conducting stakeholder-based evaluations for state agency/federal evaluation studies projects* (Contract #300-87-0155, U.S. Department of Education's Office of Special Education Programs): Rockville, MD: Westat.

Blomberg, T.G., Wald, G.P., & Bullock, C.A. (1989). An assessment of victim service needs. *Evaluation Review, 39,* 598–627.

Bradshaw, J. (1972). A taxonomy of social need. In G. McLachlan (Ed.), *Problems and progress in medical care essays on current research. Seventh series* (pp. 69–82). London: Oxford University Press.

Calsyn, R.J., & Klinkenberg, W.D. (1995). Response bias in needs assessment studies. *Evaluation Review, 19,* 217–225.

Centers for Disease Control and Prevention. (1994). *HIV/AIDS surveillance report, June 1994.* Atlanta, GA: Author.

Chambers, D.E. (1993). *Social policy and social programs. A method for the practical public policy analyst* (2nd ed.). New York: Macmillan.

Cheung, K.M. (1993). Needs assessment experience among Area Agencies on Aging. *Journal of Gerontological Social Work, 19*(3/4), 77–92.

Ciarlo, J.A., Tweed, D.L., Shern, D.L., Kirkpatrick, L.A., & Sachs-Ericsson, N. (1992). Validation of indirect methods to estimate needs for mental health services: Concepts, strategy, and general conclusion. *Evaluation and Program Planning, 15,* 115–131.

Cramer, J. C. (1995). Racial and ethnic differences in birthweight: The role of income and financial assistance. *Demography, 32*(2), 231–247.

Dean, P.G. (1992). Identifying a range of performance improvement solutions—high yield training to systems design—through evaluation research. *Proceedings of Selected Research and Development Presentations at the Convention of the Association for Educational Communications and Technology.*

Fairfax Area Agency on Aging. (1984). *Assessing the well-being of the Fairfax area elderly, 1984.* Fairfax, VA: Author.

Feuz, K. (1989). *Enabling communities to respond to the needs of young women at risk.* Funded as a Demonstration Grant by Health and Welfare Canada (4559-1-69).

Fleiss, J. (1981). *Statistical methods for rates and proportions* (2nd ed.). New York: Wiley.

Florida Department of Commerce. (1993). *Florida county comparisons: 1993.* Tallahassee, FL: Division of Economic Development, Bureau of Economic Analysis.

Florida Administrative Code. Rules of the Department of Health and Rehabilitative Services State Health Program Office. ch. 10-D /113.

Florida Statutes 383.216(2)(a) 1.–5. (1991).

Fordyce, J. E., Balanon, A., Stoneburner, R., & Rautenberg, E. (1989). *Women and AIDS: A survey of knowledge, attitudes and behaviors.* New York: New York City Department of Health.

Gadsden Citizens for Health Babies, Inc. (1995). *Service delivery plan for maternal and infant health 1995–1997.* Quincy, FL: Author.

Gallagher, K. (1988). *Methods to increase the participation of minority elderly in programs funded under the Older Americans Act. Final Report for the Gerontological Society of America.* Denver, CO: Aging and Adult Services Division, Colorado Department of Social Services.

Garner, L. H. (1989). *Leadership in human services. How to articulate and implement a vision to achieve results.* San Francisco: Jossey-Bass.

Gilmore, E. D. (1977). Needs assessment processes for community health education. *International Journal of Health, 20,* 164–173.

Golant, S.M. (1990). The metropolitanization and suburbanization of the US elderly population: 1970–1988. *The Gerontologist, 30,* 80–85.

Green, L. W., & Kreuter, M.W. (1992). CDC's planned approach to community health as an application of PRECEED and an inspiration for PROCEED. *Journal of Health Education, 23*(3), 140–147.

Grimm, R. E., & Parker, D.F. (1992). *Key maternal and child health status indicators* (2nd ed.). Tampa: University of South Florida Press.

Guba, E. G., & Lincoln, Y.S. (1981). *Effective evaluation.* San Francisco: Jossey-Bass.

Harel, Z., McKinney, E., & Williams, M. (1987). Aging, ethnicity, and services: Empirical and theoretical perspectives. In D.E. Gelfand & C.M. Barresi (Eds.), *Ethnic dimensions of aging* (pp. 196–210). New York: Springer.

Harlow, K.S. (1992). Research and the politics of decision making: Planning services for elders. *The Journal of Applied Gerontology, 11,* 22–37.

Harlow, K. S., & Turner, M. (1993). State units and convergence models: Needs assessment revisited. *The Gerontologist, 33*(2), 190–199.

Hobbs, D. (1987). Strategy for needs assessments. In D. Johnson, L. Meiller, L. Miller, & G. Summers (Eds.), *Needs Assessment: Theory and methods* (pp. 20–24). Ames: Iowa State University Press.

Hutsell, C. A., Meltzer, C.R., Lindsay, G.B., & McClain, R. (1992). Creating an effective infrastructure within a state health department for community health promotion: The Indiana PATCH experience. *Journal of Health Education, 23*(3), 164–170.

Institute of Medicine. (1985). *Preventing low birthweight: A summary.* Washington, DC: National Academy Press.

Institute of Medicine, Committee for the Study of the Future of Public Health. (1988). *The future of public health.* Washington, DC: National Academy Press.

Institute of Medicine. (1989). *Prenatal care: Reaching mothers, reaching infants: A summary.* Washington, D.C.: National Academy Press.

Iutcovich, J.M. (1993). Assessing the needs of the rural elderly. An empowerment model. *Evaluation and Program Planning, 16,* 95–107.

Johnson, D., & Meiller, L. (1987). Community level surveys. In D. Johnson, L. Meiller, L. Miller, & G. Summers (Eds.), *Needs assessment: Theory and methods* (pp. 126–141). Ames: Iowa State University Press.

Kahn, H. A., & Sempos, C.T. (1989). *Statistical methods in epidemiology.* New York: Oxford University Press.

Karsten, S., & Kasab, D. (1990). *Dissemination by design* (Award #9OPDO129). Washington, DC: The Administration on Aging.

Kaufman, A.V. (1990). Social network assessment: A critical component in case management for functionally impaired older persons. *International Journal of Aging and Human Development, 30,* 63–75.

Kaufman, R., & Bowers, D. (1990). Proactive and reactive planners: An even closer look at needs assessment and needs analysis. *Performance and Instruction, 29*(5), 7–10.

Kerr, M. (1989). *Developing services for pregnant teens and young parents: A community planning process.* Vancouver: Health and Welfare Canada.

Kimmel, W. (1977). *Needs assessment: A critical perspective.* Washington, DC: U.S. Department of Health, Education, and Welfare.

Kreuter, M. W. (1992). PATCH: Its origin, basic concepts, and links to contemporary public health policy. *Journal of Health Education, 23*(3), 135–139.

Laffrey, S., Meleis, A.I., Lipson, J.G., Solomon, M., & Omidian, P.A. (1989). Assessing Arab-American health care needs. *Social Sciences in Medicine, 29,* 877–883.

Lareau, L., & Heumann, L. (1982). The inadequacy of needs assessments of the elderly. *The Gerontologist, 22*(3), 324–330.

Lareau, L. (1983). Needs assessment of the elderly: Conclusions and methodological approaches. *The Gerontologist, 23*(5), 518–526.

Marin, B., & Marin, G. (1990). Effects of acculturation on knowledge of AIDS and HIV among Hispanics. *Hispanic Journal of Behavioral Sciences, 12*(2), 110–121.

Markides, K., & Mindel, C. (1987). *Aging and ethnicity.* Newbury Park, CA: Sage.

Martinez-Brawley, E. E., & Blundall, J. (1991). Whom shall we help? Farm families' beliefs and attitudes about needs and services. *Journal of Social Work, 36*(4), 315–321.

Maslow, A. (1954). *Motivation and personality.* New York: Harper & Row.

McKillip, J. (1987). *Need analysis: Tools for the human services and education.* Newbury Park, CA: Sage.

McLain, R. (1992, August). *Needs assessment and service utilization data: Met needs as a measure of unmet needs.* Paper presented at the meeting of the American Sociological Association, Pittsburgh, PA.

Miles, M.B., & Huberman, A. M. (1994). *Qualitative data analysis: An expanded sourcebook* (2nd ed.). Thousand Oaks, CA: Sage.

Morgan, D.L. (1988). *Focus groups as qualitative research.* Newbury Park, CA: Sage.

National Community AIDS Partnership. (1993). *Evaluating HIV/AIDS prevention programs in community-based organizations.* Washington, DC: Author.

Neuber, K., Atkins, W.T., Jacobson, J.A., & Reuterman, N.A. (1980). *Needs assessment: A model for community planning.* Newbury Park, CA: Sage.

Newcomer, K.E. (1994). *Effective utilization and dissemination of study findings* (Contract #HS92035001, U.S. Department of Education's Office of Special Education Programs). Rockville, MD: Westat.

New York City Department of Health. (1994). *AIDS surveillance update, second quarter 1994.* Office of AIDS Surveillance, New York City Department of Health.

New York State Department of Health. (1994a). *AIDS surveillance quarterly update for cases reported through June 1994.* Bureau of HIV/AIDS Epidemiology, New York State Department of Health.

New York State Department of Health. (1994b). *Community need index for New York City.* Division of HIV Prevention, AIDS Institute, New York State Department of Health.

Norris, F. (1987). Affects of attrition on relationships between variables in surveys of older adults. *Journal of Gerontology, 42,* 597–605.

Ong, B.N., Humphris, G., Annett, H., & Rifkin, S. (1991). Rapid appraisal in an urban setting, an example from the developed world. *Social Science in Medicine, 32,* 909–915.

Oriol, W. (1989). "Peter Pan" suburbs—Mellowing with age? *Perspectives on Aging, National Council on Aging, 23,* 4–5.

Pancer, S. M., & Westhues, A. (1989). A developmental stage approach to program planning and evaluation. *Evaluation Review, 13*(1), 56–77.

Patton, M.Q. (1990). *Qualitative evaluation and research methods* (2nd ed.). Newbury Park, CA: Sage.

Peterson, J. L., Card, J. J., Eisen, M. B., & Sherman-Williams, B. (1994). Evaluating teenage pregnancy prevention and other social programs: Ten stages of program assessment. *Family Planning Perspectives, 26*(3), 116–121.

Posavac, E. J., & Carey, R.G. (1989). *Program evaluation: Methods and case studies* (3rd ed.). Englewood Cliffs, NJ: Prentice-Hall.

Prochaska, J. O., Redding, C. A., Harlow, L. L., Rossi, J. S., & Velicer, W. F. (1994). The transtheoretical model of change and HIV prevention: A review. *Health Education Quarterly, 21*(4), 471–486.

Public Health Service. (1986). *The 1990 health objectives for the nation: A midcourse review.* Washington, DC: Government Printing Office.

Public Health Service. (1991). *Healthy people 2000: National health promotion and disease* (DHHS Publication No. PHS 91-50213). Washington, DC: Government Printing Office.

Reichardt, C. S., & Rallis, S.F. (1994). The relationship between the qualitative and quantitative research traditions. In C. S. Reichardt & S. F. Rallis (Eds.), *The qualitative-quantitative debate: New perspectives* (pp. 5–13). San Francisco: Jossey-Bass.

Reviere, R. (1990). *Longitudinal and minority-focused needs assessments in an Area Agency on Aging: Fairfax County, Virginia.* Final report to Fellowship program of Gerontological Society of America, Washington, DC.

Robins, B. J. (1982). Local response to planning mandates: The prevalence and utilization of needs assessment by human service agencies. *Evaluation and Program Planning, 5*(3), 199–208.

Rothman, J., & Tropman, J. (1987). Models of community organization and macro practice perspectives: Their mixing and phasing. In F. Cox, J. Erlich, J. Roghman, & J. Tropman (Eds.), *Strategies of community organization* (4th ed.). Itasca, IL: F.E. Peacock.

See, C.J., Ellis, D.N., Spellman, C.R., & Cress, P.J. (1990). Using needs assessment to develop programs for elderly developmentally disabled persons in a rural setting. *Activities, Adaptation and Aging, 15* (1–2), 53–66.

Shock, N., Greulich, R., Andres, R., Arenberg, D., Costa, P., Lakatta, E., & Tobin, J. (1984). *Normal human aging: The Baltimore Longitudinal Study of Aging.* Washington, DC: National Institute of Health (No. 84-2450).

Shryock, H. S. & Siegel, J.S. (1973). *The methods and materials of demography* (Vol. 1). Washington, DC: Government Printing Office.

Solomon, P., & Evans, D. (1992). Services needs of youths released from a state psychiatric facility as perceived by service providers and families. *Community Mental Health Journal, 28,* 305–315.

Sorkin, D.L., Ferris, N.B., & Hudak, J. (1985). *Strategies for cities and counties: A strategic planning guide.* (Cooperative Agreement #HA-5543, U.S. Department of Housing and Urban Development). Washington, DC: Public Technology.

Stanford, E. P. (1978). *Suburban black elderly.* Los Alamitos, CA: Hwong.

Stanford, E. P. (1980). *Minority aging: Policy issues for the 80's.* San Diego: Campanile.

Stewart, D. W., & Shamdasani, P. N. (1990). *Focus groups: Theory and practice.* Newbury Park, CA: Sage.

Stoller, E. P. (1984). Self-assessments of health by the elderly: The impact of informal assistance. *Journal of Health and Social Behavior, 25,* 260–270.

Strauss, A., & Corbin, J. (1990). *Basics of qualitative research: Grounded theory procedures and techniques.* Newbury Park, CA: Sage.

Sung, K.T. (1992). Identification and prioritization of needs by families by multiple groups: Residents, key informants, and agency directors. *Social Indicators Research, 26,* 137–158.

Thomas, S. B., So'Brien van Putten, J. M., & Chen, M. S. (1991). *A program planning and evaluation manual for HIV education programs: A primer for ethnic and racial minority community based organizations.* Columbus, OH: The Ohio Department of Health.

Thompson, B. (1981, November). *Communication theory as a framework for evaluation use research: Evaluation as persuasion.* Paper presented at the meeting of Evaluation Network/ Evaluation Research Society, Austin, TX.

Thompson, D. R., Freeman, K., & Steele, J. (1993). *Developing a prenatal risk criteria for florida.* Unpublished manuscript.

Thompson, D. R., Hopkins, R.S., & Watkins, S.M. (1993). Using the birth record to develop a screening instrument for infant mortality and morbidity. *Florida Journal of Public Health, 5*(1), 4–7.

Tufte, E. R. (1990). *Envisioning information.* Chesire, CT: Graphics Press.

Twible, R.L. (1992). Consumer participation in planning health promotion programmes: A case study using the nominal group technique. *Australian Occupational Therapy Journal, 39,* 13–19.

United Hospital Fund of New York. (1994). *New York City Community Health Atlas.* New York: Author.

United Way of America. (1982). *Needs assessment: The state of the art.* Alexandria, VA: Author.

U.S. Bureau of the Census. (1989). *Population profile of the United States, 1987. Current Population Reports,* Series P-23, No. 159.

U.S. Bureau of the Census. (1993). *A guide to state and local census geography* (Publication 1990 CPH-I-18). Washington, DC: Government Printing Office.

U.S. Bureau of the Census. (1994). *Geographic areas reference manual.* Washington, DC: Government Printing Office.

Warheit, G., Bell, R., & Schwab, J. (1979) *Needs assessment approaches: Concepts and methods.* Rockville, MD: National Institute of Mental Health, U.S. Department of Health, Education, and Welfare.

Wiener, R.L., Wiley, D., Huelsman, T., & Hilgemann, A. (1994). Needs assessment: Combining qualitative interviews and concept mapping methodology. *Evaluation Review, 18,* 227–239.

Williamson, J., Karp, D., & Dalphin, J. (1977). *The research craft: An introduction to social science methods.* Boston: Little, Brown.

Wolcott, H. F. (1994). *Transforming qualitative data: Description, analysis and interpretation.* Newbury Park, CA: Sage.

York, R. O. (1982). *Human service planning: Concepts, tools, and methods.* Chapel Hill, NC: University of North Carolina Press.

Zajonc, R. B. (1968). The attitudinal effects of mere exposure. *Journal of Personality and Social Psychology, 9*(2), 1–27.

Zervigon-Hakes, A., Byers, J., Terrie, E.W., Harris, D., & Sanderson, N. (1994). *Comprehensive community assessment of health care needs of pregnant women and infants in Gadsden County.* Tallahassee, FL: Florida State University, Center for Prevention and Early Intervention.

Zervigon-Hakes, A., & Lockenbach, R. (1991). *Florida's children, their future is in our hands.* Tallahassee, FL: Florida State University, Center for Prevention and Early Intervention.

Suggested Additional Readings

Converse, J. M. (1986). *Survey questions: Handcrafting the standardized questionnaire*. Newbury Park, CA: Sage.

Frey, J. (1989). *Survey research by telephone*. Newbury Park, CA: Sage.

Hall, M. S. (1988). *Getting funded: A complete guide to proposal writing* (3rd ed.). Portland, OR: Continuing Education Publications.

Hansen, M. (1993). *Sample survey methods and theory* (Vol. I). New York: Wiley.

Kalton, G. (1983). *Introduction to survey sampling*. Newbury Park, CA: Sage.

Kish, L. (1965). *Survey sampling*. New York: Wiley.

Lavrakas, P. (1993). *Telephone survey methods: Sampling, selection and supervision*. Newbury Park, CA: Sage.

Lehtonen, R., & Pahkinen, E. (1995). *Practical methods for design and analysis of complex surveys*. New York: Wiley.

Locke, L.F., Spirduso, W.W., & Silverman, S.J. (1993). *Proposals that work. A guide for planning dissertations and grant proposals* (3rd ed.). Newbury Park, CA: Sage.

Miner, L.E., & Griffith, J. (1993). *Proposal planning and writing*. Phoenix. AZ: Oryx Press.

Reif-Lehrer, L. (1995). *Proposal planning and writing*. Boston: Jones & Bartlett.

Sudman, S. (1982). *Asking questions: A practical guide to questionnaire design*. San Francisco, CA: Jossey-Bass.

Index